Railway Heritage and Tourism

TOURISM AND CULTURAL CHANGE

Series Editors: Professor Mike Robinson, *Ironbridge International Institute for Cultural Heritage, University of Birmingham, UK* and Dr Alison Phipps, *University of Glasgow, Scotland, UK*

TCC is a series of books that explores the complex and ever-changing relationship between tourism and culture(s). The series focuses on the ways that places, peoples, pasts and ways of life are increasingly shaped/ transformed/created/packaged for touristic purposes. The series examines the ways tourism utilises/makes and re-makes cultural capital in its various guises (visual and performing arts, crafts, festivals, built heritage, cuisine etc.) and the multifarious political, economic, social and ethical issues that are raised as a consequence.

Understanding tourism's relationships with culture(s) and vice versa is of ever-increasing significance in a globalising world. This series will critically examine the dynamic inter-relationships between tourism and culture(s). Theoretical explorations, research-informed analyses and detailed historical reviews from a variety of disciplinary perspectives are invited to consider such relationships.

Full details of all the books in this series and of all our other publications can be found on http://www.channelviewpublications.com, or by writing to Channel View Publications, St Nicholas House, 31–34 High Street, Bristol BS1 2AW, UK.

Railway Heritage and Tourism

Global Perspectives

Edited by
Michael V. Conlin and Geoffrey R. Bird

CHANNEL VIEW PUBLICATIONS
Bristol • Buffalo • Toronto

Library of Congress Cataloging in Publication Data
A catalog record for this book is available from the Library of Congress.
Railway Heritage and Tourism: Global Perspectives/Edited by Michael V. Conlin and
Geoffrey R. Bird.
Tourism and Cultural Change: 37
Includes bibliographical references and index.
1. Heritage tourism. 2. Railroad travel. I. Conlin, Michael V.
G156.5.H47R35 2014
338.4'791–dc23 2013048905

British Library Cataloguing in Publication Data
A catalogue entry for this book is available from the British Library.

ISBN-13: 978-1-84541-438-2 (hbk)
ISBN-13: 978-1-84541-437-5 (pbk)

Channel View Publications
UK: St Nicholas House, 31-34 High Street, Bristol BS1 2AW, UK.
USA: UTP, 2250 Military Road, Tonawanda, NY 14150, USA.
Canada: UTP, 5201 Dufferin Street, North York, Ontario M3H 5T8, Canada.

The policy of Multilingual Matters/Channel View Publications is to use papers that
are natural, renewable and recyclable products, made from wood grown in sustainable
forests. In the manufacturing process of our books, and to further support our policy,
preference is given to printers that have FSC and PEFC Chain of Custody certification.
The FSC and/or PEFC logos will appear on those books where full certification has been
granted to the printer concerned.

Typeset by R. J. Footring Ltd, Derby
Printed and bound in Great Britain by Short Run Press Ltd

Contents

Figures

Tables

Contributors

Geoffrey R. Bird is Associate Professor and Program Head for the Master of Arts in Tourism Management at Royal Roads University, Victoria, British Columbia, Canada. He has worked in the public and private sectors in the areas of tourism human resource development, heritage, sustainable tourism and community-based tourism, both overseas and in Canada, for 23 years. For the past 10 years, he has taught courses related to globalization, sustainability, cultural tourism and product development. His academic interests include heritage tourism as it relates to sites of memory such as battlefields as well as industrial heritage tourism. He recently completed his PhD focusing on the relationship between tourism, remembrance and landscapes of war. He has begun his academic publishing with a chapter in *Dark Tourism and Place Identity* (Routledge, 2013), with several other research initiatives underway related to the heritage of World War I.

Philipp Boksberger is Chief Operating Officer and Senior Associate Dean at the Lorange Institute of Business, Zurich, Switzerland. He was Head of School of Tourism at HTW Chur for six years. In this period it became the biggest research facility in this area in Switzerland and gained international reputation not only for its research and consulting work but also for its degree programmes and continuing education. In addition to that, he gained professional experience with private companies, associations and non-profit organisations, as well as with regional and local corporate bodies in Switzerland, Spain and Australia. As Professor for Tourism Management he lectured various courses at Bachelor, Master and EMBA level. His research interests cover consumer behaviour and marketing in tourism, as well as destination management issues, on which he has published various research papers and book chapters.

Blanca A. Camargo is the Director and Associate Professor of the International Tourism Program at Universidad de Monterrey, Mexico. She received her doctorate in sustainable tourism from Texas A&M University. Her research interests are in the area of sustainability, cultural heritage, justice and equity.

Ian Chaplin is Research Associate with the Department of Tourism at Flinders University, Adelaide, Australia. He holds a PhD in Cultural Tourism from this Department and has been engaged in tourism transport research in the Asia region for more than 30 years, with a special interest in railway transport and infrastructure planning and its impact on community development. The focus of his research is on the preservation and restoration of railway industrial heritage and its potential for the revitalisation of 'railway communities' through cultural tourism. His passion for railway heritage can be ascribed to the fact that he was born in the birthplace of the railway phenomenon, Stockton-on-Tees, UK.

Fredrick M. (Fred) Collison is Professor Emeritus of Travel Industry Management (Transportation and Marketing) at the School of Travel Industry Management of the University of Hawai'i at Manoa, where he was on the faculty from 1983 through to 2006. He received his PhD in Business Administration (Marketing and Transportation) from Michigan State University in 1982, his MBA from the University of Delaware in 1976 and his BSE (Naval Architecture) from the University of Michigan in 1969. He also taught at Central Michigan University, the University of Minnesota, Duluth, and Michigan State University. He served as a principal investigator on a number of grant-funded research projects, including ones on trans-Pacific aviation, air service between Hawai'i and both Hong Kong and East Asia, sustainable tourism development for the Pacific islands, and the cruise industry in the Pacific. He most recently completed funded research on sustainable tourism development and marketing for Bikini and Rongelap Atolls in the Republic of the Marshall Islands. He has articles published in journals such as *Annals of Tourism Research*, the *International Journal of Culture, Tourism and Hospitality Research*, *Journal of Transportation Management*, *Tourism Management* and *Transportation Journal*.

Michael Conlin is a Professor at the Okanagan School of Business in Kelowna, Canada, and an Adjunct Professor at Royal Roads University and the University of Guelph. He is the author of over 40 refereed articles, professional papers, case studies and book chapters, and is the co-editor of the first book on island tourism, *Island Tourism: Management Principles* *and Practice* (Wiley, 1996), with Dr Tom Baum (Strathclyde). He is also the co-editor of the first book on mining heritage tourism, *Mining Heritage and Tourism: A Global Synthesis* (Routledge, 2010) with Dr Lee Jolliffe (UNBC). He is currently working on *Motoring Heritage and Tourism: People, Places, and Products*, the first edited book on motoring heritage and tourism with Dr Lee Jolliffe and anticipates publication by Channel View Publications in 2015.

William (Bill) C. Found is University Professor Emeritus in the Faculty of Environmental Studies and the Department of Geography at York University, Toronto, Canada. Over a period of 50 years he has conducted research in 34 different Caribbean islands, as well as East Africa and South Asia. His publications and documentary films focus on landscape change, environmental management, heritage resources, community-based planning and the use in multimedia technology. Many of his consultant reports concern the implementation and assessment of development projects. His past administrative posts include Vice President (Academic Affairs) (1979–85) of York University. He holds university degrees from McMaster (BA), Florida (MA and PhD) and Umeå (Honorary Doctorate), and has held visiting posts at Harvard, Toronto, Umeå and the Academic of Sciences of Cuba.

Carla Conceição Lana Fraga graduated in tourism (2004) and MBA in Management and Enterprise (2005) at Universidade Federal de Juiz de Fora (UFJF), Brazil, and MSc and DSc in Transportation Engineering at PET/COPPE/UFRJ (2011). She is an Adjunct Professor at Universidade Federal do Estado do Rio de Janeiro (UNIRIO) and a Professor at Universidade Estácio de Sá, at both of which she runs the tourism courses. She is responsible for the Transportation and Tourism Research Group at CNPQ. She has a scholarship from CAPES/UAB as coordinator of transportation studies on the Undergraduate Tourism Course (EAD), Fundação CECIERJ/Consórcio CEDERJ. Her expertise is in railway tourism and transportation engineering in relation to planning.

Warwick Frost is an Associate Professor in Tourism and Events at La Trobe University, Melbourne, Australia. His research interests are in heritage, nature-based tourist attractions, events and the interaction between tourism and the media. With Jennifer Laing, he is the author of *Books and Travel: Inspiration, Quests and Transformation* (Channel View Publications, 2012); *Commemorative Events: Identity, Memory, Conflict* (Routledge, 2013) and *Explorer Travellers and Adventure Tourism* (Channel View Publications, 2014).

Claudia Gabriela Garzar received her bachelor´s degree in International Tourism with a specialisation in Tourism Trends at Universidad de Monterrey, Mexico. She graduated at the top of her class and received the *summa cum laude* distinction. Currently, she coordinates the Promotion and Admissions Department at Facultad Libre de Derecho de Monterrey, Mexico.

Joan Henderson is an Associate Professor at Nanyang Business School at Nanyang Technological University in Singapore where she has worked since 1997. Prior to this, she lectured in Travel and Tourism in the United Kingdom after periods of employment in the public and private tourism sectors there. Her PhD thesis, completed at the University of Edinburgh, was on the subject of social tourism and she also holds an MSc in Tourism and a BSc.Econ (Hons) in Politics and History. Current research interests include crisis management and tourism, heritage as a tourist attraction and tourism in the Asia Pacific region.

Bradford T. Hudson is Senior Lecturer in Marketing and Assistant Chair of the Marketing Department in the Carroll School of Management at Boston College, Massachusetts, USA. Previously he was Associate Professor of the Practice of Marketing and Business History in the School of Hospitality Administration at Boston University. He holds a PhD in business history from Boston University and a master's degree in hotel administration from Cornell University. He recently completed a Fulbright fellowship in Canada, where he conducted research into the historic railroad hotels that are currently operated by Fairmont.

Carla Jellum has a PhD in tourism and marketing from the University of Otago, New Zealand. Her current research interests include recreation and tourism, natural resource management, research methods, rail trail development, marketing and event management.

Lee Jolliffe, a Professor of Hospitality and Tourism at the University of New Brunswick, Canada, has an academic background in sociology, museum studies and tourism, and a research interest in the intersection between culture and tourism. Her edited publications with Channel View Publications include *Tea and Tourism: Tourists, Traditions and Transformations* (2007), *Coffee Culture, Destinations and Tourism* (2010), *Sugar Heritage and Tourism in Transition* (2013) and *Spices and Tourism* (2014). She sits on the editorial boards for a number of international hospitality and tourism journals and is the Resource Editor (museums) for *Annals of Tourism Research*.

Rhonda Koster is the Director, School of Outdoor Recreation, Parks and Tourism, Lakehead University, Canada. Her research interests focus on working with and for rural communities in examining the contribution of various forms of tourism to rural sustainability. In these areas she has conducted research and published on: determinants of success in rural tourism planning; experiential tourism development as a niche for rural communities; the role of Appreciative Inquiry in tourism development; the opportunities for gateway communities in relationship to protected areas; the role of rural tourism in the Canadian urban fringe; and frameworks for evaluating tourism as a community economic development endeavour. A specific research interest is the role of and capacity for community-based tourism in First Nations communities in Canada. As a result of an ongoing, multi-year project with the Red Rock Indian Band, her research collaboration was recognised with an Aboriginal Partnership Research Award in 2010. Her current work examines the intercommunity and governance-level networks with an aim to determine how these interactions can contribute to and impede a regional approach to tourism development in rural resourced based regions.

Jennifer Laing is a Senior Lecturer in the Department of Marketing and Tourism and Hospitality at La Trobe University, Victoria, Australia. She undertook her PhD at La Trobe, looking at the motivations behind adventure travel to the peripheries. Her research interests include: travel narratives; the role of myth in tourism; extraordinary tourist experiences; the role of events in society; and heritage tourism. She has published in journals such as *Annals of Tourism Research*, *Tourism Analysis* and the *Journal of Sustainable Tourism*. She has co-authored two academic books with Warwick Frost: *Books and Travel: Inspiration, Quests and Transformations* (Channel View Publications, 2012) and *Commemorative Events: Memory, Identities, Conflict* (Routledge, 2013). She was the recipient of the 2010 CAUTHE (Council for Australian Tourism and Hospitality Education) Fellows Award for Tourism and Hospitality Research. She is a member of the editorial board for the *Journal of Travel Research*, *Tourism Analysis* and *Tourism Review International*. With Warwick Frost, she is co-editor of the Routledge 'Advances in Events Research' book series.

Kim Lemky has worked for the Environment Canada and at various universities across Canada, teaching both geography and recreation and tourism courses. She also coordinated tourism infrastructure development for the Cabot Trail for five years. She is currently teaching in the Tourism and Hospitality Program at the University of New Brunswick Saint John as well as in the MBA program. Her research interests are in destination management and in community-led tourism initiatives, as well as souvenir research on cruise ship passengers.

Marel Morales received her bachelor´s degree in International Tourism with a specialisation in Tourism Trends at Universidad de Monterrey, Mexico. She graduated at the top of her class and received the *summa cum laude* distinction. Her professional experience is in the area of event planning.

James D. Porterfield is the Director of the Center for Railway Tourism at David and Elkins College in West Virginia, USA. He is also an author, columnist and the contributing editor for *Railfan & Railroad* magazine, as well as the creator and host of 'Journeys for a Railroad Tourist', a website and blog from the National Trust for Historic Preservation's Heritage Travel division. He is the author of six books focusing on railway heritage in the USA and writes a column for *Railroad Museum Quarterly*, the journal of the Association of Railroad Museums. He graduated from Edinboro University of Pennsylvania and taught marketing at Penn State University for 25 years prior to moving to David and Elkins College.

Bruce Prideaux holds the position of Professor of Marketing and Tourism Management at the Cairns campus of James Cook University, Australia, and works with a team of six PhD students. He has a wide range of research interests, including rail heritage, agri-tourism and climate change. Other active areas of research include military heritage, tourism transport, tourism aviation, crisis management, heritage and ecotourism. He holds Visiting Professorships at Bournemouth University in the UK and Taylors University, Malaysia, and has authored over 250 journal articles, book chapters and conference papers on a range of tourism-related issues.

Josephine Pryce is a Senior Lecturer in the School of Business, Faculty of Law, Business and Creative Arts and a Fellow of the Cairns Institute. Her research interests and professional activities focus around the quality of working lives of people from various sectors and industries. As a Fellow of the Cairns Institute, she is undertaking research to pursue this area of interest. Through this, she feels that she can contribute to and influence sustained and satisfactory working lives of individuals, labour policies and sustained labour markets in the region and beyond. In addition, she has an interest in hospitality and tourism, having worked in the hotel industry for over 10 years and conducted relevant research within this context. Her particular areas of interest are quality of service delivery, attitudes, service predispositions, organisational culture, occupational culture and heritage railways.

Arianne C. Reis is a Research Fellow in the School of Tourism and Hospitality Management, Southern Cross University, Australia. Her research interests lie within the broad theme of sustainability of tourism and leisure practices, with a particular emphasis on social and environmental justice. More specifically, her research focuses on leisure and tourism experiences in natural environments and sport tourism. The relationship between tourism development and environmental and social impacts on local communities has been a central part of her work.

Sergio de Castro Ribeiro graduated in tourism in 1998 at Universidade Estácio de Sá, Brazil, postgraduated in University Teaching Skills at Universidade Cândido Mendes in 2000 and MSc in Transportation Engineering at PET/COPPE/UFRJ (2011). He is Professor of Tourism Course at FAETEC-RJ and Universidade Estácio de Sá, and Coordinator of the tourism course at Faculdades Integradas Hélio Alonso (FACHA). His areas of expertise are transportation engineering in relation to planning, regional development and tourism.

Marcio Peixoto de Sequeira Santos graduated in Civil Engineering at PUC/RJ (1976), MSc in Transportation Engineering at PET/COPPE/UFRJ (1980), MSc in Transport Planning at University of London (1981) and PhD Transport Engineering at University of London (1987). He is Associate Professor of Transportation Engineering Program at COPPE, Universidade Federal do Rio de Janeiro (UFRJ), Brazil, and Coordinator of PLANET (Strategic Transportation Planning) and MTB - Executive Post-Graduation Course in Transportation Engineering. His areas of expertise are transportation engineering in relation to planning, regional development and policies on public transportation.

Kyle Stefanovic has a Masters in Environmental Studies from the Nature Based Recreation and Tourism Program at Lakehead University , Ontario, Canada. His research interests focus on the development of niche market tourism, more specifically 'railfan tourism'. In this area, he has conducted research on: the demographic profile of railfans as part of his honours thesis; and the process and development of railfan parks as part of his master's thesis. Currently he is the Director of Leisure Services for the Town of Wynyard, Saskatchewan, Canada. As the Director of Leisure Services, he is responsible for the management and development of recreation opportunities for the residents of Wynyard. He is also responsible for the management and development of tourism in the area. Wynyard is located in the Quill Lakes International Bird area, an internationally recognised birding spot. He is currently in the process of developing a demographic profile of visitors to the region, which is the first step in developing a Town of Wynyard Community Based Tourism Plan.

Martin Sturzenegger has been Chief Executive Officer of Zurich Tourism since March 2013. Zurich Tourism is the second largest tourism organisation in Switzerland, after Switzerland Tourism. Between 2010 and 2013 he was engaged at Rhaetian Railway (Glacier Express and Bernina Express) as Head of Sales and Marketing and a member of its executive board. Before that, he held various senior management positions at Swiss Federal Railways and Swissair. He has accomplished an MBA at Manchester Business School.

Leanne White is a Senior Lecturer in Marketing in the College of Business at Victoria University in Melbourne, Australia. Her doctoral thesis examined manifestations of official nationalism and commercial nationalism at the Sydney 2000 Olympic Games. Her research interests include: national identity, Australian popular culture, advertising, commercial nationalism, destination marketing and cultural tourism. She is the author of more than 40 book chapters and refereed journal articles, and co-editor of the Routledge tourism-research books *Tourism and National Identities: An International Perspective* (2011), *Dark Tourism and Place Identity: Managing and Interpreting Dark Places* (2013) and *Wine and Identity: Branding, Heritage, Terroir* (2014). She is a reviewer for academic journals, doctoral thesis examiner and a member of professional associations in marketing, tourism and sport.

Xingcheng Zhuang is Associate Professor of History, College of Humanities, Honghe University, Yunnan, People's Republic of China. His research interests cover history and tourism. He has published a book on source materials for historical studies of the Yunnan-Vietnam Railway (two volumes, in Chinese).

Libo Yan is Assistant Professor of Tourism Management, Faculty of Hospitality and Tourism Management, Macau University of Science and Technology, Macau, China. His research interests include cultural tourism, ethnic tourism and tourism history.

Acknowledgements

The idea for this book germinated between your editors, both of whom enjoy several common scholarly interests, including tourism and railways. Clearly this interest is shared by many others who responded to our call for participation and who have contributed excellent chapters to this book. We would therefore like first to thank the 27 authors whose insight, thought and effort have made this book what it is – a valuable contribution to the literature of industrial heritage tourism generally and heritage railway tourism specifically. It goes without saying that without their involvement, there would be no book. We are particularly appreciative of their patience and commitment to this project as it developed and moved to completion over a three-year period.

We would also like to thank sincerely our respective institutions for their tremendous support for this book. Okanagan College and the Okanagan School of Business provided your first editor with financial and scholarly release time over the three-year period, both through the College's Extended Study Leave Program and the Grant-in-Aid Program, as well as the School's professional development fund and scholarly release from teaching. In particular, the support of Dr Andrew Hay, Vice-President Academic of the College, and Dr Heather Banham, Dean of the Okanagan School of Business, has been particularly central to the success of this project. At Royal Roads University, Dr Brian White, Director of the School of Tourism and Hospitality Management, and Dr Deborah Zornes, of the Office of Research, have also provided support and mentorship for your second editor throughout this project.

On a personal level, we appreciate the support of our respective spouses, Roxi Alix and Katharine Geddes. They have stood by us with words of encouragement and thoughtful interest in the book through the long three years. We would like to specifically recognize the contribution of Roxi, who has quietly and effectively worked as our de facto manuscript manager for this book, a critical yet often unheralded task. To Roxi, thank you for keeping the wheels turning on this project.

Very importantly, we want to thank Sarah Williams, the commissioning editor for the Tourism and Cultural Change series at Channel View for her unstinting support and guidance throughout this project. Indeed, everyone at Channel View has been tremendous in both their support and expertise. And finally, we want to recognize the contribution of the series editors, Mike Robinson and Alison Phipps, who provided expert advice about the scope and theme of the book, all of which has made it a more valuable resource for scholars and students.

Michael V. Conlin
Kelowna, British Columbia

Geoffrey R. Bird
Victoria, British Columbia

February 2014

Part 1
Introduction

1 Railway Heritage and Tourism: Themes, Issues and Trends

Michael V. Conlin and Geoffrey R. Bird

Introduction

> *Ever since childhood, when I lived within earshot of the Boston and Maine,*
> *I have seldom heard a train go by and not wished I was on it.*
> Theroux (1975: 7)

It would be difficult to summarize our fascination, love and even obsession with trains and train travel any better than Paul Theroux did in his seminal work *The Great Railway Bazaar: By Train Through Asia*. As a child in England after World War II, one of your editors would sit for hours on pedestrian bridges spanning the great railway marshaling yards in Stockton, County Durham, England, covered in soot and grime and meticulously marking off steam locomotives in a trainspotting book. Growing up in Canada, your other editor remembers travelling from Ottawa to Vancouver in the comfort of a Canadian National sleeping car, venturing outside at whistle stops to have a good look at the engine pulling his family across Canada's immense landscape. Beginning in our childhoods, like Theroux, we have had a fascination with trains and particularly steam trains, a fascination that predates the withdrawal of steam locomotives from regular service – at least in Europe and North America – but which seems to grow stronger the longer we move beyond their presence in everyday life.

This book, with its collection of chapters about heritage railways from around the world, seeks to understand and explain our relationship with these relics of another age. From both a practical and a theoretical perspective, the history, growth, challenges and future of heritage railways within the context of tourism will be explored. In doing so, the following chapters will consider the principal issues which define and challenge railway heritage and its relationship with tourism. They will look to some well known and some not so well known examples of railway heritage to illustrate these issues. In doing so, they will inexorably focus on what seems to work with railway heritage and, inevitably, what does not. The book will end with a summary of the key issues and some lessons about success and failure in the railway heritage field in the context of tourism, which may offer insights into how to make this specialized and costly tourism experience sustainable.

What is Railway Heritage?

Like so much of our world, things which seem fairly simple are usually significantly more complex than they appear. This is true of railway heritage and its relationship with tourism. Unlike some other forms of industrial heritage tourism, such as motoring heritage, the very scale and immensity of railway infrastructure militates against private ownership and operation of heritage railways. In this sense, heritage railways have a lot in common with mining heritage attractions. Many of the issues facing heritage railways mirror those in the mining heritage niche (Conlin & Jolliffe, 2011: 3–6), including but not limited to:

- preservation versus commercialization and the related issues of com-modification and replication;
- the financing of heritage attraction development and the operation and maintenance of the attractions;
- skill retention and training in vanishing trades and crafts;
- land and infrastructure ownership;
- health and safety of employees, volunteers and visitors;
- and the now ubiquitous focus on sustainability in all its varied facets.

These practical considerations are critical elements in the development, maintenance and operation of successful heritage attractions and especially heritage railway attractions. But they are not the only considerations for professionals and enthusiasts, planners and volunteers. All of these practical considerations must be viewed through the theoretical and very real prism of the visitor and her or his motivations, expectations and experiences.

As a starting point for our exploration of this topic, defining heritage railway tourism will provide a framework for examination. Hudson in his discussion of railway hotels in Chapter 2 provides a framework to explain the role of hotels in the development of early railway travel and their current role in heritage railway tourism. In doing so, he highlights the expansive nature of the niche; it is not simply locomotives but the entire range of infrastructure that supports the building and operation of railways. Stefanovic and Koster in Chapter 3 seek to define 'railfans', their characteristics, their motivations and, importantly, their impact and influence on railway tourism development. Porterfield in Chapter 8 explores the further commercialization of train travel by defining the unique culinary experience which is a large part of many heritage railway attractions. In varying ways, the other authors also provide examples of railway heritage which explain the movement and its role in tourism.

Industry and professional associations also provide definitions of railway heritage. The European Federation of Museum and Tourist Railways (FEDECRAIL) defines heritage railways as including:

> historic or preserved railways, museum railways and tramways, working railway and tram museums and tourist railways, and may extend to heritage trains operating on the national network and other railways. (FEDECRAIL, n.d.)

The Heritage Railway Association in the UK defines the niche to include heritage and tourist railways, tramways, stations and maintenance buildings, museums, railway preservation groups, rail cableways, and steam centers and cliff lifts (Heritage Railway Association, n.d.). These definitions and frameworks, drawn as they have been from the development of the heritage railway movement over the past 60 years, serve to remind us just how broad, complex and fascinating the world of heritage railways is. This perspective is well supported by the range of heritage railway attractions discussed in the following chapters.

The Origins of Railway Heritage

The origins of the modern heritage railway movement can be traced back primarily to the technological development of diesel electric motive power by most railroads in developed economies, a period which ironically parallels the switch from propeller-driven aircraft to jet propulsion, namely the 1950s and the early 1960s. During this period, these two major transportation modalities changed dramatically, both in terms of technology and, it can be argued, in terms of culture. Two early examples of a recognition of this momentous change and the consequent rise in interest in preserving the past for both modalities can be found with the preservation movement directed at saving the Puffing Billy line in Australia in the 1950s and the impetus to preserve locomotives and other railway infrastructure in the UK in the early 1960s. The Puffing Billy Preservation Society was founded in 1955 and over the past six decades has grown into a successful management structure which underlies what is arguably one of the world's most successful heritage railways (Puffing Billy Preservation Society, n.d.). The development of the modern UK heritage railway movement was motivated in no small part by the Beeching report of 1963 – what was known colloquially as the 'Beeching axe' – which led to the demise of the steam era in the UK.

None of these frameworks and definitions, however, explains fully our fascination with heritage railways. There is a sense of nostalgia and romance associated with steam train travel that has not translated into modern railway travel. Collison's discussion of the downturn in ridership on the Grand Canyon Railway (Chapter 12) can be linked, at the very least anecdotally, with that line's move away from steam to diesel propulsion. As the following discussion shows, there is clearly more to this experience than vintage equipment, infrastructure and artefacts. As we have said above, these are important, and without them we would not have heritage railways. But by themselves, these collections of locomotives, passenger cars, stations and hotels, bridges and railway rights of way, documents and posters would simply be rich and interesting but nonetheless static displays of this specific aspect of our industrial transportation heritage. Underlying this broad focus on what are essentially management issues is another purpose of the present volume: to consider the meaning of railways to the human condition as a way to gain insight into why many are attracted to railways and, indeed, some might argue, entranced by them.

As this book demonstrates, the static display of equipment, infrastructure and artifacts is not sufficient to satisfy our fascination with this aspect of our heritage. We need to see the equipment in motion, we seek the sounds of the train whistle and the clanking of passenger cars being coupled, and we crave the unique smells of heritage railways and most particularly, the smell and sensation of steam. Above all, we desire the impact of the railway journey, if only for a short and fleeting time. It is this journey that captures the past for us and rekindles the nostalgia for rail travel that is the fundamental sustaining factor in this experience. In short, this final part is what fully defines heritage railways and explains in large part, our fascination with them.

The Railway Visitor's Experience

In their account of the relationship between landscape, tourism and meaning, Knudsen et al. (2008) argue that it is important to understand the attraction, those who are attracted, and the meaning they associate with a place. This theoretical perspective is adapted here in terms of railways as the tourist attraction, a product involving the train and associated buildings and artifacts as well as the passing landscapes that are viewed along the journey.

This conceptualization allows us to consider the experience of the railway traveler as shaped and defined by the experience and the landscape, not only with regard to gaining insights into visitor motivations and product positioning, but at a deeper level: what does he or she strive to capture with this experience that is distinct from other heritage experiences? For the mindful tourist (Moscardo, 1997), train travel may involve nostalgia, or a flight of childhood imagination, as Frost and Laing explore in Chapter 4. As Stefanovic and Koster note in Chapter 3, there are many different personas of tourists attracted to railways, including those seeking nostalgia. In addition, there are passengers who enjoy the opportunity to live in the present, gazing through the carriage window while grazing on a sandwich from a backpack or something more sumptuous in the dining car, as Porterfield examines in Chapter 8. The experience involves physical movement, sightseeing at a leisurely pace and allowing one to dwell in the present. Traveling by rail provides the unique opportunity to do nothing but reflect while watching the world go by, no small matter in the 21st century, characterized by speed and detachment.

What is most distinct about trains is the journey itself, the seemingly effortless movement offering passing vistas that capture the sense of adventure that is travel. Flying from Singapore to Paris, one can leave in the late evening and 14 hours later enjoy a croissant and coffee for breakfast in France – quite magical indeed. And yet the gradual geographical and cultural transition from Asia to Europe, the essence of 'the journey', will have been missed. In his epic four-month round trip train journey from Europe to Southeast Asia, Theroux (1975) captured this contrast magnificently in *The Great Railway Bazaar*. Reading the book nearly 40 years since it was first published, one can skip through time to peek not only into the world of rail travel in the 1970s, but the places, vistas and cultures of that era. In short, rail travel is a mode of travel celebrating as much the experience of motion, the passengers aboard as well as the passing landscapes and peoples as it is about reaching the destination. This may well explain why heritage railways attract such a widespread and devoted following, whereas the fascination with propeller-powered aviation prior to the introduction of jet propulsion, while vibrant, nostalgic and significant, has never reached the levels of interest in and commitment enjoyed by heritage railways.

Railways as Heritage Tourism

As is the case with other aspects of cultural heritage and industrial heritage development, railway infrastructure is often seen as an economic panacea for destinations with depressed or declining economies (Hospers,

2002; see also Firth, 2011). Many railway sites have been rejuvenated or converted to alternative tourist use, such as bike and walking trails, a topic explored by Reis and Jellum in relation to the development of the Otago Central Rail Trail in New Zealand in Chapter 7. Issues relating to economic viability (Orbaşli & Woodward, 2008; see also Firth, 2011), market and product development and management (Hughes & Carlsen, 2010) and sustainable development (Landorf, 2009) abound in the field of railway tourism. This book examines a number of them: Collison discusses the recent ridership and financial challenges faced by the Grand Canyon Railway in Chapter 12; Yan and Xingcheng's examination in Chapter 16 of the economic, social and political process currently underway with respect to the Yunnan–Vietnam Railway illustrates the complex web of interests and constituencies challenging heritage railway development; and Found's discussion of myriad challenges faced in establishing the St Kitts Scenic Railway and its subsequent success in Chapter 17 are all excellent examples.

In contrast, other jurisdictions struggle to create or even maintain a foothold in establishing an economically viable operation without ongoing government support, leaving rail projects economically vulnerable to cutbacks. Conlin and Prideaux in Chapter 18 bring the reader's attention not only to the early successes enjoyed by the West Coast Wilderness Railway in Tasmania but, perhaps more importantly, the urgency of continued government support for the project after a decade of what seemed like a very successful operation. Investment is a challenge, and without investment in infrastructure and maintenance there is little chance of establishing a railway as a tourism product. Such issues of economic viability and funding are directly or indirectly linked to the list of critical success factors (CSFs) drawn up by Hughes and Carlsen (2010: 21) for commercially viable heritage tourism sites. Their nine CSFs are:

(1) agreed objectives and clear concepts (for the organization);
(2) financial planning for budgeting, capital raising and price setting;
(3) effective marketing strategies based on sound market research;
(4) monitoring of proximity to major markets and visitor flows;
(5) effective human resource management, including paid staff and volunteers;
(6) planning for product differentiation, life cycles and value adding;
(7) quality and authenticity of products and experiences;
(8) engagement of cultural heritage and tourism expertise in conservation and promotion;
(9) interpretation as an integral part of the heritage tourism experience.

To that list, we could add the role of volunteers in sustaining heritage railway operations. Several chapters in this book offer further insight into the range of opportunities and challenges facing heritage railways.

As an industry, tourism is aware of the general fascination with train travel, highlighted by epic journeys such as the Ghan (Adelaide to Darwin, Australia), the Blue Train (Pretoria to Cape Town, South Africa), or the Trans-Siberian (Moscow to Vladivostok, Russia). Railways have provided escape to the picturesque countryside from industrial and urban growth since the mid-1800s (Atkinson, 2012). Often regarded as the first major form of mass transport, railways hastened the formation of tour operators such as Thomas Cook and Son in 1841 (see Williamson, 1998). Worldwide, railways initiated the development of destinations marked by momentous architecture in the form of stations and grand hotels (see Hart, 1983; Minnis, 2011). As Hart argues, the Canadian Pacific Railway was fully engaged in tourism as early as the 1880s, when William Cornelius Van Horne stated 'If we can't export the scenery, we'll import the tourists' (Hart, 1983: 7). The construction of railways involves epic stories in themselves, as in the case of Australia's railway employing camels (see Adam-Smith, 1974), or the traversing of canyons and valleys in British Columbia's Cascade Mountains by Andrew McCulloch and the Kettle Valley Railway (Sanford, n.d.) and, of course, Van Horne's hotel creations examined by Hudson in Chapter 2.

Weaving throughout this book is a story that speaks to the formation, sustenance and growth of communities, regions and nations. In this way, railways are often seen as an extension of the nation's ambition, their steel and iron embodying industrial power and geographic reach. As a heritage attraction, Graham *et al.* (2000) note the railway's continued significance in conveying national identity. Whereas many preservation railways may be seen as benign, there are those that do speak to the issue of nationalism. Henderson's exploration of the interesting issues surrounding the Singapore and Malayan railways in Chapter 13 illustrates this point. Yan and Xingcheng's discussion of the Yunnan–Vietnam Railway makes this point even more dramatically and in a clearly historical context. Even so, wondering who controls railway heritage may be seen to be a lost leader, so it is not typically such a concern as finding the resources and support to maintain it. Nonetheless, if we think back to the notion that many of our heritage railway attractions have, do and will continue to rely to varying degrees on public funding and support, this issue is not irrelevant.

The concept of tourism as a world-making agent (Hollinshead, 2009) is useful here. The term refers to the role tourism plays in defining, making, shaping or creating places, sometimes flawed, sometimes false, but nevertheless the lens through which the world understands a culture and its heritage. Railways as attractions – be they the Puffing Billy train ride that White writes about in Chapter 15, the Vietnam–Kunming Railway presented by Yan and Xingcheng in Chapter 16 or the grand railway hotels of North America as explored by Hudson in Chapter 2 – provide a unique world-making lens through which to view heritage and culture. Certainly, the heritage–railway–tourism nexus is an interesting focus for many authors in this book. Railways can represent a certain past, perhaps described as a time of early adventure, exploration, expansion or colonization. Authors Fraga, Santos and Ribeiro in their account of Brazilian railways (Chapter 10) and Collison in his account of Grand Canyon Railway (Chapter 12) illustrate the railway as a dominant symbol representing the culture of the nation, embodying emotional, social and even ideological meanings. Turner (1967: 31) defines a dominant symbol as a shrine. A 'forest' of instrumental symbols forms a collective of 'significata' that can be unified to form a dominant symbol (Turner, 1967: 28). In the context of this book, instrumental symbols are the trains, buildings, uniforms, signage, timetable boards, even ticket stubs that make up a railway heritage experience.

Whereas scenery offered from dome cars and open carriages is often a major attraction, the trains themselves are also a magnet for visitors. Unlike the globally mass-produced automobiles and aircraft, vintage locomotives differ from nation to nation in terms of their physical design, as if a reflection of their society and its culture. For example, the massive steam engines of China are compelling for their grandeur as well as their power, in contrast to the diminutive character of a shunting engine. Much of a discussion on the technical elements will be perhaps only fully understood and mesmerizing to a niche audience but, as with many tourism experiences, there is a range of motivations and meanings that are co-constructed by train travelers.

Rees *et al.* (2010: 102) argue that it is important to preserve and operate steam engines, as opposed to putting them only on static display, as a way to maintain the association and meaning of the railway. They note that, as with many heritage sites, there is a juxtaposition between authenticity and conservation, on the one hand, and the operational uses of the artifact for tourist purposes, on the other. They argue that the way to avoid mitigating heritage integrity is by addressing interrelated combinations of maintenance, preservation, restoration, reconstruction, adaptation and interpretation. The issue of authenticity also gains some important practical discussion here, as Josephine Pryce examines the relationship between this ubiquitous concept in tourism studies and safety in Chapter 6.

This romanticization of heritage railways, the making and connecting of places as well as building commerce engendered by railways, must also acknowledge its dark heritage. As vividly described by Yan and Xingcheng in

Chapter 16, the construction of the Yunnan–Vietnam line was accomplished by the use of cheap and slave labor, working in horrifying conditions; the line was blasted through mountains and it traversed valleys and canyons and plains at a significant cost to life and limb. The St Kitts Scenic Railway described by Found in Chapter 17 is tangentially guilty by association with its somewhat sinister origins in slavery in the Caribbean. This dark tourist legacy can be very prominent in the heritage of a railway, such as at Kanchanaburi province, Thailand, the site of the bridge over the River Kwai and a condensation site for the story of the Burma Railway. For an account of the prisoners' conditions, see Wright (2008). This railway, known colloquially as the 'Death Railway', is often described in terms of the number of sleepers that form the rail bed along the 415 km line, equal to the number of prisoners of war who died in its construction. Braithwaite and Leiper (2010) raise some of the classic concerns with regard to dark tourism sites, defined as sites associated with death, tragedy and the macabre, such as heritage dissonance (Tunbridge & Ashworth, 1996), and the unique challenges associated with managing such sites (see Seaton, 2009). This topic is noted only to reflect the broad spectrum of heritage narrative embodied in these artifacts, and to point to an area for future research.

Our nostalgia can also blind us to the pollution associated with railways. The inefficiencies of the steam engine, the soot and grime eroding building facades, the lung-damaging air quality as well as the line of human waste strewn along the tracks are all aspects that are left out of the imagery of calendars and picture books. To address this concern, preservation railways have adapted. For example, the Grand Canyon Railway (Chapter 12) has achieved ISO 14001 certification for its environmental management practices, including the operation of its 90-year-old steam engine, adapted to run on used vegetable oil (see 'environmental initiatives' at www.thetrain. com). Many have also moved to enclosed septic systems, minimizing the negative impact on the environment.

The Future of Heritage Railway Tourism

As we have discussed above, railways have heralded the exploration of continents and the development of towns, cities and nations, enabled the peaceful movement of commodities and ideas, and supplied the humanity and materiel for growth, warfare and profound cultural and social change in the past two centuries. In addition, the railway has facilitated expansion of our own individual worlds, both real and imaginary. On this last point, if given the opportunity, to what stories would trains and stations speak? They could no doubt offer witness to the love, laughter, drama and tragedy of passengers, the historic events and the passing of eras that have transpired on platforms and onboard trains journeying from place to place all over the world.

Imbued in the engines, carriages and architecture is a heritage that connects with us on many levels and in many ways with the past as well as with who we are. Many authors have captured the fascinating history of the railway, such as Simmons (1991) on the Victorian railways, or more recently the thorough account by Cossons (2010) of the history, revitalization and influence of St Pancras Station, London; there are simply too many to list here. Aside from historical accounts, our cultural memory of railways and rail travel, often described as founded on nostalgia, is fed in part by literary works. Classics such as *Murder on the Orient Express* (Christie, 1934), *The Railway Children* (Nesbit, 1906) and the Harry Potter series (Rowling, 1997–2007) have continued to capture the magic of railways in both book and film. This point is substantially expanded on by Frost and Laing in Chapter 4.

In his book exploring railways from the perspectives of landscape, land use and society, Turnock (1982: ix) noted that the subject area was 'relatively untouched'. Over 30 years later, and as with many books, we may be apt to say the same thing in an attempt to lay claim to some untouched territory of research. Of course, there have been many valuable contributions to the subject of this book. Railway enthusiasts would be quick to note the thousands of popular history books, magazines and small-run editions about little-known stations, the intricacies of timetables and railway operations, certain classes of steam engine, railway companies, electric and diesel engines and the characters who worked on the railway. Whereas many books exist, we stand in a different place and time in terms not only of railway evolution but also of the growing fascination with railway heritage. A glance at the references used in various chapters in this book will support the rich variety of materials that our authors employ. We do, though, recognize the need to expand the scope of railway literature, if only to support the numerous efforts around the world to take advantage of railway heritage in the name of economic benefit, as well as of supporting local culture and heritage.

References

Adam-Smith, P. (1974) *Romance of Australian Railways*. London: Hale.
Atkinson, N. (2012) 'Call of the beaches': Rail travel and the democratisation of holidays in interwar New Zealand. *Journal of Transport History* 33 (1), 1–20.
Braithwaite, R.W. and Leiper, N. (2010) Contests on the River Kwai: How a wartime

tragedy became a recreational, commercial and nationalistic plaything. *Current Issues in Tourism* 13 (4), 311–332.

Christie, A. (1934) *Murder on the Orient Express*. London: W. Collins, Sons & Co.

Conlin, M.V. and Jolliffe, L. (2011) What happens when mining leaves? In M.V. Conlin and L. Jolliffe (eds) *Mining Heritage and Tourism* (pp. 3–10). London: Routledge.

Cossons, N. (2010) Oubliez Waterloo: The St Pancras effect. *Industrial Archaeology Review* 32 (2), 129–142.

FEDECRAIL (n.d.) The Riga Charter. See http://www.fedecrail.org/en/index_en.html (accessed 3 April 2013).

Firth, T.M. (2011) Tourism as a means to industrial heritage conservation: Achilles' heel or saving grace? *Journal of Heritage Tourism* 6 (1), 45–62.

Graham, B.J., Ashworth, G.J. and Tunbridge, J.E. (2000) *A Geography of Heritage: Power, Culture, and Economy*. London: Arnold.

Ha, I.S. and Grunwell, S.S. (2011) The economic impact of a heritage tourism attraction on a rural economy: The Great Smoky Mountains railroad. *Tourism Analysis* 16 (5), 629–636.

Hart, E.J. (1983) *The Selling of Canada: The CPR and the Beginnings of Canadian Tourism*. Banff: Altitude Publications.

Heritage Railway Association (n.d.) http://heritagerailways.com (accessed 31 March 2013).

Hollinshead, K. (2009) The 'worldmaking' prodigy of tourism: The reach and power of tourism in the dynamics of change and transformation. *Tourism Analysis* 14 (1), 139–152.

Hospers, G-J. (2002) Industrial heritage tourism and regional restructuring in the European Union. *European Planning Studies* 10 (3), 397–404.

Hughes, M. and Carlsen, J. (2010) The business of cultural heritage tourism: Critical success factors. *Journal of Heritage Tourism* 5 (1), 17–32.

Knudsen, D.C., Metro-Roland, M., Soper, A.K. and Greer, E. (eds) (2008) *Landscape, Tourism, and Meaning*. Aldershot: Ashgate.

Landorf, C. (2009) A framework for sustainable heritage management: A study of UK industrial heritage sites. *International Journal of Heritage Studies* 15 (6), 494–510.

Minnis, J. (2011) *Britain's Lost Railways: The Twentieth-Century Destruction of Our Finest Railway Architecture*. London: Aurum.

Moscardo, G. (1997) Mindful tourists: Heritage and tourism. *Annals of Tourism Research* 23 (2), 376–397.

Nesbit, E. (1906) *The Railway Children*. Harmondsworth: Penguin (1960).

Orbaşli, A. and Woodward, S. (2008) A railway 'route' as a linear heritage attraction: The Hijaz railway in the Kingdom of Saudi Arabia. *Journal of Heritage Tourism* 3 (3), 159–175.

Puffing Billy Preservation Society (n.d.) http://www.puffingbilly.com.au/puffing-billy-preservation-society (accessed 31 March 2013).

Rees, J., Jarman, P. and Gwyn, D. (2010) The conservation of operational steam locomotives. *Industrial Archaeology Review* 32 (2), 91–102.

Sanford, B. (n.d.) McCulloch's wonder. The story of the Kettle Valley railway. At http://www.nald.ca/library/learning/okanagan/history/2railway.pdf (accessed 14 April 2013).

Seaton, A.V. (2009) Purposeful otherness: Approaches to the management of thana-tourism. In R. Sharpley and P. Stone (eds) *The Darker Side of Travel: The Theory and Practice of Dark Tourism* (pp. 75–108). Bristol: Channel View Publications.

Simmons, J. (1991) *The Victorian Railway*. London: Thames and Hudson.

Theroux, P. (1975) *The Great Railway Bazaar: By Train Through Asia*. London: Penguin Books (2008).

Tunbridge, J.E. and Ashworth, G.J. (1996) *Dissonant Heritage: The Management of the Past as a Resource in Conflict*. Chichester: Wiley.

Turner, V.W. (1967) *The Forest of Symbols: Aspects of Ndembu Ritual*. Thaca: Cornell University Press.

Turnock, D. (1982) *Railways in the British Isles: Landscape, Land Use and Society*. London: Black.

Unwin, P. (1981) *Travelling by Train in the Twenties and Thirties*. London: Allen and Unwin.

Williamson, A. (1998) *The Golden Age of Travel: The Romantic Years of Tourism in Images from the Thomas Cook Archives*. Peterborough: Thomas Cook Publishing.

Wright, P. (2007) *The Men of the Line: Stories of the Thai–Burma Railway Survivors*. Melbourne: Miegunyah.

Part 2

Issues, Themes and Trends

2 Railway Hotels: From Infrastructure to Destination

Bradford T. Hudson

Introduction

Railroads and hotels have been intertwined since railroads were first conceived in the early 19th century. At the simplest level, railroads offered transportation to travelers, who subsequently needed accommodation away from home. Any town with a significant railroad station also had a hotel within a short distance. A deeper historical examination reveals an integrated system of development and ownership, in which railroads or railroad investors built hotels throughout the United States and Canada.

Hotels as Infrastructure

Railroad hotels performed several functions. First, they served as warehouses to inventory passengers within the transportation production system. Travelers would arrive in the vicinity of a railroad station individually, at various times and by various means of conveyance. They would wait at the hotel until the designated boarding time, when they would be loaded quickly and collectively aboard the train. Railroad hotels were an important tool for managing the flow of passengers at interim stops along a route, when timing was critical, and for managing large quantities of customers at urban termination points.

Second, hotels offered basic services to railroad passengers on extended journeys and railroad employees in remote locations. During the early years, sleeping cars and dining cars did not exist. Even after such onboard services were introduced, practical considerations sometimes precluded their use. In some cases, railroads established extensive support operations in previously isolated areas, resulting in large numbers of people traveling for business purposes related to the railroad.

Third, hotels were important strategic resources and investment vehicles. Railroads were the largest and most financially sophisticated business entities in the United States during the 19th century (Chandler, 1977). As such, they commanded vast amounts of capital and pioneered a variety of strategic approaches, including vertical integration. Hotels represented an excellent opportunity for investment and diversification. Although railroad companies received significant financial support from private investors, they also benefited from government land grants intended to encourage and accelerate railroad development (Taylor, 1951). As a result, railroad companies often had significant land holdings adjacent to their tracks, which could be developed to produce additional returns. This contributed to the construction of hotels, either by the railroad companies themselves or by their partners and leaseholders.

All three purposes – warehousing passengers, providing basic services to passengers and employees, and serving as investment vehicles – could be categorized as infrastructural. Hotels were components within integrated and complex transportation systems, which complemented and facilitated basic railroad operations. They were also important elements in the financial and strategic structure of railroads as business entities. The basic nature and function of railroads in North America cannot be fully understood without considering the role of their subsidiary and allied hotels.

The first major railroad company in the United States was the Baltimore & Ohio Railroad, which was chartered in 1827 and began operating in 1830. The first lodging property associated with a railroad was the City Hotel in Baltimore, which opened in 1826 with financial backing from an investor who would subsequently serve as the first treasurer of the Baltimore & Ohio (Sandoval-Strausz, 2007). The hotel was intended to serve the existing needs of travelers in Baltimore, but it was also envisioned as the point of origin for the railroad being planned. As the Baltimore & Ohio expanded westward, the company also developed its own network of hotels, located within or adjacent to its stations. Among the first was a hotel in Grafton, Virginia (now West Virginia), which opened in 1852.

The pattern of railroad companies building hotels adjacent to their operations continued as the 19th century unfolded. Other early examples included the Susquehanna House in Susquehanna, Pennsylvania (built by the Erie Railway in 1865) and the Laramie Hotel in Laramie, Wyoming (built by the Union Pacific Railroad in 1868). Logan House (built by the Pennsylvania Railroad in 1854) in Altoona, Pennsylvania, was intended to support an adjacent repair and maintenance complex for locomotives. Mount Stephen House (built by the Canadian Pacific Railway in 1886) in Field, British Columbia, was originally a dining station, so the railroad could avoid pulling heavy dining cars through the mountain passes between Alberta and British Columbia (Chisholm, 2001).

By the early 20th century, railroad hotels in major cities had become significant business entities in themselves. These included the Hotel Pennsylvania in New York City (built by the Pennsylvania Railroad in 1919 and operated by Statler Hotels) and the Château Laurier in Ottawa (built by the Grand Trunk Railway in 1912). The Canadian Pacific Railway became well known for its portfolio of impressive urban hotels, including the Hotel Vancouver in Vancouver (1888), the Place Viger in Montreal (1898), the Royal Alexandra in Winnipeg (1906), the Empress Hotel in Victoria (1908), the Palliser Hotel in Calgary (1914) and the Royal York Hotel in Toronto (1929).

Hotels as Destinations

The railroad sector expanded rapidly during the second quarter of the 19th century and the existing population centers in the United States were connected by 1850 (Taylor, 1951). As the industry matured, railroad companies searched for new ways to increase revenues, to differentiate themselves from competitors, to overcome saturation and to sustain their financial growth. The generic solutions were to build new routes or increase revenue along existing routes. The former could be accomplished by expanding westward, while the latter could be achieved by encouraging discretionary travel.

The macroeconomic conditions were especially conducive to increasing discretionary travel for leisure purposes. On the supply side, the railroads were improving on virtually every measure of performance, including capacity, affordability, convenience, speed and safety (Taylor, 1951). On the demand side, the economic multiplying effects of the Industrial Revolution were resulting in significant increases in income levels and wealth. Average people were increasingly able to indulge in leisure activities that were previously reserved only for the aristocracy. This included travel to the mountains and the seashore, which offered more pleasant summer temperatures in the age before air conditioning. It also included travel to exotic locations, not only along the established route of the Grand Tour in Europe, but also in the western regions of North America.

As a result, many railroad companies adopted a destination strategy for the consumer sector. They constructed rail lines to isolated locations and then developed grand hotels at the termination points. Assuming that demand for such a hotel would emerge, the railroad could then collect revenues not only from the operation of the hotel itself, but also from transportation fees that would be generated by hotel guests and the surrounding community. The railroad companies were not building these hotels to respond to existing demand conditions, but rather were creating entirely new routes to induce demand.

Among the first such destinations was the Deer Park Hotel in Deer Park, Maryland (which was built by the Baltimore & Ohio Railroad in 1873). This became a favorite vacation destination for affluent consumers in the mid-Atlantic region, and the property subsequently hosted an array of dignitaries, including several Presidents of the United States.

Other railroads quickly followed this model. Early destination resorts built by railroad companies included the Grand Hotel on Mackinac Island, Michigan (built by a consortium that included the Michigan Central Railroad and the Grand Rapids & Indiana Railroad in 1887), the Old Faithful Inn at Yellowstone Park in Wyoming (built by the Northern Pacific Railroad in 1904), El Tovar Hotel at the Grand Canyon in Arizona (built by the Atchison, Topeka and Santa Fe Railroad in 1905 and operated by the Fred Harvey Company) and the Greenbrier Hotel in West Virginia (built by the Chesapeake & Ohio Railroad in 1913).

Although railroads often built more than one destination property, several railroads became associated with portfolios of multiple celebrated hotels. The Florida East Coast Railway built the Hotel Ponce de León in St Augustine (1888), the Royal Poinciana Hotel in Palm Beach (1894), the Breakers in Palm Beach (known as the Palm Beach Inn upon opening in 1896) and the Royal Palm Hotel in Miami (1897). The Great Northern Railway built the Glacier Park Lodge in Montana (1913), the Many Glacier Hotel in Montana (1915) and the Prince of Wales Hotel in Alberta (1927). The Union Pacific Railroad built the Bryce Canyon Lodge in Utah (1925), the Zion Lodge in Utah (1925), the Grand Canyon Lodge in Arizona (1928) and the Sun Valley Lodge in Idaho (1936). The Canadian Pacific Railway was involved in building the Château Frontenac in Quebec (1893), which it subsequently acquired outright. Canadian Pacific also built the Château Lake Louise in Alberta (1894) and the Banff Springs Hotel in Alberta (1888).

Hotels as Icons

Many of the later railroad hotels were large and picturesque, with architecture or settings that were intended to impress guests and generate publicity. Some adopted architectural styles that were reminiscent of grand European palaces, such as the Canadian château hotels derived from French and Scottish influences (Kalman, 1968; Liscombe, 1993). Others were more modest, with stylistic elements borrowed from wilderness log cabins, but these were nonetheless extraordinary in reflecting the quintessential character of their natural surroundings.

Over time, these impressive hotels became embedded in the popular imagination. They were preferred destinations for travelers, required stops for sightseers, familiar images for regional tourism promotions and focal points for local community identity. As retrospection and nostalgia developed into widespread phenomena, railroad hotels served as instruments of historical utopianism related to a golden age of travel. These hotels became icons of special geographic locations, important historic eras and meaningful cultural narratives.

In many cases, the importance of such hotels has been officially recognized. In the United States, several former railroad hotels have been designated National Historic Landmarks, including the Bryce Canyon Lodge, the Grand Canyon Lodge, the Grand Hotel, the Greenbrier Hotel and the Hotel Ponce de León. In Canada, several former railroad hotels have been designated National Historic Sites, including the Banff Springs Hotel, the Château Laurier, the Empress Hotel and the Prince of Wales Hotel. Many of the other railroad hotels are listed on the National Register of Historic Places in the United States or the Canadian Register of Historic Places.

Railroads Eclipsed

As a financial and transportation phenomenon, the American railroads reached their peak at the beginning of the 20th century. Thereafter they experienced steady declines in financial performance, while aircraft and motor vehicles increasingly assumed a dominant position in passenger travel. By 1960, nearly half of all commercial long-distance passengers traveled by air and another quarter traveled by bus (Stover, 1997).

As a result, none of the major railroads achieved profitability in passenger operations after 1945. Similar problems in freight operations led to the collapse or merger of several major railroads. The largest of these occurred when the New York Central Railroad and the Pennsylvania Railroad combined to form the Penn Central in 1968, which subsequently declared bankruptcy in 1970. This signaled the end of the railroad era (Stover, 1997).

The situation in Canada was little different. The Canadian National Railway was formed in 1918, as an amalgamation of several bankrupt or struggling railroads. It then absorbed the Grand Trunk Railway in 1920. Meanwhile, the Canadian Pacific Railway was experiencing similar problems in its passenger operations (Lamb, 1977). During the period 1946–75, the number of rail passengers throughout Canada declined about 45%, despite a corresponding population increase of about 85% (Statistics Canada, 1999:

tables A1 and T39–46). This led to the formation of the nationalized Via Rail organization, which in 1978 assumed all passenger operations from both the Canadian National and the Canadian Pacific Railways.

There were two general effects on railroad hotels during the period of railroad decline. First, many were sold. They were purchased by hotel companies, insurance companies, pension funds and investment syndicates. The final chapter in the story of railroad hotels was written in Canada at the turn of the millennium, when the last major railroad company to own hotels divested its portfolio. The Canadian Pacific Railway acquired several hotels from the rival Canadian National Railway in 1988 and then acquired Fairmont Hotels in 1999. The railroad division was then separated from the hotel division when the Canadian Pacific conglomerate was broken apart in 2001, and the former hotel division subsequently adopted the Fairmont brand for its new independent corporate identity (Fairmont, n.d.).

Second, as railroad passenger traffic declined, the majority of hotel visitors eventually arrived by other modes of transportation. As an example, consider the Banff Springs Hotel in Alberta. A transportation study conducted for the Town of Banff in 1998 found that 81% of visitors arrived by single-occupancy vehicle, 17% by motorcoach (bus) and 2% by all other types of transportation (Banff, 1998). This phenomenon was a catalyst for a major reconstruction of the hotel in 2001. The main entrance was moved from the valley side of the building, a grand new lobby was built to accommodate tour groups and a huge arrival ramp with multiple lanes was constructed for motorcoaches (Hudson, 2011).

As the more impressive station and destination hotels became famous in their own right, and as railroad travel and railroad ownership of them decreased, the identities of such hotels eventually became separated from their railroad heritage. During the past decade, the author has conducted hundreds of informal interviews of guests at numerous former railroad hotels in the United States and Canada. Most leisure travelers, and the vast majority of business travelers, were completely unaware of any railroad history connected to these hotels. The value proposition for most guests was related to an appreciation of the historic architecture, enthusiasm for the surroundings of the hotel or practical consumer issues such as price and location.

Heritage Tourism in Canada

Although the current identities of many former railroad hotels are disconnected from their railroad heritage, a notable exception is the group of Canadian railroad hotels currently managed by Fairmont. Many of these remain together in a portfolio of historic properties, which has been supplemented by the addition of similar hotels built by other transportation companies, such as Le Manoir Richelieu in Quebec (built by Canada Steamship Lines in 1929). The heritage of these hotels is actively promoted by the current operators.

The author recently conducted site visits to numerous former railroad hotels in Canada (Hudson, 2011). These included the Château Frontenac in Quebec, the Château Laurier in Ottawa, the Royal York Hotel in Toronto, the Palliser Hotel in Calgary, the Banff Springs Hotel in Alberta and the Château Lake Louise in Alberta. All these hotels refer to their railroad heritage by displaying historical photographs of trains in their lobbies or adjoining public areas. In many cases, the hotels also exhibit vintage travel posters that were used to promote trains, hotels or destinations under the railroad brand (Choko & Jones, 2004).

At four of these hotels – the Château Frontenac, the Royal York Hotel, the Banff Springs Hotel and the Château Lake Louise – the lobby retail stores feature multiple items related to the era of ownership by the Canadian Pacific Railway. These include books about the history of the railroad and its hotels, reprints of vintage travel posters and souvenirs featuring images from the posters. In all cases, the Canadian Pacific brand is featured prominently in memorabilia, despite the current use of the Fairmont brand by the hotels.

The author conducted informal interviews of guests at these four hotels, probing for knowledge about railroad heritage (Hudson, 2011). As elsewhere, most guests traveling for business purposes were completely unaware of any railroad connection. This was especially true at urban hotels in the group, such as the Royal York Hotel and the Palliser Hotel. The results were dramatically different at hotels with a significant proportion of leisure travelers, such as the Banff Springs Hotel and the Château Lake Louise. Almost half of the leisure travelers were aware of the railroad heritage of these properties and most could identify the Canadian Pacific brand without prompting. A surprising number, representing more than one-quarter of all leisure travelers, could discuss some aspect of the history related to the railroad itself. It should be noted that none of the knowledgeable guests identified themselves as railroad enthusiasts, and none were engaged in any type of railroad tour, either independently or as a group. Despite their awareness about railroad heritage, these visitors were apparently attracted to the hotels for other reasons. However, it should also be noted that the author conducted these interviews during the winter and spring months. According to staff at the Banff Springs Hotel, the number of guests with an explicit interest in railroads increases during the summer months (Hudson, 2011). This undoubtedly relates to the sightseeing trains that still travel through western Canada, including those operated by Via Rail and the Rocky Mountaineer Company.

A particularly notable railroad experience is that currently offered aboard the Royal Canadian Pacific, which is the only passenger train still operated by the Canadian Pacific Railway. This leisure travel experience has a threefold value proposition for consumers. First, it offers stunning views as it travels through the Canadian Rocky Mountain region from its base in Calgary. Second, it offers a luxury hospitality experience with accommodation, meals and service similar to the current Orient Express trains in Europe. Third, it offers a historical experience beyond the anachronistic nature of railroad travel itself. The train comprises 10 passenger cars from the period 1926–31, and two diesel locomotives from the period 1946–60. All have been immaculately restored, with exterior livery from their respective eras. The website features a section about the heritage of the train and its equipment, famous passengers who have traveled aboard similar trains in the past and the history of the Canadian Pacific Railway (Royal Canadian Pacific, n.d.).

Tour packages include the Canadian Rockies Experience, a train journey through several Parks Canada sites, including Banff National Park. The route includes the town of Field in British Columbia, where the track passes the location of the (now demolished) Mount Stephen House, which was the first hotel built by the railroad. This tour also includes a visit to the Banff Springs Hotel. As such, the Royal Canadian Pacific offers a glimpse of the full evolution of railroad hotels in Canada, from the era of infrastructure to the era of destination to the era of icons.

Conclusion

During the 19th century, hotels were built near railroad stations throughout North America. In many cases, they were constructed by the railroad companies themselves to facilitate interchange related to rail travel, in manner similar to modern airport hotels. Subsequently, the companies realized that hotels built in spectacular locations could generate additional demand for rail travel and the destination resort was born. Eventually, these hotels became famous in their own right, with identities separate from the railroad companies that built them. Many of these hotels survive today and serve as symbolic reminders of the past. These different eras, which overlapped as they progressed, together represent a continuous evolution of railroad hotels, from elements of operational infrastructure to icons of a bygone era.

Today, the transportation history of such hotels has been largely forgotten, but a few have modern identities that are inseparable from their railroad heritage. Among these are the former hotels of the Canadian Pacific Railway. The railroad origins of these hotels are featured in lobby exhibits and retail memorabilia, and a surprising number of visitors are aware of this heritage. The interplay of transportation and tourism comes full circle in the province of Alberta, where the modern Canadian Pacific Railway operates the nostalgic Royal Canadian Pacific train for tourists, with sightseeing journeys that are seamlessly integrated with former Canadian Pacific properties such as the Banff Springs Hotel.

Many of the existing railroad hotels will probably survive through the next century, especially those built as magnificent destination resorts, which continue to fascinate and attract leisure travelers. Some properties may even maintain elements of railroad history in their modern identities. As such, these hotels may contribute to the creation of a new generation of railroad heritage enthusiasts, from a population lacking personal experience as railroad passengers. The public memory of these railroads may continue through their hotels.

References

Banff (1998) *Integrated Transportation Plan Final Report*. Banff, Alberta: Town of Banff.

Chandler, A.D. (1977) *The Visible Hand: The Managerial Revolution in American Business*. Cambridge, MA: Belknap Press.

Chisholm, B. (ed.) (2001) *Castles of the North: Canada's Grand Hotels*. Toronto: Lynx.

Choko, M.H. and Jones, D.L. (2004) *Posters of the Canadian Pacific*. Richmond Hill, Ontario: Firefly Books.

Fairmont (n.d.) 'The birth of the brand', on the corporate website, Fairmont Hotels & Resorts, http://www.fairmont.com/about-us/ourhistory (accessed 2012).

Hudson, B.T. (2011) Site visits to various Fairmont hotels in Canada. Unpublished field research.

Kalman, H.D. (1968) *The Railway Hotels and the Development of the Château Style in Canada*. Victoria, British Columbia: University of Victoria.

Lamb, W.K. (1977) *History of the Canadian Pacific Railway*. New York: Macmillan.

Liscombe, R.W. (1993) Nationalism or cultural imperialism? The château style in Canada. *Architectural History* 36, 127–144.

Royal Canadian Pacific (n.d.) Corporate website, http://www.royalcanadianpacific.com (accessed 2012).

Sandoval-Strausz, A.K. (2007) *Hotel: An American History*. New Haven, CT: Yale University Press.

Statistics Canada (1999) *Historical Statistics of Canada*. Ottawa: Government of Canada.

Stover, J.F. (1997) *American Railroads*. Chicago, IL: University of Chicago Press.

Taylor, G.R. (1951) *The Transportation Revolution, 1815–1860*. Armonk, NY: M.E. Sharpe.

3 Railfans and Railway Heritage Tourism

Kyle Stefanovic and Rhonda Koster

Introduction

Across North America (and other parts of the Western world), many rail enthusiasts are engaged in watching and photographing trains. Most often these aficionados go unnoticed, but increasingly small cities and towns are accommodating these 'railfans' by developing and building 'railfan parks'. A review of resources reveals that although there are many books, websites and magazines dedicated to railfans, virtually no academic research has been conducted on who railfans are, what their economic impact is and how communities seek to exploit this niche market. The purpose of this chapter is to address this void; it is based on Stefanovic's 2009 undergraduate and 2011 graduate research. We begin by examining the demographic profile of railfans, where they go and what they look for in a particular location. We then examine the development and economic impact of railfan tourism. We conclude by providing a summary of what has been examined to date and what future railfan tourism research could be conducted.

What is a Railfan? Determining a Definition

There are different terms used throughout the world to describe a railfan, such as a trainspotter, foamer, railnut and train enthusiast. The term 'railfan' is difficult to define because of the varied activities railfans engage in. For example, there are those who photograph, video or simply watch trains, while others build model trains, study rail history or collect train-related memorabilia. Each of these types can be further subdivided; for example, rail photographers can be broken down into subgroups who photograph only trains in scenic locations or who select locomotives associated with a particular roster, unique trains or those with special paint schemes. Clearly, the term 'railfan' involves many different variations and finding a single definition is further complicated by the fact that interest in trains is worldwide and is expressed in various ways reflective of geographic location. Stefanovic (2009: 12), reporting research into the demographic profile of railfans, offers this definition:

> A railfan is someone who has an overall interest in trains and who enjoys watching the day-to-day activities of the railway either during their leisure time or while on vacation.

There are many products and services available to railfans, such as videos, magazines, books, railfan guides, computer programs, radio scanners, computer games, model trains and railfan websites, along with several festivals and museums that are focused on trains. Such products and events help to illustrate the range of interests of this group and help to provide an indication of the number of train enthusiasts. For example, *Trains Magazine* estimates there are approximately 175,000 railfans in the US alone (Chen, 2009).

Who is a Railfan? Behavioral and Demographic Characteristics

During 2008, a research project to determine the demographic and behavioral characteristics of railfans was conducted (Stefanovic, 2009). Data were gathered through an online survey, available for three months, at the end of which there was a total of 1,475 usable surveys. A profile of railfans (including motivation, demographic characteristics, activities, destinations and expenditures) was created from analysis of the data.

In the survey, railfans were predominantly male (98%), mostly over 50 years of age (47%) and had an average income of between US$41,000 and $80,000. The research determined that railfans are distributed throughout the world but are predominantly from Western nations.

Although a number of motivations for becoming a railfan were reported, most individuals did so because of a general interest in trains, which they pursued in a variety of forms, the most popular of which was watching and photographing trains. Railfans tended to commit to this hobby for most of their adult life (averaging 35 years). They spent a great deal of time on the activity, on average taking pictures or watching trains approximately 22 times per month. Railfanning was also found to be very important to respondents, with the majority indicating that how they organized their life was affected by railfanning, and it was something that they considered as central to their personality and relationships.

When railfanning, 47% of respondents indicated that their preference was to railfan alone. Among the other 53% who undertook the activity with someone else, 32% of the total favoured the company of other railfans and 21% preferred to go with their family. Accompanying family members tended to visit local attractions or to go retail shopping while the respondent was railfanning.

The railfans incorporated railfanning as part of their vacation regardless of the primary purpose. However, they would select specific railfan destinations based on three criteria: the number of trains that can be viewed within a 24-hour period; a unique view from which to photograph and watch trains; and the variety of railroads in one location. The vast majority (over 93%) of respondents were willing to travel at least three hours to get to a railfan destination, with 54% of these willing to travel six or more hours. While at railfan destinations, they almost exclusively engaged in railfanning, but they also visited local attractions and occasionally went shopping. Based on responses, the following characteristics of railfan vacations were determined:

- the average distance traveled (in) was 1200 miles;
- there was an average of five people involved per trip;
- the average number of days spent on vacation was 6.84;
- the average amount spent was $1447.

Given the average length of time people indicated they had been railfanning (35 years) and the level of commitment they had, it is clear that respondents to the survey were a highly specialized group, and likely not representative of the broader railfan population. Despite this fact, Stefanovic's (2009) research illustrates the potential of this niche market for communities that possess the favorable attributes for railfans, and railfan parks offer one option.

Where Do They Go? Railfan Parks: Development and Impact

The development of railfan parks speaks to the tourism potential of this niche market. In 1998, Rochelle, Illinois, was the first North American community to build a site specifically for train watching (R. Freier, personal communication, 2011). Rochelle had been a popular railfan destination for years prior to the park's establishment, but in 1998 Rochelle's economic development officer (EDO) noticed there were many people loitering around the town's train tracks and realized that these people 'weren't bums or anything – they had fancy cameras, cars and radio scanners' (K. Wise, personal communication, 2011). The EDO felt that the City of Rochelle had an obligation to create a place for these railfans to watch trains safely, rather than having them sprawl all over the community. As a result, the city agreed to build a railfan platform, with a covered area and gift shop, at a main intersection in town where approximately 100 trains could be seen daily. Since its development, the park has hosted some 30,000–40,000 people per year (R. Freier, personal communication, 2011).

To further understand the development and economic impact of railfan tourism, a two-phase sequential mixed-methods research project was undertaken from 2009 to 2011 (Stefanovic, 2011). In phase 1, members of different communities were contacted and asked to complete an online survey. In phase 2, interviews were conducted in two case study communities: Rochelle, Illinois, which has an established railfan park, and Fostoria, Ohio, where a park was being established. The following paragraphs provide a summary of both phases of this research to contextualize the discussion that follows, regarding the economic potential of railfan tourism for communities choosing to embrace this niche market.

Results and discussion: The survey

Ingles (2001: 29) identifies the top 100 locations in North America where the highest number of trains can be viewed. These sites were selected as the target sample for an online survey, as previous research (Stefanovic, 2009) had indicated that railfans select locations based on the number of trains that can be seen in one day and this provided a way to standardize the sample. Of the 100 locations identified in the guide, 79 were identified as a discrete location and were therefore deemed to be 'contactable', given that a community was associated by proximity to the railfan location; 11 were identified as a railfan route (for example the Thompson River Valley, British Columbia), which involved numerous communities along the route and as a result were not contacted; the other 10 were identified as a railfan location not located close to or within a community and so not contactable.

Of the 79 contactable communities, three were in Canada and the remainder in the United States. The economic development officer or tourism director associated with each community was first emailed directly, informed of the research and requested to participate in the research project; follow-up telephone calls were also made. The email included a direct link to the survey, with questions focused on: determining whether or not the community was aware of railfan tourism, identifying how they catered to this niche market; and ascertaining an estimation of the economic impact that railfans had on the community and local business. The survey was implemented using Survey Monkey, an online survey tool. Of the 79 communities contacted, 49 completed the survey (response rate of 62%). Based on an analysis of the survey data, it is possible to gain a broad understanding of what has been developed for railfans in North America as well as an estimation of the economic impact. These results are summarized next.

While 40 of the 49 respondents indicated that they had noticed railfans in their community, only 24 communities (49%) indicated they had done something to provide a specific service; all these communities were in the United States. These respondents were then asked to identify what they had done to cater to this market (Figure 3.1), with 17 of the 24 participants providing multiple answers to this question. For example, a single community could have developed signage, built a railfan park and advertised to this niche market.

As illustrated in Figure 3.1, 12 of the 24 communities (50%) stated that they had developed signage to show railfans where to go in their community, 8 (33%) had created and distributed a map of railway locations in their town and 13 (54%) had advertised to this niche market via railfan-related

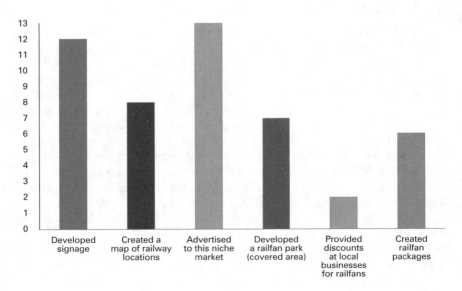

Figure 3.1 Railfan tourism development initiatives among 24 surveyed communities

magazines and websites and by attending railfan festivals. Two communities (8%) stated that local businesses provided discounts for railfans while they were in town and 6 (25%) stated that they had created railfan packages (i.e. put together and distributed information packages about their community, its railway history and its other attractions). Of the 24 communities, 7 (29%) stated that they had created a railfan park or covered area for railfans. An additional community stated in the 'other' category that they had cleared an area for future railfan park development. Communities also stated in the 'other' category that they hosted rail-related events or gatherings (5), had built a railway museum (2) or had created a website with live webcam to advertise their attractions (2).

Of the 24 communities stating they did provide services specifically for railfans, the majority indicated that they got the idea to do so from a local railfan. Creating the various services to accommodate railfans (including park creation) required various levels of governmental approval, especially related to funding. Fourteen communities (58%) stated they had needed local government approval, 8 (33%) had required community endorsement, 3 (13%) had needed state/provincial support and 1 (4%) stated that federal authorization was involved. Further examination reveals that 9 of the 24 communities (38%) needed approval from a single source, most often from the municipal government (5 communities) followed by community (2), state/provincial (1) and federal (1). Municipal and community approval was the most often indicated combination of approvals, with 4 of the 24 communities (17%) reporting needing both.

Funding for the railfan projects required financial investment from federal government in 3 communities, while 7 received money from their state/provincial government and 11 from their municipal government. Private organizations provided funding in 8 communities, while in another 8 communities it was a historical society; 12 communities received their funds through donations. In total, 14 of the 24 communities (58%) reported requiring two or more funding sources to complete their railfan tourism projects; only 5 projects were funded by a single source.

Of the 24 participants that had stated they catered to railfans, 21 (90%) indicated that railfan attractions were not their main tourism product, but part of a suite of tourism offerings.

Participants were asked to indicate the economic impact railfan tourism had had on their community. Many indicated that they had no way of being able to track the activities of railfans and as a result they provided best-guess estimates. They were asked to supply these estimates on a series of indicators, including the number of railfans visiting, length of their stay, spending, jobs supported by railfan tourism and tax revenues generated. A

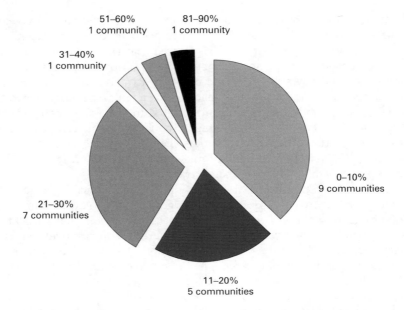

Figure 3.2 Economic impact of railfan tourism: Estimation of the proportion of the community's overall economic structure that was accounted for by railfan tourism among 24 surveyed communities

more general economic impact measure was an estimation of the proportion of the community's overall economic structure that was accounted for by railfan tourism. Figure 3.2 shows that 21 of the relevant 24 participating communities (88%) reported that railfan tourism made up less than 30% of their total economic structure.

As illustrated in Figure 3.3, total estimated railfan expenditures per year varied widely. Six (25%) communities reported railfans spending over $100,000, while another six reported spending estimates of $0–10,0000 per year.

The number of jobs generated by railfan tourism was estimated by 22 (92%) communities to be between 1 and 100. It appears that for most communities (17 of 24 or 71%) the taxes generated were low ($0–$10,000). However, three communities (13%) reported tax revenues of approximately $100,000 per year.

The estimated number of railfans visiting these communities ranged from a high of over 1000 per year for 7 of the 24 communities (29%); an

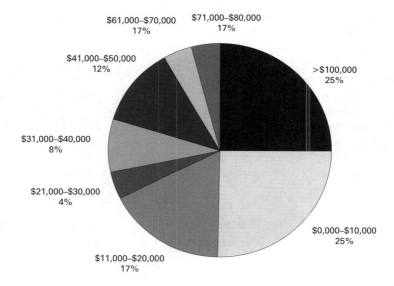

Figure 3.3 Estimates of total railfan tourism spending per year among 24 surveyed communities (note that no community reported a range of $51,000–$60,000)

additional three estimated the figure at 900–1000. On the other end of the spectrum, 14 of the 24 communities (58%) estimated receiving 0–400 railfans per year.

Twelve of the 24 (50%) communities estimated that railfans spent two days in their community, 8 (33%) communities stated that they spent one day, 3 (13%) communities three days and 1 community reported railfans spending five days. Thus, two-thirds of the communities reported that railfans stayed more than one day, which is significant in terms of the dollars that can be generated.

The seven communities that had developed railfan parks indicated that they received the greatest economic impact due to higher levels of visitation, length of stay and associated spending. Not surprisingly, these were also the communities that had created specific services for railfans, such as direct advertising, signage, railway maps of locations and railfan packages with local businesses. Although the communities with railfan parks were the ones that identified the greatest economic 'success', railfan tourism did provide some economic diversification in most communities, as it generated additional business for hotels and motels and food establishments, which in turn increased tax revenues generated in the area.

Railfan tourism is still an emerging tourism niche market, as the first railfan park was created in Rochelle, Illinois, only in 1998. Other communities have slowly become aware of the railfans visiting their area and have begun to develop services to better accommodate their needs. Respondents to the survey indicated that they were planning to do more in the future. The 25 communities contacted that were not aware of railfans suggested that if they were to gain more information about this niche market and its potential economic impact, they would consider development options to attract railfans.

Results and discussion: The case study

While the survey provided general information about what types of services had been developed for railfans and the consequent economic impact, it did not allow for a detailed understanding of the process of railfan park development. As a result, semi-structured interviews were conducted in two case study communities, Rochelle, Illinois, and Fostoria, Ohio, with 11 community officials involved in the development of railfan tourism in their community. The intent of these interviews was to explore how the railfan parks had been developed and what economic impacts the community had experienced as a result. Table 3.1 summarizes the way in which each community developed and funded its railfan tourism projects, along with an illustration of the economic impact.

When examining the common themes and differences across the cases, it is obvious that railfan parks in both communities were created to enhance tourism and economic development, based on the rail infrastructure and consequent variety and number of trains present within the communities. Fostoria chose railfan park development as an economic solution during a time of need, as the community had been experiencing significant economic decline since the 1990s in its automotive sector (D. Fligor, personal communication, 2011). In contrast, the local economy of Rochelle was strong when the idea to develop a railfan park emerged as part of an economic diversification strategy, specifically targeted at enhancing the retail and service sectors.

Both communities had conducted limited research regarding their railfan visitors. Visitor logs/sign-in books were used in both communities. Rochelle tracked visitors' license plates to get a sense of who was coming and a rough estimate of how many. Fostoria had done a short survey of

Table 3.1 Comparison of case study communities

	Rochelle, Illinois	Fostoria, Ohio
Park completed	1998	At time of case study, anticipated completion summer 2012
Idea	Noticing railfans blocking driveways	Noticed railfans and created train tourism group to understand these people and to discuss accommodating them
Research	Initially visitor data gathered from license plate count and through talking with railfans; visitor data now obtained through logbook at railfan park. Before the park was created, Horseshoe Curve had been visited to see what had been done there	Visitor data collected in survey included in railfan packages distributed at local hotel and to railfans sitting by the tracks. Rochelle had been visited to see what had been done there
Purpose	To generate tourism and get more money in the local tax base; park viewed as opportunity to diversify economy	To generate tourism and get more money in the local tax base; park viewed as opportunity to diversify economy
Development	By the Town of Rochelle for photography and to create a safe place for railfans to go	By the Town of Fostoria and the Fostoria Rail Preservation Society to create a safe and accessible place for railfans
Funding	New hotel/motel tax to support railfan park development, plus grant monies from the Illinois state government	Enhancement grant from the Ohio Department of Transportation (ODoT), plus grade separation monies and the use of hotel/motel tax to support railfan park development
Cost	$250,000 to build the park, which came from an Illinois state tourism grant and hotel/motel tax; $32,500–$35,000 per year from hotel/motel tax to run gift shop and visitor center, to advertise and to maintain park	$1.7 million to build. $1.36 million from the ODoT enhancement grant, $68,000 from grade closures, $253,000 from the town (to be covered by hotel/motel tax); not known how much it would cost per year to run, but costs to be covered by hotel/motel tax

Table continues over

Community support (based on participant opinions)	Limited in the beginning, but community had started to realize its potential; tried to sell it to the community by incorporating local history	Fostoria Rail Preservation Society attempted to educate the local community (a largely lue-collar community not well versed in tourism) about railfan tourism. Consultation with community on parks design
Partnership with railway	Railways did not want the railfan park, due to safety concerns; railway had since come to see the railfan park as a safe place for railfans to go	Constant communication with both the NS and CSX railways to make sure that it was something they were okay with
Economic impact	Hard to track, as business did not track railfan expenditures, although it was estimated that 30,000–40,000 railfans per year from all over the world visited; railfan tourism was estimated to make up approximately 10% of overall economic revenue	It was hoped that it would be significant, with estimates that at least 5000 railfans per year would visit from all over the world, and that railfan tourism would make up approximately 11–20% of overall economic revenue
Future	Plans for future development to increase parking, improve access and to make it a year-round destination.	Plans for future development into a destination for the whole family

visitors in 2006 and was able to determine that railfan tourism generated extra income for existing business, thus contributing to the local tax base, but it had not created or supported many jobs. Since the development of the park in Rochelle and train-related services and events in Fostoria, anecdotal evidence from business owners and event organizers suggests that visitation has increased in both communities.

While these methods provide some general visitor information, they do not provide consistent data on how long they stay, where they are spending their money, if they are satisfied with their experience or whether they will return. In addition, local businesses do not keep track of railfan expenditures, and places of accommodation are able only to estimate how many guests are railfans. The difficulties of tracking visitors is well documented in the literature (English *et al.*, 2000; Ennew, 2003) and these become especially problematic in smaller destination areas (Wilson *et al.*, 2001). However, having estimates of visitor activities and expenditures is critical for economic development officers and local businesses, as they provide important information about who the market is and what their needs are. Such information helps entrepreneurs create businesses to fill these needs and businesses to be profitable (Douglas *et al.*, 2001; Fleischer & Felsenstein, 2000; Gartner, 2004; Kokkranikal & Morrison, 2002; Russell & Faulkner, 2004; Wall, 1999; Wilson *et al.*, 2001). In addition, visitor and economic impact data are important elements in a planner's toolkit, as they aid in explaining the economic benefits and potential for creating tourism infrastructure and products to community residents (Butler *et al.*, 1998; Gartner, 2004; Reid *et al.*, 1993). Participants in both case study communities indicated that they had struggled to gain local citizens' support for their rail-related initiatives. Fostoria had undertaken familiarization tours during its annual rail festival, in an effort to inform residents of the importance of the railroad and railfans to the community.

Although both railfan parks in this case study were developed for tourism and economic purposes, there were variations, as one might expect, in terms of cost, funding and economic impact. Despite these differences, they appeared to have followed a similar development trajectory:

(1) a community member (often a railfan, but sometimes just a resident who notices people watching trains in the community) begins discussions with local groups and/or government officials on how they might be able to capitalize on the visitors' presence;
(2) land is purchased where the most trains can be seen, to develop a park;
(3) funding is sought from various sources (different levels of government, private bodies, not-for-profit societies etc.) to support the development;
(4) a development plan is decided upon and construction is undertaken;
(5) the community businesses and local government begin to recognize the economic impact in the form of increased tax dollars being spent and local business getting new customers.

A railfan park is the largest infrastructural undertaking, but these communities also cultivated partnerships between the city, local businesses and organizations to develop a range of services and products to support railfans, such as creating a map of railway locations and associated signage, providing discounts for railfans, and developing railway themes in restaurants and places of accommodation.

The fact that railfans were present before the creation of any development, including railfan parks, provides an interesting point of discussion.

Both case study communities built their infrastructure based on a 'build it – they are already coming' philosophy. This begs the question of whether creating a railfan park has the potential to increase the number of railfans who travel to a particular community, or are the same number of railfans still coming that were coming before? There is generally no way of knowing if visitation increases due to a railfan park's existence, as the baseline information of the number of railfans coming before the parks' creation often does not exist. Furthermore, accurate estimates of the numbers of railfans who are currently coming are not gathered. As a result, it is difficult to determine the return on investment and, in turn, the direct economic impact of creating a railfan park.

Data from the surveys indicated that railfans visit locations based on the number and variety of trains, and do so regardless of the presence of special infrastructure. Evidence from the case studies indicated that, as a result, railfans frequently watch trains from parking lots, railway crossings and private property, and in some cases this had caused conflict with residents and local authorities. In creating railfan parks, communities can not only develop safe physical spaces for railfans to undertake their pastime, but can also create safe social spaces. Railfanning is a pastime often misunderstood and therefore hidden from the public. Having infrastructure created to accommodate railfans makes their interests more socially acceptable and, by extension, makes the destination more attractive to railfans.

Regardless of process, cost, funding sources and economic impact, those interviewed in both communities were in agreement that the creation of a park had been of benefit to their community. The construction of the park had cleaned up derelict parts of each town, and created a safe place for visitors and residents alike to enjoy the trains. It had also put each town 'on the map' and had illustrated that although they did not think they were a location with a viable market, railfans worldwide now know the names of Rochelle and Fostoria as desirable destinations.

Conclusion

This chapter began by providing a demographic profile of railfans, and suggested that railfans have a general interest in trains, pursue the activity for the majority of their lives and they tend to be older, middle-class males. Most railfans are avid photographers, and spend a great deal of time each month viewing trains. They tend to participate in the activity alone, and are willing to travel significant distances; they often incorporate railfanning into a trip regardless of its primary purpose. They are attracted to locations with a high number of trains and a unique view, and to particular railways.

This chapter has further reported that railfan tourism has been under-taken in various forms, funded in various ways and, as a result, has had varying economic impacts. While a majority of the survey participants were aware of people taking pictures of trains in their community, only 24 of 49 communities had catered to this niche market. Further examination revealed that those communities that had developed railfan parks in con-junction with developing other train-related services received the greatest economic benefit. However, results also indicated that any additional services that recognize the presence of railfans had contributed in some way to the economy of most communities, as it generated increased business for hotels/motels and food establishments, which in turn increased tax revenues generated in the area.

Although the development of railfan parks has occurred in various ways, there seems to be a common process of first noticing railfans and beginning a discussion of how to provide services, then purchasing land to develop a park on a site where the most trains are visible, and finally obtaining the necessary funding to support the development.

As a niche market, railfan tourism has a limited economic impact and should be considered only as part of an economic diversification strategy. Even for those communities that have created parks and are anecdotally aware of its economic benefits, railfan tourism does not make up a large portion of their overall economic structure, although it does contribute to the retail, service and accommodation sectors. Clearly, there is a need to understand more precisely the economic impact of railfan tourism through conducting extensive tourism expenditure studies: not only prior development studies to aid in accurately understanding the market and the development requirements, but also ongoing data collection to aid in moni-toring the visiting population, to allow adjustments to be made to services and to ascertain whether current investments were obtaining appropriate returns.

There are numerous areas of future research required to build on the foundation of the research reported here. First, these communities are creating railfan infrastructure based on current observed visitation – 'build it – they are already coming'. Not only does this beg the question of whether the creation of the park actually increases visitation, it raises inquiry into whether it changes the kind of railfan who is coming. Building on Butler's (1980) tourism area life cycle, does the initial railfan visit an area because there are fewer people, but then move on elsewhere once it becomes popular (through the development of a railfan park)? Does Plog's (1991) psychographic typology have relevance in understanding the range of railfans' location and attribute preferences as they specialize or become more serious? These issues have yet to be explored and the current data-set does not provide this information.

More precise research on the economic impact of railfan tourism is clearly required. Knowing the economic impact will help communities understand what effect railfan tourism has on their community, allowing them to determine the 'success' of catering to this niche market. Such understanding not only provides a better basis for planning and management, but also allows for education of and support from the local community.

Research to date has specifically focused on the development and economic impact of railfan tourism, but equally important areas for consideration include its social and environmental impact. While not explicitly examined, it is evident that railfan tourism has social impacts in terms of crowding, as well as environmental impacts, as parks are being developed on brown-field sites. Future research should be undertaken to examine the impacts of railfan tourism outside of a purely economic focus.

References

Butler, R.W. (1980) The concept of a tourist area cycle of evolution: Implications for management of resources. *Canadian Geographer*, 24 (1), 5–12.

Butler, R.W., Hall, M. and Jenkins, J. (1998) *Tourism and Recreation in Rural Areas*. Chichester: John Wiley.

Chen, S. (2009) Trains are life for avid railfans, at http://www.cnn.com/2009/TRAVEL/05/08/railfan.train.watching/index.html (accessed 13 January 2011)

Douglas, N., Douglas, N. and Derrett, R. (eds) (2001) *Special Interest Tourism: Context and Cases*. Toronto: John Wiley.

English, D.B.K., Marcouiller, D.W. & Cordell, H.K. (2000) Tourism dependence in rural America: Estimates and effects. *Society and Natural Resources*, 13, 185–202.

Ennew, C. (2003) Understanding the economic impact of tourism. Som Nath Chib Memorial Lecture, 14 February, at http://fama2.us.es:8080/turismo/turismonet1/economia%20del%20turismo/analisis%20del%20turismo/understanding%20the%20economic%20impact%20of%20tourism.pdf (accessed 20 July 2011).

Fleischer, A. and Felsenstein, D. (2000) Support for rural tourism: Does it make a difference? *Annals of Tourism Research*, 27 (4), 1007–1024.

Gartner, W.C. (2004) Rural tourism development in the USA. *International Journal of Tourism Research*, 6 (3), 151–164.

Ingles, D.J. (2001) *Guide to North American Railroad Hot Spots*. Waukesha, WI: Kalmbach Publishing Co.

Kokkranikal, J. and Morrison, A. (2002) Entrepreneurship and sustainable tourism: A case study of the houseboats of Kerala. *Tourism and Hospitality Research*, 4 (1), 7–20.

Plog, S. (1991) *Leisure Travel: Making It a Growth Market ... Again!* Chichester: John Wiley.

Reid, D., Fuller, A., Haywood, K. and Bryden, J. (1993) *The Integration of Tourism, Culture and Recreation in Rural Ontario: A Rural Visitation Program*. Toronto: Queen's Printer, Ontario Ministry of Culture Tourism and Recreation.

Russell, R. and Faulkner, B. (2004) Entrepreneurship, chaos and tourism area life cycle. *Annals of Tourism Research*, 31 (3), 556–579.

Stefanovic, K. (2009) Railfan tourism. Unpublished honours thesis, Lakehead University, Thunder Bay, Ontario, Canada.

Stefanovic, K. (2011) Build it and they will come railfan tourism in North America. Unpublished masters thesis, Lakehead University, Thunder Bay, Ontario, Canada.

Wall, G. (1999) The role of entrepreneurship in tourism. In K. Bras, H. Dahles, M. Gunawan and G. Richards (eds) *Entrepreneurship and Education in Tourism* (pp. 15–24). Bandung: ATLAS Asia Inauguration Conference.

Wilson, S., Fesenmaier, D.R., Fesenmaier, J. and van Es, J.C. (2001) Factors for success in rural tourism development. *Journal of Travel Research*, 40 (2), 132.

4 The Magic of Trains and Travel in Children's Stories

Warwick Frost and Jennifer Laing

Introduction

> *'Oh, never mind about the garden now!' cried Peter ... 'Let's get to the railway.'*
> E. Nesbit, *The Railway Children* (1906)

Trains play a prominent role in a number of children's stories. Sometimes they are the main characters, such as the engines in the Reverend Awdry's Thomas the Tank Engine series, and sometimes they are an important plot device, such as the train taken by pupils to Hogwarts School in J.K. Rowling's Harry Potter series. The use of steam trains in children's stories plays on the idea that steam train travel is mysterious and romantic, with wreaths of smoke, mysterious small compartments and a loud whistle warning of danger. An interesting paradox exists whereby most trains in children's stories are steam-powered, yet no one travels by steam train any more. The exceptions are tourists. They travel on steam trains, journeying back to the world of childhood.

This love of steam trains is increasingly used by destinations to boost interest in and visitation to heritage railways. Children's stories about steam trains, whether in books, film or television, provide compelling examples of the *mediatization* of tourism. This mediatization occurs where media sources and tourism converge, both working upon each other to stimulate interest and awareness in potential tourists (Mansson, 2010). This is well illustrated by the book *The Railway Children*, originally published in 1906. In the 1950s and 1960s it was filmed four times for BBC Television and then in 1970 as a feature film. The latter was filmed on location at the Keighley and Worth Valley Railway in Yorkshire. Since then this heritage tourism steam railway has very effectively used its connection with the film in its marketing (Shipley, 2010). A play of *The Railway Children* was developed at the Railway Museum in York and was so successful it shifted to the former Eurostar terminal at Waterloo Station in London. We viewed a performance in 2011. The set was a recreated platform of an Edwardian railway station, built atop a modern railway platform. Real tracks allowed the movement back and forth of trucks and, in the finale to the first act, the arrival of a real steam engine. The chief sponsor of the play was Yorkshire Tourism. Advertising brochures at the venue encouraged the audience to visit Yorkshire for its two railway museums and six heritage steam railways. The link with the Keighley and Worth Valley Railway was particularly emphasised.

Another example of media-inspired steam tourism operations is the Sierra Nevada Railway at Jamestown, California. It has been used in over 130 Hollywood productions, including the films *Go West*, *High Noon* and *Back to the Future III* and the television series *Casey Jones* and *Petticoat Junction*. The revenue raised through film encouraged the railway to maintain its steam operations and it is now a State Historic Park, providing steam train rides and tours of its historic roundhouse and engine works (Frost, 2009).

The role of media in encouraging tourists to visit specific featured places is well known. Our aim is to go further than this, and to explore how fictional media implants ideas that travel in general will be exciting and inspirational, even magical and transformative (Laing & Frost, 2012). In this chapter we examine six children's stories, which illustrate the travel images and experiences involving steam trains that are promised to children.

Our six choices are divided into three broad periods:

(1) *Stories from the 19th and early 20th centuries*. These establish a pattern of an attractive and glamorous image for steam. Trains are new and full of adventure and open up opportunities for travel. Examples covered are E. Nesbit's 1906 *The Railway Children* and *Around the World in Eighty Days*, by Jules Verne, published in 1873.

(2) *Stories from the mid-20th century*. The train is a symbol of nostalgia, even conservatism, as we look back at a golden age that is fast disappearing. The stories recognise that tourists are now taking steam trains for recreational day trips. Travellers are searching for authenticity, particularly that lost world of the past. Examples are *Thomas the Tank Engine*, which also introduces anthropomorphism and trains, and *The Titfield Thunderbolt*.

(3) *Steam in a new century*. The steam train is magically endowed, allowing fantastic journeys which enable self-transformations. We examine *The Polar Express* and *Harry Potter*.

Our choices are subjective, though we justify them as classics enjoyed by many generations. Their popularity is demonstrated by five of the six being both books and films or television programmes. Indeed, four have been filmed in the 21st century. We present them as children's stories, though we recognise that *Around the World in Eighty Days* and *The Titfield Thunderbolt* were originally produced for adult audiences. However, illustrating the link between steam trains and children, they both strongly appeal to children.

Railways as Adventure

Both the books from the late 19th and early 20th centuries depict train travel as exciting, dangerous and accompanied by surprises. The steam train was cutting-edge technology in its time and thus represented the height of modernity (Smith, 2001), contrary to the way we view it today.

Around the World in Eighty Days

Englishman Phileas Fogg gets into an argument while playing cards at his club. A story in the *Morning Chronicle* explains that now the Great Indian Peninsula Railway has been opened, it is possible to travel around the world in 80 days. As his friends dispute this, Fogg enters into a wager of £20,000 that he will undertake the journey within that time frame.

This classic Verne adventure is a tale of a race against time. Fogg should be able to win his bet, but there are unexpected obstacles. What is striking is that only about 15% of his itinerary is by train, but it is this modern technology which provides the bulk of the problems. The whole wager is based on a newspaper article announcing that India has been spanned by a railway. However, once on the train, Fogg learns that the line has not been completed. This is the first time he falls behind schedule, as he is forced to hire an elephant to finish this leg of his journey.

More adventures come as he crosses the United States. The Union-Pacific had been completed only in 1869 and obstacles abound. A herd of buffalo force an unscheduled stop. An unstable bridge threatens to waylay them. The reckless driver decides the only way to cross is at full speed and the bridge collapses immediately after they pass. Indians attack the train and there is a fierce fight. Fogg's servant – Passepartout – is captured. Fogg leads the cavalry to the rescue, though this delays him even further.

The Railway Children

E. Nesbit wrote a number of enduring classics for children, but *The Railway Children* is arguably her most famous work. It has never been out of print since it was first published in 1906. The inspiration behind it was her own childhood, growing up beside a railway cutting. The story involves three children, Roberta (known as Bobbie), Peter and Phyllis, who have grown up in privileged circumstances in London. They are aware of trains, but only as a means of travel to the treats they enjoy – visits to the zoo, the pantomime and Madame Tussauds. Trains are associated with fun and they are taught by grown-ups that stations are only places 'from which to get away'. Then they move to the country, after their father is imprisoned for espionage. The children are not aware of the circumstances of their move, just that they are now poor and their mother is harassed and often absent. The nearby railway station becomes a sort of refuge for them – 'the centre of their new life'. They begin to think of themselves as the 'railway children' and trains are at the forefront of most of the plot developments.

The train becomes a magical object to the children, something that helps them to forget their worries about their missing father and their lack of money. They liken it to a 'great dragon', with snorts of hot steam, coming out of its 'lair' of a tunnel. For Peter, the station represents a treasure trove – of coal – which he takes to replenish their dwindling stocks. He is caught, but the station master lets him off with a caution. The railway is also something stable and reliable in a world full of upheaval (Anderson, 2007). The staff at the station become their friends, particularly Mr Perks, the porter.

The train is their last link with their life back home, breaking up the silence of the country in a comforting way, like the cabs and omnibuses of the London streets, but also leading to where they believe their father to be. The children wave to the 9.15 train every morning, which they christen the Green Dragon, to send their love back to their father. An old gentleman who regularly takes that train waves back. He becomes very important in the children's lives. The children slip a message to him at the station when the train arrives one morning, asking him to help with some goods that their mother needs to recover from serious illness. The train also brings a Russian dissident to their village, who has been searching for his wife and child. The railway thus acts as a messenger and a conduit to the wider world outside. It is 'the emblem of connectivity' (Anderson, 2007: 308).

The children learn quickly, however, that trains can be dangerous. Their mother tells them not to walk on the tracks in case they get hurt. They persuade her to allow them to do so, but learn the risks posed by the railway at first hand. Several adventures occur to them, linked to the train, when they must act selflessly to save the lives of others. The first involves a landslide that falls on the railway tracks. The children warn the approaching train with flags made from the girls' red flannel petticoats, and receive watches for their bravery. In another instance, they save the old gentleman's grandson, who has broken his leg during a school cross-country run and lies helpless in a railway tunnel. Two of the children run to a nearby signal box and find the signalman asleep. They wake him in time to operate the signals and avoid a catastrophe.

The return of the children's father also involves a train. When the children wave at the 9.15 train one day, *all* the passengers wave back. The children observe that 'it almost seemed as though the train itself was alive, and was at last responding to the love that they had given it so freely and so long'. Bobbie goes back to the station and waits without really knowing why. Something important is about to happen. Her father steps off the train and into her arms, and her scream 'Oh my Daddy, my Daddy!' entered 'like a knife into the heart of everyone in the train'. The passengers share in this intimate moment, as their lives and the children's have become inextricably linked through their communal dramas. In the film, this moment is marked by the father emerging from a cloud of engine smoke. The train provides a momentary sense of mystery, before revealing all.

Steam as a Symbol of Modernity

Train travel encapsulated the marvels of the industrial age for the readers of Jules Verne's adventure novels, opening up frontiers and linking empires. *Around the World in Eighty Days* was at the forefront in documenting this development, given the railroad across North America was completed only in 1869, four years before the book's publication.

Around the World in Eighty Days is more than a mere travelogue or ripping yarn. It is about Fogg's personal journey. He is introduced as a man obsessed with order, following a clockwork schedule. Passepartout calls him 'a real machine'. His bet reflects his view that the world can be tamed by technology. His journey demonstrates that this is not so. Fogg's routines and schedules mask deep emotional problems. As with many Verne heroes, his obsession with modern machinery is at the expense of his humanity – reflecting Verne's arguments with his father over his choice of writing as a career instead of law (Butcher, 1990; Martin, 1990). When the railways go wrong, they provide Fogg with the opportunity to be more human. Both of his train trips are interrupted by dangerous incidents in which Fogg voluntarily departs from his quest in order to rescue people. In India it is Aouda; in America it is Passepartout. It is the uncertainty of the supposedly clockwork trains which provide the tests of Fogg's humanity.

The Railway Children is also about personal transformation. By the Edwardian era, the steam train was more commonplace, although it still had symbolic resonance. The children liken it to a mythical beast, instead of merely representing the inexorable march of progress. Interestingly, early locomotives were labelled 'the iron horse', in an attempt to see this new development in more naturalistic terms. While the railway had its critics, this technology is not depicted as soulless, nor alienating, in these books. Its dangers are real, but so are its benefits. *The Railway Children* extols the marvels of railway engineering and is full of passages detailing the intricate workings of the train, as well as how it *feels* to ride on a train. The layout of the station and its operations are also explained to young readers. The children learn to respect the steam train's capacity to connect people and places (Anderson, 2007).

The book imparts a strong sense of the importance of the railway to the lives of its protagonists and the society of the time, although some prefer a more 'nostalgic reading' of the text (Anderson, 2007). Others critique the work for focusing on a 'middle-class subject who benefits from, but does not have a close bodily association with, mechanized urbanity' (Boone, 2007: 93). This is a difficult argument to sustain, given the children's physical and emotional interaction with the railway and its workers and passengers. They literally stand on the line to warn an oncoming train of danger and make themselves intimately acquainted with the mechanics of rail travel. These children are not disinterested bystanders. While 'the world of locomotion was a gendered domain' (Smith, 2001: 127), *The Railway Children* is unusual in having its heroine, Bobbie, dream of being an engine-driver when she grows up. Her father does not discourage her ambitions, perhaps echoing Nesbit's Fabian philosophies of equality of opportunity (Mickenberg & Nel, 2005).

Railways as Heritage

In the two stories from mid-20th century England, steam trains are viewed nostalgically and as worthy of preservation.

Thomas the Tank Engine

Thomas started life as a bedtime story the Reverend W. Awdry told to his son Christopher. Encouraged by his wife, the Reverend sought a publisher and the first of what became known as the Railway Series appeared in 1946. They recounted the adventures of a variety of steam locomotives, chief of these being the diminutive Thomas. The trains and their lines were mainly based on real ones but Awdry constructed the imaginary Island of Sodor as a setting. It was based partly on the Isle of Man. Clergyman Awdry took the name from the Bishop of Man and Sodor.

The engines were represented anthropomorphically. They had faces, could talk and while they had drivers, they could also move by themselves. In essence they were children, excitable and full of energy, keen to show off and subject to tantrums and grumpiness. As might be expected from an English vicar, Awdry imbued his stories with moral lessons. The trains (and the readers) learnt the value of teamwork, respect for others, working hard and knowing one's place.

In 1984 a television series took these stories to a new audience. Using models and animation, great detail was possible and the train-set atmosphere was part of the programmes' immense popularity. The series was a great success and is still in production. Furthermore, it spawned a massive merchandising empire, with books, videos, toys, playsets and even the licensing of heritage railways to run special Thomas rides.

The Titfield Thunderbolt

One of the best of the Ealing comedies, this feature film was released in 1953. The inhabitants of the village of Titfield are devastated when they are informed that their local branch line is to be closed. Traffic and revenue are not sufficient to justify its conversion to diesel. The local squire (John Gregson) and vicar (George Relph) come up with a scheme to take over and run the railway themselves. Finance comes from the eccentric Valentine (Stanley Holloway), who is attracted by the prospect of a bar on the morning train.

The authorities allow them a limited trial. With strong community support, the line is a success. In an inversion of their normal roles, the vicar becomes the driver, his bishop the fireman and the squire the conductor. Large numbers of tourists are attracted, the train is packed and after years of losses the villagers are horrified that they are making profits. Now viable, they could be nationalised! On the night before the final inspection, the engine is sabotaged by the local bus operator, who wants to remove the competition. Facing defeat, the resourceful villagers utilise a vintage engine from the local museum. They successfully complete the inspection and receive a permanent licence.

Steam in a Changing World

Within a very short period of time after World War II, the steam train shifts from being a symbol of modernity to obsolete technology valued for its nostalgia. Diesel replaces steam and the automobile displaces the railway. Paralleling this transformation in transport are massive social changes. The old social order is swept away as Western societies quickly become more urbanised, consumerist and egalitarian.

Interest in heritage is often a reaction to modernity. Faced with rapid changes, it is tempting to long for a supposed golden age, a period in history when life was simpler and better (Lowenthal, 1985). Accordingly, the trappings and artifacts that were modern in that earlier era become valued as heritage worthy of preservation. In the case of steam trains, their rapid replacement by diesel and the widespread closure of small lines led to their elevation as intrinsic to and symbolic of this idyllic past.

The sample of children's stories provide two variants of this quest to keep the past alive. Thomas, his fellow engines and the Sodor Railway are frozen in time. In both the books and television series, people are dressed in 1930s clothing. Sodor is mainly rural, though quarries and ports exist to provide varied work for the railway. There are no rail closures, no supplanting by cars or trucks. When some diesels arrive expecting to take over, they are rebuffed. The world is content and unchanging. This gap becomes even greater in the television series, released when steam had completely disappeared. It promotes a similar nostalgia to that created by the modern versions of *The Railway Children*.

In *The Titfield Thunderbolt*, the clash between the old social order and modernity is the key element of the story. The campaign to save the railway is led by the squire and village vicar. The squire certainly is an anachronism in post-war Britain. The vicar may also be seen in this light; seemingly he has little work to do and spends all his time fantasising about trains. Indeed, his ambition is to be a train driver. The squire and the vicar represent a middle-class fascination with trains. As Wallace (2006) has noted, there is a paradox that the hard, dirty and mechanical work of running heritage railways is particularly appealing to those in white-collar jobs.

Representatives of the old order, the vicar and squire lead the resistance to modernity. This is not just about their love of trains, as the squire passionately pleads to the government enquiry:

> Don't you realise you are condemning our village to death? Open it up to buses and lorries and what's it going to be like in five years' time? Our lanes will be concrete roads, our houses will have numbers instead of names. There will be traffic lights and zebra crossings and that will be twice as dangerous.

To the modern viewer this might just seem to be conservative longing for the past. However, we need to realise that the squire is complaining about recent innovations. Concrete roads, house numbers and traffic lights were new. His innocuous reference to zebra crossings was very timely: they had been introduced only in 1951 and their safety impact was a contentious issue. While lamenting the loss of the character of the English village was hardly new, *The Titfield Thunderbolt* broke new ground in firmly including the steam train as intrinsic to its heritage nature and appeal. There is an interesting contrast with H.V. Morton's quest to find the vanishing rural world in his book *In Search of England* (1927). For Morton, the car and bus are the villains, but the train had not yet been elevated to heroic status.

Both stories drew heavily on the establishment of the Talyllyn Railway in Wales. In 1951 it had become the first volunteer-operated heritage railway in the world. Awdry worked on it as a volunteer and used it as the basis for the narrow-gauge Skarloey line on Sodor. Like Talyllyn, it ran to a slate quarry and had been converted to a tourist railway. The writer T.E.B. Clarke had also come across the story of Talyllyn and pitched it to Ealing. Clarke had just won the Academy Award for Best Screenplay for *The Lavender Hill Mob* and had the clout to gain Ealing's support for his idea and screenplay. A number of real occurrences on the Talyllyn Railway were woven into *The Titfield Thunderbolt*. For example, the scene where passengers save an overheating engine from exploding by taking a line of buckets to a stream had happened at Talyllyn. The sad irony was that *The Titfield Thunderbolt* was filmed on a recently closed railway. This was the Bristol and North Somerset Railway branch line between Limpley Stoke and Camerton. It received no fairy-tale ending; it remains closed today.

The Magic of Railways

In recent times, steam trains have undergone another evolution in the way they are depicted in children's narratives. They are now the setting for magical adventures, and the characters are often seen to change as a result of their experiences on a railway.

The Polar Express

This short children's book by Chris Van Allsburg (1985) was made into a feature film directed by Robert Zemeckis in 2004. It involves a fantastic, impossible train journey to the North Pole on Christmas Eve. The little boy at the centre of the story is awake in his bed 'many years ago' and listening intently to hear the bells of Santa's sleigh. He is at that age when he is sceptical about the reality of Father Christmas, yet not confident enough to voice his disbelief out loud to his parents. To his astonishment, he hears the rattle of a train, its smoke whooshing and its whistle madly blowing. Intrigued, the boy goes outside and is greeted by a guard, who calls 'All aboard'. The boy is fearful at first, but jumps aboard as the train starts to move off; lights shining amidst the falling snow.

Other boys and girls are onboard. A 'know-it-all' child asks the others if they can identify the train. One girl answers: 'It's a magic train'. The 'know-it-all' is bemused – after all, 'it's a Baldwin 284 53 Class steam locomotive, built in 1931 at the Baldwin Locomotive Works'. He is wrong. The children discover that it is indeed a magical journey, with the train slipping and sliding off the rails and even becoming a form of roller-coaster at times. This theme park allusion is an obvious one, given that trains feature in a number of rides at Disneyland (the Disneyland Railroad runs around the perimeter of the park and the Big Thunder Mountain Railroad takes visitors on a wild ride on a runaway 'train' through a mine) and a replica of the Hogwarts train is located at the entrance to The Wizarding World of Harry Potter at Universal Studios in Florida.

The boy meets a mysterious figure on the top of the train, dressed like a vagrant and warming his hands over a fire. He echoes the boy's cynicism over Christmas, noting 'Seeing's believing', before saying to him cryptically: 'Do you believe in ghosts?' The vagrant then disappears, and one is left with the feeling that he is playing the role of the ghosts in Charles Dickens's *A Christmas Carol*, acting as the boy's conscience. This is reinforced by a marionette who calls the boy 'Scrooge' and uses the latter's famous epithet – 'Humbug!'

The children are not passive during this thrill of a ride. Two of them end up driving the train at one point, applying the brakes when the train threatens to hit a herd of caribou. This is an inversion of real life, echoing the supernatural occurrences. The train ends up at Santa's workshop and the boy learns that 'The most real things in the world are the things we can't see'. He can finally hear the bells and we are told that he continues to do so, as long as he continues *to believe*. This is another literary reference, this time to *Peter Pan*, and the exhortation to children to 'clap your hands if you believe in fairies', to avert the death of Tinkerbell.

Harry Potter

At the start of each school year, Harry Potter and his friends take a steam train to Hogwarts, their school of witchcraft and wizardry. The Hogwarts Express in *Harry Potter and the Goblet of Fire* is described as a 'gleaming scarlet steam engine ... clouds of steam billowing from it, through which the many Hogwarts students and parents on the platform appeared like dark ghosts'. This description immediately put us on our guard; the train is slightly sinister and mysterious. It departs London's King's Cross Station from platform nine and three-quarters, which can only be reached by walking 'straight at the barrier between platforms nine and ten'. This must be done without attracting attention from the non-magical (Muggle) commuters, and thus subterfuge is required. Like *The Polar Express*, things are not as they seem on this railway and appearances can deceive (Duriez, 2007). The platform is effectively a portal to another world (Duriez, 2007), a transition to magic and make-believe.

J.K. Rowling uses the steam train as a device to advance the plot in Harry Potter, allowing Harry and his friends Ron and Hermione the opportunity to meet various new characters or to discuss the latest news in the magical world. In *Harry Potter and the Prisoner of Azkaban*, they share a compartment with the new Dark Arts Teacher, Professor Lupin, who becomes an ally in their fight to defeat Lord Voldemort. They also encounter the Dementors for the first time, nightmarish and wraith-like figures who suck the soul out of a person. The books become darker as the series progresses, and the train reflects this. Harry is nearly left for dead on the train in *Harry Potter and the Half-Blood Prince*, as he has made himself invisible with a magic cloak and then been paralysed by an evil spell cast by a fellow student. Even a seemingly ordinary event on the train, such as the comical introduction of Ron's pet rat, Scabbers, on their first journey to Hogwarts, becomes significant down the track, when we learn that he is actually a human in disguise, the man who betrayed Harry's parents to Lord Voldemort.

The Hogwarts Express also represents freedom to Harry, as it allows him to escape from his dreary home life with the Dursleys in the evocatively named town of Little Whinging. We are told that 'Harry inhaled the familiar smell [of the train] and felt his spirits soar ... he was really going back [to Hogwarts]'. The last book in the series is the only one that does not commence with a train journey, which emphasises the danger Harry faces. He is no longer protected by his school and familiar routines and rituals, but must venture out into the world and kill Voldemort.

Harry becomes a sacrificial victim to save his friends and family, and ends up in a kind of limbo world which resembles King's Cross Station, 'a place of meetings and potential journeys' (Duriez, 2007: 30). He is given the choice to return and continue the fight – to 'board a train'. The station is a 'spiritual' crossroads, which marks 'a borderland between worlds' (Duriez, 2007: 85). Harry chooses life and the continuation of the struggle. The ultimate defeat of his nemesis is symbolised by another train journey, 19 years later, this time taken by Harry's sons, Albus and James, and Ron and Hermione's daughter, Rose, to Hogwarts. The next generation is now free to board the train. As the final words of the book observe: 'All is well'. The familiar train trip is now bitter sweet, a farewell to beloved children.

Steam Trains and Magical Transformations

Modern children's narratives depict the steam train as a magical environment which facilitates the transformation of the protagonist. Harry meets his two best friends, Ron and Hermione, on the train, and their loyalty and support will be instrumental in overcoming the threat posed by Lord Voldemort. Unlike his experiences during his early childhood, Harry learns that he is not alone. The train is also the setting for Harry's rite of passage to adulthood. He experiences stirrings of first love and pangs of jealousy, first over Cho Chang and then Ginny Weasley. Harry also undergoes various 'testings and trials' (Duriez, 2007: 169), which he must successfully withstand, in a form of hero's journey (Campbell, 1949). He learns, for example, to overcome the power of the Dementors, who threaten him during a train journey. Harry moves from a state of innocence to the knowledge of what he must do to defeat evil and the awakening of his 'moral consciousness' (Behr, 2005: 114). Each train journey sees Harry a little wiser and warier. The choice he makes at King's Cross Station not to give up and abandon others exemplifies his courage and 'character development' (Behr, 2005: 117).

The Polar Express is also concerned with a child on the cusp of adulthood. In this case, the boy wants to put fantasy behind him, but also paradoxically yearns to retain the magic of childhood. The train journey teaches him not to see life so literally, and to retain a sense of wonder and awe. His transformation is thus not so much a moral one as emotional – taking on a worldview that is open to new experiences and environments. The Harry Potter series also echoes these themes. The world created by Rowling is finely etched and lovingly detailed, right down to the magical sweets sold off a trolley on the train, yet the importance often lies in the things that cannot be seen, like the hidden railway platform and Harry's invisibility cloak. We marvel at the imaginary world Rowling conjures up and the train is a central part of this narrative, at once a solid reminder of the real world, yet with magical elements that take us beyond the everyday. An ordinary express train would not do for this. It must be a steam train, redolent of mystery and intrigue, which gives us the sense that anything is possible.

A Concluding Note

The six stories considered here demonstrate how powerfully steam trains figure in children's stories. There is a consistent promise that trains are exciting, adventurous and magical. Such ideas are absorbed in childhood and contribute to the motivation of experiencing steam heritage railways.

No longer practical in the modern world, steam trains provide a portal to once again experiencing the stories and adventure of childhood.

References

Anderson, S. (2007) Time, subjectivity and modernism in E. Nesbit's children's fiction. *Children's Literature Association Quarterly* 32 (4), 308–322.

Behr, K.E. (2005) 'Same-as-difference': Narrative transformations and intersecting cultures in Harry Potter. *Journal of Narrative Theory* 35 (1), 112–132.

Boone, T. (2007) 'Germs of endearment': The machinations of Edwardian children's fictions. *Children's Literature* 35, 80–101.

Butcher, W. (1990) *Verne's Journey to the Centre of the Self: Space and Time in the Voyages Extraordinaires*. Basingstoke: Macmillan.

Campbell, J. (1949) *The Hero with a Thousand Faces*. Princeton, NJ: Princeton University Press (1993).

Duriez, C. (2007) *The Unauthorised Harry Potter Companion*. Stroud: Sutton.

Frost, W. (2009) Projecting an image: Film-induced festivals in the American West. *Event Management* 12 (2), 95–104.

Laing, J. and Frost, W. (2012) *Books and Travel: Inspirations, Quests, Tranformations*. Bristol: Channel View Publications.

Lowenthal, D. (1985) *The Past Is a Foreign Country*. Cambridge: Cambridge University Press.

Mansson, M. (2010) Negotiating authenticity at Rosslyn Chapel. In B.T. Knudsen and A.M. Waade (eds) *Re-Investing Authenticity: Tourism, Place and Emotions* (pp. 169–180). Bristol: Channel View Publications.

Martin, A. (1990) *The Mask of the Prophet: The Extraordinary Fictions of Jules Verne*. Oxford: Clarendon.

Mickenberg, J.L. and Nel, P. (2005) What's left? *Children's Literature Association Quarterly* 30 (4), 349–353.

Morton, H.V. (1927) *In Search of England*. London: Methuen (1934).

Nesbit, E. (1906) *The Railway Children*. London: Penguin (2010).

Shipley, J. (2010) *The Making of the Railway Children*. Haworth: Keighley & Worth Valley Railway Preservation Society.

Smith, S. (2001) *Moving Lives: Twentieth Century Women's Travel Writing*. Minneapolis, MN: University of Minnesota Press.

Verne, J. (1873) *Around the World in Eighty Days*. Ware: Wordsworth (1994).

Wallace, T. (2006) Working on the train gang: Alienation, liminality and communitas in the UK preserved railway sector. *International Journal of Heritage Studies* 12 (3), 218–233.

5 Railway Heritage for the Cruise Market

Kim Lemky, Lee Jolliffe and Michael V. Conlin

Introduction

This chapter explores the connection between railway heritage transportation and cruise tourism, and specifically examines the incorporation of heritage railway infrastructure as shore-based attractions for cruise tourists. The focus is on three examples of this transportation-based interconnectivity: the White Pass and Yukon Railway for passengers arriving at Skagway, Alaska, USA (WPYR); the St Kitts Scenic Railway operation on the island of St Kitts in the Caribbean (SKSR); and the Bay of Fundy Scenic Railway experience for cruise passengers arriving at Saint John, New Brunswick, Canada (BFSR). In all three cases, the heritage railway component is part of the destination's attraction for cruise tourists.

Because of the historical linkage between water-based and rail-based travel well into the mid-21st century, it is not surprising that a resurgence in heritage railway tourism has been part of the growth of cruise tourism in the past half century. The primary infrastructure supporting both forms of travel is invariably linked both physically and in terms of synergistic operation. Most ports were historically connected to railway networks and many still are, notwithstanding innovations in cargo handling. As a result, the growth in cruise tourism has been a key driver in the resurgence of railway heritage attractions.

Cruise lines use ports of call as intermediate stops on a cruise where passengers can spend a few hours, usually from 4 to 8 and on average under 10 hours (Gibson, 2008). Ports should be interesting, culturally stimulating, safe and non-threatening, friendly, accessible and user-friendly, according to passenger feedback (Gibson, 2006). At a port call, passengers may visit the port city or town independently, or take a local shore excursion provided by a local tour company normally pre-purchased onboard through the cruise company. The cruise lines or their representative companies work with local suppliers to design shore excursions that will provide unique experiences, designed and operated just for ship passengers, while generating revenue and profits for the cruise lines. Some researchers have found that shore excursions are a major source of revenue for the cruise lines (Teye & Leclerc, 1998). These excursions are normally available as half-day or full-day tours, fitting in with typical cruise schedules.

Research has shown that the provision of well run cruise excursions contributes to cruise satisfaction (Marti, 1992). The shore excursion is thus considered to be a key element of the cruise product, along with transportation, accommodation, dining, entertainment and ports of call (Teye & Leclerc, 1998). A large percentage of cruise passengers will therefore purchase a shore excursion onboard from the cruise line prior to a particular port of call. A 2002 survey of cruise passengers in Bar Harbor, Maine, found that over half (56%) of those surveyed took a tour sponsored by the cruise line while in port (Gabe *et al.*, 2003). Cruise industry reports indicate that shore excursions may be a key to generating repeat cruise business (Dooley, 2010).

Railway Heritage and Shore Excursions

The romance of travel by cruise ship is complemented by the nostalgia of a train ride. A number of railroad preservation projects have nurtured the repurposing of historic train lines and their emergence as tourist railroads (Halsall, 2001). Railway heritage is part of the visitor experience for those riding these trains. Rail heritage is acknowledged as an asset for heritage tourism (Henderson, 2011). Rail transport, especially in the case of heritage railroads, can also be a tourism attraction in its own right (Dallen, 2007). Combining a train tour as a shore excursion thus potentially complements the experience provided on the cruise ship. Such a trip allows passengers to experience another mode of historic transportation in a local setting, viewing the local scenery, landscape and attractions from onboard the train.

Rail shore excursions exist at a number of ports of call around the world (see Table 5.1). These tours utilize existing railroad lines, often built and/or operated for industrial purposes, to provide cruise passengers with a scenic train ride. The rail cruise excursion is in fact often a combination rail and bus tour, as the combination allows more flexibility in getting the passengers to the train, adds value by permitting them to view additional attractions such as historic city centres, and accommodates tight time lines for shore excursions. Since the excursions are for the most part available only for cruise passengers, there is also an element of exclusivity in these tours.

Table 5.1 Examples of international rail cruise shore excursions

Port of call	Name	Tour operator/ railroad	Date estab-lished	Description
Colon, Panama	Two Oceans Journey	Panama Canal Railway Company	2001	Journey (47 miles) parallels the canal from port of Colon on the Atlantic to city of Balboa on the Pacific (up to 300 passengers)
Porte Zante, St Kitts	St Kitts Scenic Railway	St Kitts Scenic Railway Ltd	2003	A 3-hour, 30-mile circular tour by narrow-gauge bus/ train trip on a historic rail line built to carry sugarcane from plantations to a central factory
Saint John, New Brunswick, Canada	Bay of Fundy Scenic Railway	Ambassatours Grey Line/ New Brunswick Southern Railway	2012	A 2-hour guided bus/rail tour on New Brunswick Southern Railway, featuring 'reversing rapids' where the Saint John River meets the Atlantic Ocean
Skagway, Alaska	White Pass and Yukon Route	ClubLink Enterprises Limited/White Pass and Yukon Railway	1988	Trains depart ship-side in Skagway for rail excursions combined with other components
Port Chalmers, New Zealand	Taieri Gorge Railway Trip	Taieri Gorge Railway	1990	Trains departing from ship-side in Port Chalmers carry cruise passengers into the Taieri Gorge

Sources: Panama Canal Railway Company website, http://www.panarail.com; St Kitts Scenic Railway website, http://www.stkittsscenicrailway.com; White Pass and Yukon Route website, http://www. wpyr.com; Taieri Gorge Railway website, http://www.taieri.co.nz.

Case Studies

The phenomenon investigated here using a research case study method-ology (Beeton, 2005) in a contemporary context is the rail-related shore excursion for cruise passengers. The context is that of the cruise products available for consumption, in particular the shore excursion and more specifically the rail and rail/bus (or bus/rail) tours as shore excursions. The case studies rely on multiple sources of evidence, including in-depth interviews with shore excursion tour operators, examination of excursion participant experience (blogs) and secondary information from the academic literature, company financial and performance reporting and the popular press.

Based on a convenience sample (access to and availability of informa-tion) we chose case studies from three different cruise regions, Alaska (the WPYR), the Caribbean (the SKSR) and New England/Canada (the BFSR). Information collected when available for each case included the duration and description of the tour, tour management, cruise ships offering the product, name of rail line/railroad used, number of passenger cars, special characteristics/experiences, marketing focus, date of foundation as a tourism product, and capacity.

White Pass and Yukon Route

The WPYR has the distinction of being the busiest tourist railway in North America, having carried just under half a million passengers in 2008 before the financial downturn occurred (Brewer, n.d.). It is also arguably the best-developed heritage railway attraction operating in close collaboration with the cruise tourism sector. Because of its location and asset holdings, the majority of its ridership is cruise tourists and the WPYR collaborates closely with that industry. Indeed, the railway operates only during the cruise season, which is on average around 130 days annually from May to September. It uses a wide range of rolling stock, including steam locomotives, offers highly popular and successful excursions and activities, and operates on one of the most geographically spectacular railways in the world.

Having been built during the Klondike Gold Rush of the late 20th century, the WPYR can justifiably boast of its historical heritage. It is also a historic engineering attraction, having in 1994 been designated by the American Society of Civil Engineers as an International Historic Civil Engineering Landmark (American Society of Civil Engineers, n.d.). The WPYR's original right of way was 107 miles long and connected Skagway, Alaska, with Whitehorse in Canada's Yukon Territory. The current usable right of way runs from the cruise docks in Skagway through the Canadian province of British Columbia and ends at Carcross in the Yukon Territory, a distance of 67.5 miles. Key destinations along the right of way include the White Pass on the border between Alaska and British Columbia, the station and depot in Fraser, British Columbia, and Bennett, British Columbia, where the historic White Pass and Chilkoot Trails from the Klondike Gold Rush era ended.

The history of the WPYR is a classic example of what has happened to many railway systems in the past century. Construction of the line began in 1898 in the context of the Klondike Gold Rush. However, by the time the railway was finished in 1900, the Gold Rush was over. Nonetheless, the WPYR enjoyed commercial success for much of the 20th century, primarily as a freight and ore transporter. However, as so often has been the case in railway history, when mining in the region collapsed in 1982, the WPYR ceased operations.

The WPYR's resurrection as a tourist attraction began in late 1988. Since 1997, the WPYR has been owned and operated by a Canadian company, ClubLink Enterprises Limited, whose primary business is the ownership and operation of private golf clubs in Ontario, Quebec and Florida. The WPYR is a commercial venture with a full-time staff of 20 people and a seasonal workforce of approximately 200 employees. According to ClubLink:

> White Pass maintains a symbiotic relationship with the cruise lines – carrying almost half of all cruise passengers – making it Alaska's most popular shore excursion and a high volume, highly rated and profitable shore excursion for the cruise lines. (ClubLink Enterprises Limited, 2012)

Indeed, the relationship between the WPYR and the cruise industry is highly synergistic. ClubLink owns and operates the cruise docks in Skagway, which the cruise industry is reliant upon. By operating what is a historic railway attraction from the docks, the company and the cruise industry are able to offer tourists a seamless and fully integrated shore excursion. The company plans to expand the docking capacity at Skagway in 2013 by adding a floating dock capable of handling Royal Caribbean's new Solstice-class ships, which can carry 2900 passengers (ClubLink Enterprises Limited, 2012).

From a ridership of 37,000 in 1988, the WPYR has grown dramatically and in 2007 ridership reached a record 461,000 passengers (Brewer, n.d.). The economic downturn negatively impacted tourism in Skagway and the WPYR and in 2008 there were 438,000 passengers. Nonetheless, the WPYR did set a one-day record of 7009 passengers on 23 July 2008. The President of the WPYR, Gary Danielson, said of this achievement:

Table 5.2 Railway ridership by cruise passengers to Skagway

Year	No. of cruise passengers	Railway ridership	Percentage ridership
2007	820,000	461,000	56.2%
2008	779,000	438,000	56.2%
2009	781,000	396,000	50.7%
2010	697,000	368,000	52.7%
2011	712,000	382,000	53.6%

Source: ClubLink Enterprises Limited (2012).

This historic milestone – breaking the 7000 passengers in one-day threshold – is truly symbolic for us. This milestone is testament to our brand, our people and our industry partners. This milestone celebrates our investment in infrastructure, service and systems.... Yesterday's feat was accomplished with all trains being on time. (White Pass and Yukon Route Railroad, 2008)

The decline in ridership continued in 2009, when 396,000 passengers were carried. In 2010, ridership had fallen to 368,000 passengers but by 2011 it had recovered to 382,000 passengers (Table 5.2). It is noteworthy that the percentage of cruise passengers coming through the Skagway and who purchased an excursion on the WPYR declined faster than the overall number of passengers arriving at Skagway (ClubLink Enterprises Limited, 2012).

Given that the life blood of the WPYR is cruise tourists, it is worth noting that the Skagway Convention and Visitors Bureau estimated in 2012 that the total number of cruise tourists likely to arrive in Skagway in 2013, based on confirmed calls by cruise ships, was 800,428 (Skagway, Alaska, 2012). However, WPYR's parent, ClubLink, indicated that, in 2011, 54.4% of its passengers were generated by three cruise lines – Carnival Cruise Line, Princess Cruises and Holland America Line – and that a loss of this customer base would be very detrimental to the WPYR and ClubLink (ClubLink Enterprises Limited, 2012).

ClubLink does not divulge the specific financial performance of the WPYR. However, it does report income and earnings for its rail, tourism and port operations. In 2011, these amounted to revenues of US$35,572,000 and income of US$17,467,000. The company's consolidated financial statements for 2011 show that the company as a whole enjoyed increased revenues, topping $200 million for the first time in the company's history.

The company also reported record net earnings of $16.4 million for 2011 (ClubLink Enterprises Limited, 2012: 3). The company has stated that:

> ClubLink's continued investment in programs to build the core operating business at White Pass & Yukon Route … has historically been the Company's key to profitability. As a standalone entity, White Pass has an experienced on-site management team and has been able to generate growth in the passenger traffic and corresponding US dollar revenue since its acquisition in 1997. Significant initiatives in this business segment have included capitalizing on historical relationships with the cruise lines, supporting investments to create one of the leading port facilities in southeast Alaska and an investment to repower our locomotive fleet to reduce both environmental emissions and on-going operating costs. These initiatives have led White Pass to become Alaska's premier shore excursion experience of the travelling public. (Clublink Enterprises Limited, 2012: 23)

Excursions on the WPYR are varied. By far the most popular excursion is the three-hour White Pass Summit Excursion, which takes passengers from the Skagway docks to White Pass on the Canadian border and back to the Skagway docks. The Yukon Adventure Excursion takes passengers past White Pass to Lake Bennett, where they enjoy a meal at the WPYR's historic Bennett Eating House before continuing on to Carcross in the Yukon Territory. The WPYR also offers a variety of excursions that allow hikers to experience the history of the Chilkoot and White Pass Trails by combining various hikes with return transportation on the railway. Passengers can ride the train from the cruise ship docks in Skagway all the way to Carcross in the Yukon Territory and return by train to Skagway. The railway also offers excursions that combine bus and train rides, including extended excursions to Whitehorse in the Yukon Territory (White Pass and Yukon Route Railroad, n.d.).

In terms of rolling stock, the WPYR has an impressive array of historic locomotives, coaches and supporting equipment, such as the rotary snowplough built in 1898 specifically for the WPYR. The locomotives include 20 diesel-electric units made by General Electric in the 1950s and by ALCO in the 1960s as well as two steam locomotives, both of which are Baldwin units, one built in 1907 and the other in 1947. The fleet also includes 79 restored and replica passenger coaches, which are on average 50 years old. The WPYR also maintains its right of way using a range of specialized equipment. Most of this equipment is on display at the railway's historic depot in Skagway, Alaska.

As a shore excursion, on its own or paired with other activities, the WPYR is a mature product, part of a very large tourism company, and an integrated operation with tracks, rolling stock and even the docks owned by the company. Extending the cruise experience by offering shore excursions, the WPYR has a considerable impact on its region (Munro & Gill, 2006). In the case of this tourist railway catering mainly to cruise passengers the international cross-border operation (USA–Canada) may provide added interest for passengers as a form of bi-national tourism and at the same time operational complexity in terms of dealing with two sets of regulations as well as cross-border issues.

St Kitts Scenic Railway

Tourism in St Kitts has become an important part of the economy, especially since the closure of the sugar industry late in 2005. In 2009, there were 235 port calls, with 450,553 cruise passengers visiting the island (Central Statistics Office, 2010). In 2011, the direct contribution of travel and tourism to gross domestic product (GDP) was 7.5% and was predicted to rise to 9.6% of GDP by 2022 (World Travel and Tourism Council, 2012). The current tourism product caters to both stay-over and cruise visitors with an emerging heritage tourism sector (Dodds & Jolliffe, 2013).

St Kitts possesses a wealth of heritage resources in the form of both built sites and material culture (Nurse, 2008). These relate to the colonization of the island by the British (Brimstone Hill World Heritage Site) and to the former sugar industry: great houses and their ruins on former estates, old sugar production facilities and the narrow-gauge railway built between 1912 and 1926 to transport sugarcane from the fields to the factory in Basseterre.

Sugar dominated the economy from the 1640s. Around 2002, that is, before the projected closure of the nationalized sugar industry (after the 2005 harvest), a tourist railway expert and entrepreneur, Steve Hites, identified the potential use of the rail line for a rail tour. As Hites later observed, besides the spectacular landscape along the route, the railway had expert staff and was used to running on tight schedules, getting the sugarcane from harvesting to production on time (Steve Hites, personal communication, January 2011). Government was keen to further diversify its tourism product and to address the impacts of the closure of the sugar industry. It was therefore possible for Hites and other investors to form a partnership with the government, leasing the rail line for a tourist attraction for a 30-year period (Office of the Prime Minister of St Kitts and Nevis, 2012). Other investors brought their expertise in building dedicated rail cars for tourist train attractions.

The rail cars were designed by Thomas Rader of Colorado Railcar and built by Hamilton Construction in Oregon (Churcher, 2008). Hites brought to the project his experience with the White Pass and Yukon Route in Alaska discussed above and developing shore excursion products for the cruise lines through ownership of Skagway Street Cars Inc., in Skagway, Alaska. His expertise contributed to the ability of the SKSR to understand cruise line requirements for shore excursions and provided contacts to approach the cruise lines with the new product proposal. With tourism being an important part of the economy in St Kitts, it was possible to enlist the support of the Prime Minister and for him to accompany Hites on a visit to the Carnival Cruise Line headquarters in Miami, to 'pitch' the new product (Steve Hites, personal communication, January 2011).

The old narrow-gauge rail line was originally designed only to haul sugarcane from the field to the factory and this infrastructure provided some challenges for the new SKSR, resulting in numerous upgrades being made to the track. It proved necessary for the SKSR to negotiate rights of way along the tracks and at crossings. The carriages of the passenger cars have two levels, allowing passengers to have both a seat and a place on the observation deck. The locomotives were purchased from Romania. The rail cruise product was tested during the 2003–04 tourist season, initially using five rail cars. Later, more cars were added, reflecting the phased development of the SKSR.

The train portion of this tour departs from Needsmust Station in Basseterre (the capital city of St Kitts) with passengers being transported to the station by bus from their cruise ship berths at Port Zante. Most passengers ride the train as part of a shore excursion, having purchased their trip as part of an excursion pre-sold aboard their cruise ship. Passengers ride the train for two hours, then complete their tour with a one-hour bus tour; 'The 18 miles by rail and 12 miles by bus make a complete 30 mile circle around the island' (St Kitts Scenic Railway, n.d.). The SKSR notes the tour can operate in reverse as a bus/rail tour. Billing the tour as the 'last railway in the West Indies', the trip is described as follows:

> The Railway hugs the Northeastern coastline where spectacular vistas of the ocean, surf, cliffs and lush vegetation surround you. The train rolls across tall steel bridges spanning deep 'ghuts', or canyons, and winds through small villages and farms. Dark green rain forests are skirted by rippling fields of sugar cane, with the volcanic cone of Mt Liamuiga rising above the railway. Your tour conductor will point out all the sights as the train passes old sugar cane estates with abandoned windmills and chimneys. (St Kitts Scenic Railway, n.d.)

The complete description also lists some local landmarks, including the Brimstone Hill Fortress. The excursion capitalizes on the varied heritage resources and landscapes of the island.

The success of the SKSR rail/bus trip as a shore excursion may be attributed in part to its being one of the few opportunities for cruise visitors to ride a train; in fact, this is the only such tourism product in the eastern Caribbean. The SKSR is noted as a good example of cultural entrepreneurship, whereby a public asset (the rail track) is leased for private development (David Rollinson, personal communication, February 2011). Evidence of success is found in the SKSR ridership increasing from 56,500 overall in 2010–11 to 60,000 out of 600,000 cruise passengers in 2011–12 (Steve Hites, personal communication, January 2011). In 2012, the SKSR constructed a new administrative and shop building at Needsmust Station and ordered a 30-inch gauge diesel hydraulic locomotive, costing US$650,000, designed to operate on the SKSR's narrow-gauge rails (Office of the Prime Minister of St Kitts and Nevis, 2012).

The initial signature SKSR rail/bus shore excursion piloted in 2003–04 led to diversification in terms of tours now being offered in addition as rail/sail and rail/fortress/great-house packages. This variety of offerings allows for different experiences, all with the rail ride as the key component. This packaging should encourage repeat customers, attracted by the possibility of experiencing new variations of the original tour. New offerings will also allow the SKSR to have a broader appeal to the stay-over market of visitors to the island.

Using existing heritage resources and railroad infrastructure, the SKSR as a public/private partnership could be a model for future heritage tourism development. With 68 employees, many being formerly employed by the sugarcane railway, the SKSR is contributing to local livelihoods in St Kitts. The railway on St Kitts, while no longer serving an industrial purpose, has been reinvented into what Baldacchino (2008: 31) calls 'cute and exotic, short-distance train services that essentially support the tourism industry and where the ride per se (rather than getting to one's preferred destination) is the attraction'.

There are some challenges for the future of this tourist rail line. They include the SKSR's dependency on the cruise market and the need to replant the cane, as that creates the attractive sugarcane landscape. As an outdoor attraction, the rail excursion is subject to weather conditions. It would therefore be desirable for related indoor attractions to be developed; for example, railway museums are known to have a positive effect on cultural tourism (Akbulut & Artvinli, 2011).

Bay of Fundy Scenic Railway

The BFSR was established in 2012 as a rail excursion based in historic Saint John, New Brunswick, Canada. It is operated by Ambassatours Grey Line, a bus tour company based in Halifax, Nova Scotia, in partnership with the New Brunswick Southern Railroad (NBSR), owned by a local business, J.D. Irving Ltd. It was billed as the first new rail experience in 25 years in North America. Given that this is the only new railroad excursion offered (for cruise passengers) on the eastern seaboard, the local tourism industry and the cruise lines as well as the NBSR were excited at being able to offer this experience to cruise passengers (Dennis Campbell, personal communication, October 2012).

Saint John is an industrial city located in southern New Brunswick, on the Bay of Fundy, at the mouths of the Saint John River and of the Kennebecasis River. It marked its 225th anniversary in 2010 and has a historic uptown core with diverse architecture. The population of Saint John itself is approximately 68,000 but when combined with the surrounding area there is a total population of 120,000 people in five communities. It is scenic, with rolling hills and spectacular waterways. It is a dynamic city with a diversified economic base. It is home to the New Brunswick Museum (Canada's oldest public museum) and Stonehammer Geopark, so designated in 2010, the first and so far only UNESCO Geopark designation in North America (Stonehammer Geopark, n.d.).

The cruise industry in Saint John started in 1989, when a hurricane diverted a ship to the port. From 2007 to 2012, 65–80 ships annually have made the city a port of call, with over 180,000 passengers disembarking each year (Hrabluk, 2012; Saint John Port Authority, 2012). Figure 5.1 shows the growth in cruise passenger numbers over time.

The initiative to develop this new product offering arose from the need to diversify the onshore excursions to cruise passengers, to meet demand for more child-friendly excursions from Disney Cruise Lines and to help to lengthen the cruise ship season in Saint John (Dennis Campbell, personal communication, October 2012). As there are a disproportionately large number of ships making a port of call from September to October, the goal is to increase the number of port calls from May through to August and new shore excursions could contribute to this objective.

The initiative was also based on the history of the rail lines in Saint John. The construction of the railway line through Saint John known as the Western Spur by Canadian Pacific Railway (CPR) began around 1885. Some smaller spur lines were also constructed, including the West Saint John Spur Line, serving the industrial west side of the Port of Saint John. These tracks

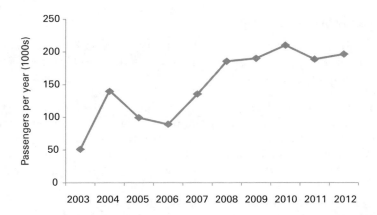

Figure 5.1 Growth in cruise passenger numbers (passengers/year) to Port of Saint John
Source: Saint John Port Authority (2012); Hrabluk (2012)

were built in the early 1870s as the Carleton, City of Saint John Branch Railroad and later acquired in the 1890s by CPR (Wallace, 1976). A unique feature of this line is the bridge that crosses the Saint John River, dating from the 1930s.

The process of developing the rail/cruise tour thus commenced with the recognition of the need for a new product, the knowledge that a railroad tour is popular with children, and an assessment of the resources in the Saint John region which would make this product offering viable without too much capital input into infrastructure. For example, the New Brunswick Southern Railroad was a willing partner, since the passenger rail cars, the locomotive, caboose, the train station, rail lines and scenic infrastructure were already in existence. An expert consultant who was brought in to assess the product subsequently confirmed its viability and was optimistic about its success. The expert was also able to provide practical advice about the operation of a tourist rail excursion for the cruise market (Dennis Campbell, personal communication, October 2012).

The BFSR experience commenced at the Port of Saint John, where 'road trains' (buses painted in a similar manner to the rail cars) picked up cruise passengers from the dock and brought them to the railroad station situated about five minutes from the port. Passengers disembarked and boarded the train in one of three passenger railcars (built circa 1953 and with a capacity of 70 passengers each), restored to their original state, for a 40-minute scenic tour. This enabled passengers to view historic parts of the 225-year-old Saint John; the trip included a stop on the bridge overlooking the Reversing Falls

Rapids. The train then passed the T.S. Simms Brush Company, Moosehead Brewery and the Irving Pulp and Paper Mill, and then continued over to Bayshore on the West Saint John Spur Line, where the interpretive focus was on the Bay of Fundy (considered one of the natural wonders of the world, with its record-breaking tides of 11.7 m or 38 feet) (J.D. Irving Ltd, 2012). At the end of the line, passengers were dropped off and made the return trip on a 'road train' and another load of passengers was picked up to make the train trip for the reverse route (the tour was also designed to operate in reverse).

In 2012 the excursion was offered to cruise passengers by three companies – Royal Caribbean International, Disney Cruise Line and Carnival Cruise Lines. The BFSR was available as a stand-alone excursion and in conjunction with a variety of other excursions: a walking tour, the Pink Bus Tour and the Saint Andrews by the Sea Tour. The pairing of the excursion with other popular tours helped to ensure that more people bought into the experience. The prices of these tours in 2012 varied from US$55 to $75 for adults (aged 9 and over) and $29.99 to $49.99 for children (aged 3–9), the higher price reflecting tours combined with other tour components (Disney Cruise Line, n.d.). This rail/bus tour was exclusive to the cruise ship excursion industry (i.e. it was not otherwise available to the public).

Figure 5.2 shows cruise passenger participation in the tour in 2012. Thirty-six ships with an average of 261 passengers each experienced the 'Bay

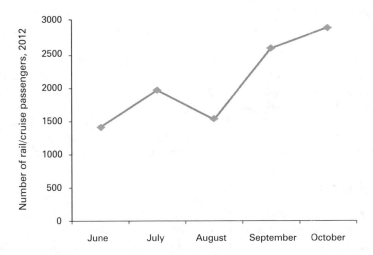

Figure 5.2 Bay of Fundy Scenic Railway, passenger numbers 2012
Source: Ambassatours Grey Line (personal correspondence, October 2012)

of Fundy Scenic Railway' product (with a total of 10,000 passengers in its inaugural year). Disney Cruise Line ships averaged closer to 350 passengers per port of call and the product was modified to reflect the higher proportion of children by making it more interactive and tripling the number of guides to enhance the experiences for the children. This included more props and more animation by the guides as well (Dennis Campbell, personal communication, October 2012).

The offering of the BFSR experience resulted in employment for the operation of the train by New Brunswick Southern Rail (conductor, switch operator) and also for the driver of the 'rail bus' and three guides and attendants from Ambassatours. Expertise from both partners was used to maximize the experience. This partnership between an experienced tour operator and an industrial railroad thus drew upon the strengths of both organizations.

In an interview, the chief executive of Ambassatours (Dennis Campbell, personal communication, October 2012) noted that the company was very pleased with the uptake of the new product, especially in its inaugural year. However, there were an unexpected number of cancellations of the tour because the tour was operating on an active industrial rail line, and a considerable increase in the commercial business on the rail line resulted in the high number of cancellations. Although the product was very well received by cruise passengers, the cruise lines may be hesitant to offer the product in future years because of these unknowns. There were plans to offer the product in 2013, but with a possible reduction in the schedule to several weeks when passenger loads could be counted on, rather than for the full season.

As a new rail/bus experience for the shore excursion cruise product the BFSR experience now has a baseline of operational experience that can be built upon in future years of operation. Amabassatours valued the experience for the company in terms of developing a quality tour product for the family market (Disney Cruise Line) and this led the company to think about offering other rail-based experiences for this market, beyond the cruise product (Dennis Campbell, personal communication, October 2012).

Discussion

The three cases differ in terms of their history and development, scale and complexity of operations, and ownership models. However, they do have common elements. All three cases use historic rail infrastructure to develop shore excursions focused on railway heritage to fulfil the cruise industry's need for quality experiences and differentiation in shore excursions.

Since railway heritage has an appeal to passengers of all ages, providing a unique experience of a scenic train ride with interpretation, the rail/bus tours that shore operators have created, often for the exclusive benefit of the cruise lines, are attractive as a product. The rail tours also contribute to destination competitiveness.

These cases represent the evolution of the development of rail tour excursions for the cruise market, the WPYR being the most mature, having been in operation since 1988. The SKSR is more recently established (2003) but now has behind it a number of years of operation, a time during which it has been able to refine its product and to extend its availability through packaging. The BFSR is more recently founded as a tour product, having just completed its first season at the time of writing (2012).

All of the rail tour excursions profiled have local economic impacts, mainly in the form of employment for the bus drivers, railroad staff and tour operators who deliver the product. In two of the cases (WPYR and BFSR) these employment impacts are seasonal. In terms of the cruise passengers participating in the tours, as they are excursionists normally in port only for the day, their spending will be limited, and the purchase of the tour will be onboard, with only a portion of the price going to the local tour operators. Passengers may also purchase items locally, such as souvenirs. There may thus be potential for the development of rail tour souvenirs as a complementary revenue stream.

The availability of heritage rail assets is important in all three cases. The WPYR has behind it a historic real line and a considerable stock of heritage locomotives and passenger cars. In the case of the SKSR only the track is historic, as this tourist railway operation has opted to use new custom-built passenger cars and locomotives purchased for the operation. On the other hand, the BFSR operation uses the historic and industrial rolling stock and tracks of its partner, the NBSR. The right of ways alongside the tracks is also important to tourist train operations: the WPYR owns its own, the SKSR is in the process of acquiring the rights of way and the BFSR uses the right of way already owned by the NBSR.

What links the three cases, beyond the use of historic rail infrastructure, is the contribution that they are making to the success of local cruise markets by offering a unique and appealing experience that is available at only a few cruise destinations. Since the operation of a tourist railway within a shore excursion has unique operational challenges, all three cases benefit from the expertise of experienced tourism railroad operators as advisers, as well as the knowledge and professionalism of the associated railway operators.

As a historic form of transportation, a ride on a railroad is ideally paired with the experience onboard the ship, providing participating cruise passengers with a memorable experience, and in both modes a unique per-spective of the landscape.

Conclusion

The chapter offers insight into the use of railway infrastructure and rolling stock for shore excursion tours as products in relation to both rail and cruise tourism. It has demonstrated through the case studies that there is an evolution of the tourist railroad excursion for the cruise market, as they become more mature product offerings. It has also identified the fact that, as shore excursions, tourist rail trips provide a unique product that is capable of attracting cruise ships to stop at particular destinations. As such, these rail products also have the ability to contribute to extending the length of traditional cruise seasons at cruise destinations.

There are lessons here for other potential rail operations as shore excur-sions. First, in planning it is beneficial to have expert advice from those who have been involved with these operations at other locations. Second, it is necessary to develop itineraries that will have both a broad appeal and a more directed appeal for specific audiences such as families (lesson from the BFSR). Third, the rail/bus shore excursion has potential to be paired with other forms of tours and transportation (evidenced by all three cases), thus offering an enriched experience of various forms of historic transport. The inclusion of rail in shore excursions for cruise lines thus has much to offer in terms of unique appeal and authentic experience, thereby enriching the offerings of the cruise lines at the few locations that are able to offer this product.

References

Akbulut, G. and Artvinli, E. (2011) Effects of Turkish railway museums on cultural tourism. *Procedia – Social and Behavioral Sciences* 19, 131–138.

American Society of Civil Engineers (n.d.) Historic Civil Engineering Landmark Index. At   http://www.asce.org/People-and-Projects/History-and-Heritage/Historic-Civil-Engineering-Landmark-Program/Historic-Civil-Engineering-Landmark-Index/ (accessed 4 October 2012).

Baldacchino, G. (2008) Trains of thought: Railways as island antitheses. *Shima: The International Journal of Research into Island Cultures* 2 (1), 29–41.

Beeton, S. (2005) The case study in tourism research: A multi-method case study approach. In B.W. Ritchie, P. Burns and C. Palmer (eds) *Tourism Research Methods: Integrating Theory with Practice* (pp. 37–48). Wallingford: CABI Publishing.

Brewer, G. (n.d.) Gold rush narrow gauge: For this little railway, the gold rush is back. At http://www.travelthruhistory.com/html/historic34.html (accessed 5 October 2012).

Central Statistics Office (2010) *St Kitts and Nevis Selected Tourism Statistics Quarterly*, Basseterre, St Kitts: St Kitts and Nevis Eastern Caribbean Bank.

Churcher, C. (2008) An update on the St Kitts Railway. Bytown Railway Society. At http://www.bytownrailwaysociety.ca (accessed 2 October 2012).

ClubLink Enterprises Limited (2012) *ClubLink Enterprises Limited Annual Report 2011*, King City, Ontario: ClubLink Enterprises Limited. At http://www.clublinkenterprises.ca/pdf/2011annualreport.pdf (accessed 5 October 2012).

Dallen, J. (2007) The challenges of diverse visitor perceptions: Rail policy and sustainable transport at the resort destination. *Journal of Transport Geography* 15 (2), 104–115.

Disney Cruise Line (n.d.) http://disneycruise.disney.go.com (accessed 8 May 2012).

Dodds, R. and Jolliffe, L. (2013) Developing sugar heritage tourism in St Kitts. In L. Jolliffe (ed.) *Sugar Heritage and Tourism in Transition* (pp. 110–127). Bristol: Channel View Publications.

Dooley, G. (2010) CLIA: Shore tours key to building repeat cruise business. *eTN Global Travel Industry News*. At http://www.eturbonews.com/17906/clia-shore-tours-key-building-repeat-cruise-business (accessed 10 February 2013).

Gabe, T.M., Lynch, C., McConnon, J. and Allen, T. (2003) *Economic Impact of Cruise Ship Passengers in Bar Harbor, Maine*. Orono, ME: Department of Resource Economics and Policy, University of Maine.

Gibson, P. (2006) *Cruise Operations Management*. London: Butterworth-Heinemann.

Gibson, P. (2008) Cruising in the 21st century: Who works while others play? *International Journal of Hospitality Management* 27 (1), 42–52.

Halsall, D.A. (2001) Railway heritage and the tourist gaze: Stoomtram Hoorn-Medemblik. *Journal of Transport Geography* 9 (2), 151–160.

Henderson, J. (2011) Railways as heritage attractions: Singapore's Tanjong Pagar station. *Journal of Heritage Tourism* 6 (1), 73–79.

Hrabluk, L. (2012) Meet and greet. *Progress Magazine* 19 (8), S7–S8.

J.D. Irving, Ltd (2012) All aboard! New Brunswick Southern Railway and Ambassatours Gray Line offer exclusive new train excursion for Saint John cruise ship visitors. At http://www.jdirving.com/article.aspx?id=3088 (accessed 22 January 2013).

Marti, B.E. (1992) Passenger perceptions of cruise itineraries: A Royal Viking Line case study. *Marine Policy* 16 (5), 360–370.

Munro, J.M. and Gill, W.G. (2006) The Alaska cruise industry. In *Cruise Tourism* (pp. 145–159). Wallingford: CAB International.

Nurse, K. (2008) *Development of a Strategic Business Management Model for the Sustainable Development of Heritage Tourism Products in the Caribbean*. Barbados: Caribbean Tourism Organization.

Office of the Prime Minister of St Kitts and Nevis (2012) St Kitts Scenic Railway to get a new US$650,000 locomotive. At http://www.cuopm.com (accessed 30 September 2012).

Saint John Port Authority (2012) *Saint John Port Authority Annual Report 2011*. At http://www.sjport.com/english/public_registry/documents/2011EnglishannualReportLR.pdf (accessed 20 January 2012).

Skagway, Alaska (2012) Skagway cruiseship calendar. At http://skagway.com/skagway-cruiseship-calendar (accessed 5 October 2012).

Stonehammer Geopark (n.d.) Stonehammer Geopark. At http://www.stonehammer geopark.com (accessed 9 February 2012).

Teye, V.B. and Leclerc, D. (1998) Product and service delivery satisfaction among North American cruise passengers. *Tourism Management* 19 (2), 153–160.

Wallace, C. (1976) Saint John boosters and the railroads in mid-nineteenth century. *Acadiensis* 6 (1), 71–91.

White Pass and Yukon Route Railway (n.d.) Alaska train excursions. Cruise ship passengers. At http://www.wpyr.com/excursions.html (accessed 1 October 2012).

White Pass and Yukon Route Railway (2008) White Pass and Yukon route sets historic new daily ridership record! At http://www.wpyr.com/news/july242008.html (accessed 2 October 2012).

World Travel and Tourism Council (2012) *Travel and Tourism Economic Impact 2012 St Kitts and Nevis*. London: World Travel and Tourism Council.

6 Safety on the Line: Balancing Authentic Experiences Against Risks and Hazards

Josephine Pryce

Introduction

Heritage railways offer opportunities to participate in recreational activities linked to historic modes of transport (Urry, 1990) and to connect with 'history and industrial archaeology' (Halsall, 2001: 152). They draw visitors who seek exciting, educational and authentic experiences in heritage places (Halsall, 2001; Tillman, 2002). The interaction of visitors with railway heritage environments inextricably exposes people to potentially harmful situations. The range of hazards and the inexperience and lack of specific knowledge of visitors heighten the potential risk from hazards and activities. Understanding, identifying and mitigating these risks are critical to ensure the safety of visitors engaged with railway heritage environments. This chapter examines the health and safety issues faced by railway attractions and explores approaches to mitigating risks and implementing standards and guidelines which balance providing a quality experience for visitors and achieving other business objectives. It presents two illustrative case studies from Australia – the Ipswich Heritage Railway Workshops (Queensland) and Puffing Billy in Belgrave (Victoria) – to provide insights into how safety can be effectively managed for all involved in the travel and leisure industry.

An Authentic Experience

Chhabra *et al.* (2003) point out that authenticity is an important attribute of heritage tourism, sought by many visitors. Li (2003: 250) adds that this can be realised 'either through environmental experiences or people-based experiences, or an interaction of the two'. MacCannell (1976: 36) reflects on the significance of visitors being exposed to 'the displayed work of others'. For visitors to industrial heritage sites, the attractiveness of the experience is often interwoven with the adventure and authenticity of the work and production process (e.g. observe the making of train parts in a workshop setting) and/or the opportunity to participate in associated activities (e.g. ride on a heritage train). As such, visits to industrial heritage sites afford learning opportunities, nostalgic interludes and 'tangible' experiences (Halsall, 2001; Taska, 2003).

Various researchers have noted the connotations of authenticity in relation to reality (Berger, 1973; Pine & Gilmore, 2011), to genuineness (Cohen, 2007), and to culture, value and integrity (Cohen, 1988). Other authors extend the usage of 'authentic' to emphasise preservation and conservation (e.g. Breathnach, 2009; Cohen, 1988; Wang, 1999). In an examination of the development of a jeep museum in Toledo (Ohio), Xie (2006) identifies authenticity as one of the six key aspects contributing to the appeal and vitality of industrial heritage sites. Building on the work of Lowenthal (1985), Cohen (1988) and Leary and Sholes (2000), Xie (2006: 1327) argues that authenticity is captured via multidimensional 'representational spaces' where various backgrounds and interests are drawn together, the past is brought to life and visitors are educated and entertained. In addition, Gelbman (2007: 153) acknowledged that industrial heritage sites play a key role in regenerating and revitalising curiosity and interest in historical industries as well as contemporary ones. He notes the reality and physical sensations that visits to such sites engender in visitors 'by way of noises, smells and experiencing the dynamics'. The vibrancy, intrigue and charm add to the appeal and enduring nature of the phenomenon of industrial heritage experiences (Longworth, 1992).

Safety on the Line

The health and safety of visitors and employees is an area of increasing priority for operators and owners of attractions. Swarbrooke (2002: 165) states that 'Legislation and the need to protect visitors and staff means that safety and security must be a major consideration in the design of any new attraction'. For managers of attractions, old and new, there is a growing need to ensure minimisation of health and safety issues and adoption of best practice. Railway attractions are environments which present particular risks in relation to health and safety.

Frew (2000) notes that one of the major considerations for companies developing and organising industrial heritage tourism sites is to ensure that issues of safety and security are addressed. More specifically, Bregman (2011) emphasises that companies which conduct tours should be mindful of the risks to safety and adopt strategies to deal with these. He suggests that striking a balance between safety and a 'real company experience' can be challenging, as higher risks may be incurred by the latter; however, solutions could include segregating visitors from hazards by avoiding areas of high risk and constructing partitions, such as glass walls. Bregman (2011) notes that risks to safety increase with higher levels of automation in production processes and that this is further amplified by non-skilled visitors, who may or may not be involved in the production process. Such is the situation for organisations involved in showcasing railway heritage sites.

In the quest to provide authentic experiences, there are risks for which the provider is responsible. There is a 'duty of care' which rests with the provider to ensure measures are taken to safeguard visitors. The British Medical Association (1990: 146) states that 'Nobody sincerely believes that all recreational activities can be made free of risk'. As the work of Bentley et al. (2001) illustrates, risk associated with adventure tourism includes several factors, some of which are beyond the control of the company: extra-organisational, management and organisational, environmental, equipment, client and mishap. In fact, Bentley et al. (2001) proposed a model for the identification of 'risk factors for adventure tourism mishaps' which considered the above factors. This model was adapted and adopted for investigation of the safety at visitor railway heritage sites. It is presented in Figure 6.1.

Bentley et al. (2001) argue that risk in adventure tourism can be reduced by intervention principally enacted at four levels: the individual visitor or tourist; the management and operators; the industry; and the government regulators. In the model above, the role of staff in ensuring safety is included. Bentley et al. (2001) note that there is a range of risk factors in adventure tourism and that injury events are multi-causal and result from the interaction of a number of contributory factors related to each of the levels in the model. Their model was intended to assist operators with risk assessment and the management of safety. It is argued that the negotiation of risk requires 'a delicate balance to be struck between ensuring that tourism businesses are not swamped by bureaucracy and red tape, while their clients are offered an experience that falls within internationally acceptable levels of risk and injury' (Bentley et al., 2001: 336).

Other authors have also discussed the relationship between risk and safety. For example, Espiner (1999) investigated visitors' perceptions of risk and the degree to which they assume responsibility for their own safety. Espiner (1999: 7) defines risk as 'the potential to lose something of value' and hazards as 'conditions which increase the possibility of loss occurring'. Interestingly, he highlights the distinction between 'real' and 'perceived' risk, noting that the latter governs individuals' behaviour. It is reasoned

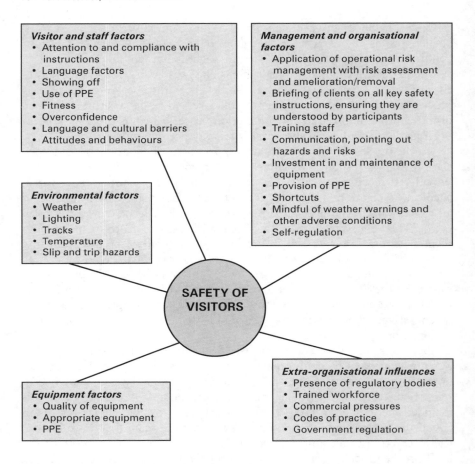

Figure 6.1 Model of risk factors for industrial railway heritage sites (PPE, personal protection equipment)

that individuals' assessment of risk is subjective and that their awareness of risk is influenced by various factors such as cultural conditioning, previous experience and personal attributes (e.g. personality, attitudes and dispositions). Espiner (1999: 12) points out that visitors may have an insulated view of the prospective experience, thinking and trusting that they are protected from risks by management and so are not as diligently mindful of risks as they should be. This incongruity between perceived and real risks is an issue of safety which is pertinent, of relevance to this study and is subsumed in Bentley *et al.*'s (2001) model, especially in relation to factors associated with visitors, staff and management levels.

While the work of Bentley *et al.* (2001) is within the context of adventure tourism, it is reasonable to propose that a similar approach to risk can be applied to industrial railway heritage attractions. Hence, this chapter uses the model presented in Figure 6.1 to evaluate the approach to safety of such attractions and, in particular at two Australian case study sites: the Ipswich Heritage Railway Workshops (Queensland); and Puffing Billy in Belgrave (Victoria).

Case Studies

The following two case studies represent different ways in which organisations have developed industrial heritage experiences. The safety issues relevant to each and the management of these are discussed in relation to the model presented in Figure 6.1.

Information was gathered from several sources, including participant observation, diary entries and document analysis. For example, company websites provided some valuable background information on experiences being offered by the two organisations. In addition, various studies were consulted to gain further insights, such as the *Profile of the Tourist and Heritage Railway and Tramway Sector in Australia* (Association of Tourist and Heritage Rail Australia, 2008). Also, field visits to the sites provided opportunities to observe operations and to glean information from brochures and other documents (e.g. from the static displays and library at the Ipswich Heritage Railway Workshops). These approaches allowed the recording of in-depth personal experiences of the participant observer and comments from workers at the organisations involved (Halsall, 2001; McIntosh, 1998). Each of the two sites was visited for two days and the information was gathered before, during and after the visits.

Puffing Billy

The modern-day Puffing Billy steam train is a legacy of one of Australia's oldest steam trains. More than a century ago, Puffing Billy was built to serve the communities in the Dandenong Ranges, 40 km east of Melbourne. Today, locomotives representing the Puffing Billy trek through the remaining railway line used to develop the remote eastern rural regions of Melbourne, taking visitors on a journey back in time. Each locomotive of the Puffing Billy Railway Line has its own identity and history. Over 900 volunteers and a small team of paid staff work to maintain and present Puffing Billy to visitors on every day of the year, except Christmas Day. The journey takes in various landmarks, including the historic Monbulk Creek Trestle Bridge, the site of a 1953 landslide, the Nobelius Packing Shed, and rest-stops at Lakeside and Gembrook. The main offices and locomotive workshops are in Belgrave. The Puffing Billy Preservation Society was set up in 1955 and its members have played an active role in the life and operation of Puffing Billy. The Emerald Tourist Railway Board acts as the statutory authority overseeing operation of the railway and ensuring appropriate training and testing of vehicles and staff are maintained. More than 5 million visitors have travelled on Puffing Billy and experienced its many delights.

The Ipswich Heritage Railway Workshops

The Ipswich Heritage Railway Workshops are an annex of the Workshops Rail Museum. The Museum is a tourist facility which is managed by Queensland Museum and presents a number of attractions and exhibitions for visitors of all ages and from all walks of life. Some of the regular features and events include: Steam Train Sunday; Platform 9; Toyland Express; Day Out with Thomas; Nippers Play and Learn; and Build It. Exhibitions include: a large model railway; Greatest Railway Journeys of Australia; equipment and stories from the Ipswich Railway Workshops; and Moving Goods. Some of these exhibitions are static, others interactive, and all have interpretive information for visitors to peruse. There is even a library on the site (the John Douglas Kerr Reading Room). Visitors to the Workshops Rail Museum can also visit the Heritage Railway Workshops, which are managed by Queensland Rail.

The Heritage Railway Workshops have played a key role in the history of Queensland Rail, with the inaugural steam journey of the first Queensland train running from the Ipswich Heritage Railway Workshops to Grandchester (formerly Bigges Camp) in 1865. The site remains an operating railway workshop, making it the oldest to be continually involved in the construction, development and maintenance of steam locomotives. At its peak, during World War II, the Ipswich Railway Workshops employed over 3000 people.

These days, tradespeople who are employees of Queensland Rail run 30-minute tours through the Blacksmith Shop and the Steam Shop. The workshop houses 50 railway workers in various trades, including boilermakers, fitters, blacksmiths and electricians. Queensland Rail realised that some of the older workers would soon retire and, with that, knowledge about heritage railways would potentially be lost. Hence, a number of apprentices make up the workshop workforce.

The tours are run several times a day. Visitors are informed that 'enclosed footwear' is a requirement and safety glasses are provided for the tour of the Blacksmith Shop, where 'sparks fly' and visitors can 'feel the heat of the furnaces and thud of massive one-tonne steam hammers'. Like the experience described by Gržinić *et al.* (2009) in relation to Muzej Labin, the Ipswich Heritage Railway Workshops provide insights into traditional engineering and manufacturing practices as well as into the skill and expertise of the workforce.

Discussion

This section presents a comparison of safety issues as they were observed and noted at Puffing Billy and the Ipswich Railway Heritage Workshops. The themes identified in Figure 6.1 are used to guide the discussion.

Management and organisational factors

Tours at the Ipswich Heritage Railway Workshops began by visitors congregating outside the workshop sheds. A sign in this area stated that it was policy for closed footwear to be worn by anyone partaking in the workshop tours, but it was observed that this was not always enforced.

Visitors are led into the workshops area and escorted onto a 'Traverser' (Figure 6.2). The Traverser is a mobile platform with integral rail lines and 100 tonne capacity, and is used to move locomotives and rolling stock from one shed to another across the railway lines. It has been modified to carry visitors to the workshops. It had been fitted with a cover, removable safety rails and closing gates at either end, enabling it to 'qualify as a tourist attraction', as mentioned by the guide.

On the first day of the research visit to the Ipswich Heritage Railway Workshops, the tour was conducted by a female boilermaker employed by Queensland Rail. She guided visitors through both the Blacksmith Shop and the Steam Shop. The visit was in January and due to this being a holiday period there was only a skeleton crew in the workshop. Visitors were informed that generally there are 50 employees from a range of trades working in the workshop. The Blacksmith Shop tour was accompanied by the tour guide, a volunteer and two people who operated the equipment. The Steam Shop tour was attended by only the tour guide.

By contrast, the trip on the Puffing Billy steam train began with an announcement over the public address system highlighting the importance of safety. It warned people of various dangers, such as walking on the track, awareness of other trains on the track and not getting too close to the hot

Figure 6.2 Traverser transporting visitors along the railway tracks down to the Blacksmith Shop at the Ipswich Heritage Railway Workshops

engine. While pertinent, it was hard to hear the speaker over the conversations in the carriage. Hence, the value of this commentary needs to be questioned. In addition, many of the travellers were international visitors who were busy conversing in their native languages while this important message was being broadcast. One assumes that commonsense does prevail and that most people will be attentive to safety issues but unruly children running around on the platforms was a good indication that ensuring safety of passengers requires more than just their commonsense. In their study on safety along rail trails, Tracy and Harris (1998) commented that visitors' use of commonsense and alertness to their surroundings was a contributing factor to mitigating risk.

Volunteers were distributed in the various carriages to provide assistance and ensure appropriate and safe behaviour of travellers. In comparison with the Ipswich Heritage Railway Workshops, the volunteers at Puffing Billy are people who have an interest in the concept of Puffing Billy and are not necessarily trained tradespeople. However, they are provided with an induction and ongoing training that cover attention to safety and customer service. Staff at the Puffing Billy were allocated such that there were a number of qualified first-aid providers on each trip. Further training included 'what to do in case of an accident on the line'. The focus on safety at Puffing Billy

Figure 6.3 Riding the Puffing Billy

was apparent in the attitude of staff, who enforced appropriate behaviour when required.

As a last action prior to the steam train leaving the station, the conductor came past every carriage checking that all the doors were closed properly and he asked passengers to ensure that their shoes were on properly (see Figure 6.3). Volunteers were positioned in every second carriage so as 'to keep an eye on things' and at every stop they moved to the next carriage. Most carriages could accommodate up to 50 people and travellers were encouraged to sit on the window rail with feet dangling out of the train (Figure 6.3). Sitting with arms and legs protruding out of the train was risky, as extremities could easily be caught by tree branches or other incursions along the railway line. Huge trees line the tracks and regular maintenance includes pruning of shrubs and trees near the tracks, ensuring that any obstructions are removed. However, occasionally obstacles are missed. As it happened, on one trip on the Puffing Billy there was a small dead branch hanging from a tree about passenger level and near enough to the train for it to injure a passenger. The train made an emergency stop and the guard promptly attended to removing the branch.

The volunteers and organisation do what they can to minimise incidents, and signage in the carriages promotes attention to safety. Despite this effort, occasionally there are incidents which compromise safety. As mentioned by one of the carriage conductors, there was an incident where a young boy opened the carriage door just as the train was passing over the Trestle Bridge. Fortunately, the boy was spotted and disaster averted.

Similar to the Ipswich Heritage Railway Workshops, it can be difficult to monitor all passengers when visitor numbers are large.

Tour groups at the Ipswich Heritage Railway Workshops were limited to 25 people. This way was a good safety strategy and afforded some control over circumstances, especially when the workshop was in full operation. Risks are easily compounded with 25 visitors walking through a workshop where 50 workers are engaged in various stages of locomotive restoration and activities such as welding, riveting and steel fabrication. Welding screens were noted and these obstructed visitors from viewing welding activities and possibly being inadvertently exposed to harmful light. Equally, if riveting activities were happening, visitors would require ear protection because riveting is very noisy. That would require 25 sets of earmuffs to be handed out. In the Steam Shop, one boiler was under construction using traditional riveting methods but with workers away on holiday the equipment remained idle.

Painted lines were used to indicate to visitors the areas they could access. It is easy to imagine that on days of full operation it could be quite a task for the tour guide (and volunteer) to keep a watchful eye on all 25 visitors and ensure that none of them strayed into dangerous areas or behaved in a manner that would jeopardise their safety. Relying on painted lines in those circumstances, especially where people are in close proximity to what amounts to heavy industrial processes, is not without risk.

An example is the steam hammer display. At present, visitors are required to stand behind a painted line at quite a distance from the steam hammer as the tradespeople demonstrate how they make a tool for the workshop. The demonstration is spectacular, with sparks flying, but the distance does detract from the experience, so much so that, during the visit, it was observed that some of the visitors gave up looking at the steam hammer and become more engrossed in their own individual conversations and walking over and touching other equipment. If visitors were perhaps positioned closer and behind a barrier of safety glass, they could feel the power and thump of the steam hammer and the authenticity of the experience would be enhanced. Admittedly, this is far more costly than painted lines but it would ensure that people are more engaged and would not get themselves into dangerous situations.

Visitor and staff factors

At the Ipswich Heritage Railway Workshops, staff consisted of professionally qualified tradespeople, and so they were adept at managing risk and would have been aware if people strayed into dangerous areas. The guides seemed to be appropriately trained but awareness of risk and responsibility differed between guides, with some guides being more attentive than others to the wanderings of visitors. In particular, if the guide was asked a question, it was noted on occasion that he or she became caught up in responding and was oblivious to what all the visitors were doing, such that a couple wandered beyond the painted lines. Fortunately, the volunteer assisting the guide was sufficiently attentive to draw the visitors back into the allocated space.

The lack of physical barriers at the Ipswich Heritage Railway Workshops meant that there was a reliance on visitors following instructions and children being kept under supervision and ensuring there was no climbing over locomotives or going into dangerous areas. Therefore, visitors' attitudes and behaviours are determinants of the effectiveness of safety measures. A physical barrier around the more active displays, such as the steam hammer, is a worthy consideration.

It is possible to imagine some young people getting a bit bored with the presentation and deciding that it would be fun to stand up on top of the Garrett locomotive or some such prank, as there was really nothing other than signs to prevent unwarranted behaviour. Without physical barriers, there is less of an impediment to pursue whimsical ideas and have a distorted perception of the associated risks.

Similarly with the Puffing Billy, it was apparent that travellers could easily become so consumed by the adventure of travelling on a real steam train that their perception of associated dangers is distorted. The boy who opening the carriage door as described above is a case in point. Equally, passengers were keen to board the train and often remained oblivious to the safety messages and associated aspects. Other visitor factors include language barriers, such that visitors do not understand safety announcements and through lack of awareness can jeopardise their safety or that of other passengers. Fortunately, the Puffing Billy was adequately staffed by people who were dedicated to providing a memorable experience for visitors and were vigilant in ensuring their safety.

Equipment factors

Overall, the whole experience at the Ipswich Heritage Railway Workshops was a passive one. There was no interaction with what was going on and that in itself is a concession to safety. For example, the steam hammer in the boiler-making shop is a piece of equipment that requires a great deal of experience to use and it is preferable not to have people standing too close to it and certainly not interacting with it and poking bits of steel underneath it. Hence, trained people provided demonstrations and visitors, wearing safety glasses, were confined to viewing from behind a safety line marked on the ground. Thus it was very much a passive experience. Of note is the presence of a first-aid room, workers with two-way radios, and modern gates and padlocks preventing people not on tour from straying into the more dangerous areas of the workshops.

By comparison, the experience at Puffing Billy was one of immersion in the experience. Visitors revel in the journey. As the steam train chuffs its way along the Dandenong Ranges, travellers are swallowed in clouds of smoke billowing out from the engine and thrill to the long shrill from the steam whistle. It is impossible to escape the sense of adventure and not to be caught up in the spirit of a bygone era as the train meanders its way through bushland, bringing history to life. The experience is educational, exciting and enlightening. Within this framework, staff from Puffing Billy had to ensure that the people and the train are safe. Locomotive drivers and engineers of international standing work to make the trains safe; fire patrol and track patrol staff effect safe tracks and surrounds; and carpenters, carriage builders and painters take care of the safety of the rolling stock.

Environmental factors

At the Ipswich Heritage Railway Workshops, there did not seem to be too many environmental hazards. Slip and trip hazards were a noticeable factor but they seemed to be well controlled. There were a number of railway lines (four to five railway lines going the length of each shed) which were level with the concrete and were crossed by visitors; where there were walkways, there were inserts to fill in the gaps and they would have been removed when the rolling stock needed to be moved. This is an effective way to control potential slip and trip hazards. As a further safety measure, visitors had to walk within yellow lines and stand behind green lines at demonstrations. This was a positive initiative but it was relying on people to follow instructions and not to go beyond the painted lines. Generally, visitors were obliging.

At the Puffing Billy, the scene seemed to be more chaotic, with visitors actually interacting with the train as they travelled in the carriages, waited on the platforms and visited the engine locomotive with the hope of sitting in the driver's seat or opportunity to shovel coal. Safety was a real concern as train engines and carriages were unlocked and moved along the tracks in preparation for the trip. Volunteers at various points along the track and platform were vigilant and ensured that travellers did not endanger them-selves. Slip and trip hazards were apparent as travellers ventured in and out of carriages and manoeuvred themselves on and off the windowsills. Travelling open to the elements was in itself part of the allure of the experience of the Puffing Billy but, equally, it left visitors exposed to a myriad of weather conditions, such as heat, cold, wind, rain and sunlight.

Temperature at the Ipswich Heritage Railway Workshops could be a consideration in mid-summer, especially where welding was being done. It was ameliorated by the fact that compressed air rather than steam was used to drive the steam hammer. When the workshop was working years ago in maintaining the rolling stock and locomotives for Queensland Railway, it would have been a very hot environment in summer, with all of the welding, forging and steam to drive the machinery, but nowadays it seemed to be very well controlled. As it was, on one visit into the Blacksmith Shop, a lady became faint but, fortunately, provision of seating at various points enabled her to sit down and regain her composure.

Lighting at the Ipswich Heritage Railway Workshops was good, especially in the sheds where visitors were taken on tours. The saw-tooth roofing, which is a legacy of the early days of the Ipswich Railway Workshops, maximised natural lighting and aeration. Originally, the saw-tooth roofing, with its large glass panels, was designed to allow light into the massive workshop sheds and improve ventilation. Recently, a safety audit found that these panels are a safety hazard. Consequently, the Blacksmith Shop and Steam Shop which constitute the Queensland Rail Workshops and are part of the Ipswich Railway Workshops Museum were temporarily closed while the saw-tooth roof was made safe. It is reassuring to know that safety process and practices are in place at industrial heritage sites which have been opened to the public. The issue of visitor safety in developing old industrial sites for purposes of public access and tourism has always been of great concern. For example, Dewar and Miller (2011) and Frew (2011) point out that visitor safety is a management issue for consideration when transforming old or operational mining sites into visitor attractions. It is encouraging to see that measures are in place to ensure visitor safety.

Extra-organisational influences

One thing which was not apparent to visitors and which would have been working in the background is that all of these procedures need to conform to regulations and codes of practice. All the items of rolling stock and locomotives are required to submit to government regulations and follow codes of practices, and they are surveyed to ensure they are fit for service. In particular, when one thinks that a steam locomotive going out in public is potentially a very large explosive device if it is not maintained and the potential for death and injury is very high. On the tour at the Ipswich Heritage Railway Workshops it was pointed out by the tour guide that steam locomotives require boilers to be renewed every 10 years, regardless of mileage, and that was from the experience in the early days of Queensland Rail, when the workshops were coming under increasing maintenance pressure and some locomotives went beyond that period and they experienced two boiler explosions within months of each other. One was in the Roma St (Brisbane) yards, where locomotives were blown right off the tracks. Fortunately, there were no fatalities in those cases but it can be imagined that on train excursions, which the Ipswich Museum runs every now and then, if there were enthusiasts clustered around the steam locomotive and taking photographs and the boiler exploded, there would certainly be fatalities. Hence, even industrial heritage rolling stock needs to be surveyed to ensure it is fit for service. This is equally pertinent in the case of the Puffing Billy, where there are mechanical and boiler inspectors, logbooks to record all maintenance, and a maintenance regime which is comparable with any state or private transport system.

Where the experience for the visitor relies on the train, proper maintenance of locomotives, rolling stock and tracks is an ongoing mission. Recently, the historic Ravenshoe Steam Railway train was derailed as it was returning from its regular weekly trip from Tumoulin to Ravenshoe. The steam locomotive, water tender and four passenger wagons were derailed. At the time, there were 108 passengers and 9 staff onboard but no one was hurt. The Rail Safety Regulation Board arrived on the following day seeking to determine the cause of the derailment but, to date, the Ravenshoe Steam Railway remains non-operational. The impact of this incident has implications for the hard-working volunteers and community who are involved in the venture and potential visitors who would avail themselves of the associated history and experience of steam railway.

Conclusion

By restoring and reviving historical industrial sites, industrial heritage tourism invigorates and preserves traditional ways of life, especially ways of doing work. Industrial heritage railway sites, with their locomotives, rolling stock and other machinery and with their static and live exhibitions occupy a valuable niche in enlightening visitors about the fascinating history of railways and the role they assumed in people's lives, communities and nations. They provide authentic experiences which range from information archived in dedicated libraries, to displays with artefacts, to demonstrations of how equipment, machines, rolling stock and locomotive engines are built (as with the Ipswich Heritage Railway Workshops), through to opportunities to journey on heritage vehicles (as with Puffing Billy). The safety of visitors at these sites is a key aspect of managing the development and presentation of these experiences to visitors. Risks to visitors' safety should not be neglected, as they represent threats to companies' images, reputations and strategies. Hence, it is paramount that frameworks, strategies, policies and practices are in place which ensure best practice in management of risk and create safe and fun experiences for visitors to heritage railway sites.

It seems that organisations do endeavour to make industrial railway heritage sites 'safe places'. They employ preventative strategies to reduce risk and accidents and injuries to visitors. They recognise the need for safety measures and identify factors to be considered in the process of doing so, while accommodating the needs of industry regulators, the business and staff, and optimising the visitor's experience. Aside from the ethical issues when it comes to providing safe environments for visitors, operators need to ensure that, in the event of litigation, they can demonstrate that they have adequately addressed the management of risk and provision of safe sites.

Ultimately, despite the efforts of management and organisations, visitors' attitudes and behaviours can place themselves and others at risk. Awareness and perceptions of hazards and risks can go a long way to compliant behaviour if organisations enforce a culture of safety at their sites. Hence, management and staff can play a key role in minimising risk and in advancing visitors' awareness, attitudes and behaviour. Espiner (1999) recognised that there is a challenge in determining a fitting balance between economic, legal and social factors with the safety of visitors and staff. This is consistent with the model suggested in this chapter, in that the challenge is to find the balance between management/organisational goals, visitors' expectations, staff training and attitudes, environmental factors, equipment utilised and extra-organisational influences. From this perspective, industrial railway heritage sites should allow visitors to participate and live in and through the vicarious and real spaces and places of museums, workshops, tours and journeys. The Ipswich Heritage Railway Workshops and Puffing Billy seek to capture authentic environments and foster experiences which vitalise the senses, expand understanding and knowledge and enrich appreciation of industrial railway heritage. They integrate preservation, interpretation and entertainment in ways which minimise risks to visitors.

In order to ensure continuous, genuine and credible attention to safety for industrial railway heritage sites, there needs to be further research into current practices from a range of both heritage and industrial sites (such as railway, mining, forestry and motor industries) and from a variety of international areas. Such research should then inform the development of relevant policies and contribute to the development of best practice in the provision of training for staff and tour guides and the management and sustainability of industrial railway heritage sites.

References

Association of Tourist and Heritage Rail Australia (ATHRA) (2008) *Profile of the Tourist and Heritage Railway and Tramway Sector in Australia.* Port Adelaide: ATHRA.

Berger, P. (1973) Sincerity and authenticity in modern society. *Public Interest* 31, 81–90.

Bentley, T., Page, S., Meyer, D., Chalmers, D. and Laird, I. (2001) How safe is adventure tourism in New Zealand? An exploratory analysis. *Applied Ergonomics* 32, 327–338.

Breathnach, T. (2009) Looking for the real me: Locating the self in heritage tourism. *Journal of Heritage Tourism* 1 (2), 100–120.

Bregman, W. (2011) Industrial tourism visits: The role of company tours within companies' strategies. Unpublished masters thesis, Department of Economics, Erasmus University, Rotterdam.

British Medical Association (1990) *Living With Risk.* Harmondsworth: Penguin.

Chhabra, D., Healy, R. and Sills, E. (2003) Staged authenticity and heritage tourism. *Annals of Tourism Research* 30 (3), 702–719.

Cohen, E. (1988) Authenticity and commoditization in tourism. *Annals of Tourism Research* 15 (3), 371–386.

Cohen, E. (2007) 'Authenticity' in tourism studies: Apres la lutte. *Tourism Recreation Research* 32 (2), 75–82.

Dewar, K. and Miller, R. (2011) Geotourism, mining and tourism development in the Bay of Fundy, Canada. In M. Conlin and L. Jolliffe (eds) *Mining Heritage and Tourism: A Global Synthesis* (pp. 203–213). New York: Routledge.

Espiner, S. (1999) *The Use and Effect of Hazard Warning Signs: Managing Visitor Safety at Franz Josef and Fox Glaciers.* Wellington: Department of Conservation.

Frew, E. (2000) Industrial tourism: A conceptual and empirical analysis (pp. 1–10). Unpublished PhD thesis, Victoria University, Melbourne.

Frew, E. (2011) Transforming working mines into tourist attractions. In M. Conlin and L. Jolliffe (eds) *Mining Heritage and Tourism: A Global Synthesis* (pp. 72–83). New York: Routledge.

Gelbman, A. (2007) Tourism in industry in the post-industrial city. In P. Duhamel and S. Knapou (eds) *Mondes urbains du tourisme* (pp. 151–162). Paris: Belin, Series 'Mappemondes'.

Gržinić, J., Zanketić, P. and Baćac, R. (2009) Industrial tourism in Istria. *Ekonomska misao i praksa* 18 (2), 211–232.

Halsall, D. (2001) Railway heritage and the tourist gaze: Stoomtram Hoorn-Medemblik. *Journal of Transport Geography* 9, 151–160.

Leary, T. and Sholes, E. (2000) Authenticity of place and voice: Examples of industrial heritage preservation and interpretation in the US and Europe. *Public Historian* 22 (3), 49–66.

Li, Y. (2003) Heritage tourism: The contradictions between conservation and change. *Tourism and Hospitality Research* 4 (3), 247–261.

Longworth, J. (1992) Heritage talking: A semiotic analysis of a major railway museum.

Paper presented at the Sixth National Conference on Engineering Heritage, Hobart, 5–7 October.

Lowenthal, D. (1985) *The Past Is a Foreign Country*. Cambridge: Cambridge University Press.

MacCannell, D. (1976) *The Tourist: A New Theory of the Leisure Class*. New York: Schocken Books.

McIntosh, A.J. (1998) Mixing methods: Putting the tourist at the forefront of tourism research. *Tourism Analysis* 3 (2), 121–127.

Pine, J. and Gilmore, J. (2011) *The Experience Economy* (updated edition). Boston, MA: Harvard Business School Publishing.

Swarbrooke, J. (2002) *The Development and Management of Visitor Attractions*. Oxford: Butterworth-Heinemann.

Taska, L. (2003) Machines and ghosts: Politics, industrial heritage and the history of working life at the Eveleigh Workshops. *Labour History* 85, 65–88.

Tillman, J.A. (2002) Sustainability of heritage railways: An economic approach. *Japan Railway and Transport Review* 32, 38–45.

Tracy, T. and Harris, H. (1998) *Rail-Trails and Safe Communities*. Washington: National Park Services.

Urry, J. (1990) *The Tourist Gaze: Leisure and Travel in Contemporary Societies*. London: Sage.

Wang, N. (1999) Rethinking authenticity in tourism experience. *Annals of Tourism Research* 26 (2), 349–370.

Xie, P. (2006) Developing industrial heritage tourism: A case study of the proposed jeep museum in Toledo, Ohio. *Tourism Management* 27, 1321–1330.

7 New Zealand Rail Trails: Heritage Tourism Attractions and Rural Communities

Arianne C. Reis and Carla Jellum

Introduction

Around the world, abandoned railways are being converted into rail trails, resulting in a range of economic and social benefits for visitors and communities alike. A major catalyst for this process and for the ample provision of these trails has been the social movement initiated by the non-profit American organization Rails-to-Trails Conservancy, established in 1986 with the explicit goal of 'working with communities to preserve unused rail corridors by transforming them into trails' where people can engage in various recreational activities (Rails-to-Trails Conservancy, 2012). Similar groups have been created in other countries and have been relatively successful in establishing a range of trails on abandoned or inoperative railway lines.

A notable contribution from this alternative use of railway lines is the preservation of heritage, which may in turn result in increased cohesion among rural communities. Although presenting a much younger history than their counterparts in North America and Europe, rail trails in New Zealand are exemplary in their development, being dedicated to preserving as much of the original railway infrastructure as possible and thus providing an experience that visitors may label as authentic. This chapter presents the Otago Central Rail Trail (OCRT) as a case study and provides evidence of the tourism potential that this rail trail embodies.

Despite the increasing recognition of the significance of rail trails as a recreational resource and tourism product, there is little research exploring the tourism experience and social and economic impacts associated with this heritage asset (for examples of available studies see: Bowker *et al.*, 2007; Hawthorne *et al.*, 2008; Moore & Graefe, 1994; Moore *et al.*, 1994a; Mundet & Coenders, 2010; Reis & Jellum, 2012; Siderelis & Moore, 1995). Moreover, the OCRT is a unique tourism product, as it combines two distinct heritage attractions: a historic, scenic excursion train on the original track, and a multiple-use rail trail on the disused track.

This chapter is organized as follows. First, we provide a brief overview of the literature on the development of the international rail trail movement. This is followed by a discussion of the conversion of 'rails to trails', specifically in New Zealand. Next we present recent research providing empirical support for the claim that rural communities, particularly businesses, perceive a positive benefit from rail-to-trail conversion. The chapter concludes with some cautions and suggestions for preserving site-specific heritage attractions unique to rail trails that may enhance the tourist experience while preserving a rural community's historic identity.

A Brief History of Rail Trail Development

Rail trails can be defined as multi-use trails that are sited on former railway lines or that run continuously beside an active railway for most of its length (Beeton, 2003; Moore et al., 1994b). Rail trails are used for transportation and/or leisure purposes. They are usually characterized by their gentle gradients, wide curves and corridors and hard surfaces, and are popular with cyclists, walkers and horse riders.

An important contribution to the rails-to-trails movement in North America and Europe was the greenway movement. Since rail trails are considered a particular type of greenway (Betz et al., 2003), the environmental and landscape planning movement of the 1980s provided extra impetus and support for the conversion of abandoned railway lines into 'ecologically significant corridors' or 'greenways with historical and cultural values' (Fábos, 2004: 322). Crucial to the movement was the 1986 report from the President's Commission on Americans Outdoors (PCAO) that recommended 'the development of a national network of greenways characterized by local, grassroots activism' (Betz et al., 2003: 79). However, the particularities of the rails-to-trails projects (e.g. landowner resistance) meant that progress was slower and opposition greater than with general greenway plans. Notwithstanding the success of such trails today, right-of-way issues still exist and legal action is still required in many cases (Bowman & Wright, 2008). Likewise, opposition from local residents is sometimes present and can hinder development (Brown, 2008; Hawthorne et al., 2008). For example, the United States has over 256,000 km of disused railway lines (Fábos, 2004); however, to date 'only' less than 10% has been converted into rail trails (Rails-to-Trails Conservancy, 2012). Therefore, there exists a great potential for an even larger rail trail network for the country.

The United States is in fact considered the first country to have established a structured social movement for rail trails. The Railroad Revitalization and Regulatory Reform Act of 1976 is commonly described as the first major driver for the rails-to-trails movement. Although the country's rails-to-trails program was not a major focus of the Act, the legislation did provide some legal support for the conversion proposals (Tiedt, 1980). The Act offered the possibility of converting abandoned railways into areas of recreation, and this argument was used to support appeals in support of their implementation. As a consequence, today the United States is served by the widest and longest web of rail trails in the world, with more than 14,000 rail trails in the country, ranging from less than 1 km to over 300 km (Jaffe, 2006; Rails-to-Trails Conservancy, 2012).

However, the greatest impulse for the movement in the United States came 10 years after the Act, with the establishment of the Rails-to-Trails Conservancy in 1986. This non-governmental organization argued for the 'reuse of a resource – the recycling of a whole transportation system' that would not only recycle the transportation system but also provide for recreation, conserve local and national heritage, and benefit the environment (Fletcher, 2006: 16). This rationale helped the organization to receive funds from government agencies that were responsible for, or dealt with, transportation issues, and broadened the scope of the movement as well as the uses of the trails. Rail trails today therefore have different purposes, some serving mainly as a transportation corridor connecting national parks and other rural areas, or urban settings and green strips, and others serving as a recreation ground for locals and domestic and international tourists (Fábos, 2004; Fletcher, 2006; Ross, 1996).

In Europe, rails-to-trails development has similarities with that in the United States, in the sense that it is part of a broader project that aims to develop greenway corridors as alternative transport routes (European Greenways Association, 2012b). The European Greenways Association was established in 1998 with its scope strictly limited to transportation systems, and with minimal attention to the recreational value of these corridors. In fact, the definition of greenways (rail trails included) used by the Association states that 'greenways are *transport corridors*' that provide 'ease of passage', 'safety', 'continuity' and 'respect for the environment' (European Greenways Association, 2012a, original emphasis).

Germany has the largest network of rail trails in Europe, with over 550 trails currently in use, followed by the UK, with almost 150 tracks. In total, Europe has more than 1300 rail trails actively used by visitors and locals, with several projects under way (Bahntrassenradeln, 2009). In the UK, the two most influential advocates of rails-to-trails programs have been the Railway

Ramblers and Sustrans. With their support and lobbying, 2000–3500 km of discarded railway lines have been converted into rail trails open to the public for recreational purposes. In Europe, however, disused railways that have not yet been sold or converted to serve other purposes are not as common as they are in Australia and New Zealand, where spatial constraint is not yet a major issue. Therefore, although greenways and cycling tourism in general are very popular, and efforts to develop them will continue to increase in European countries, rail trails have not as much scope for expansion when compared with these less populated countries.

In Canada, rail trail developments were slightly slower than in the United States. The official opening of the Trans Canada Trail in 2000 is considered a benchmark in the history of the rails-to-trails movement in the country, although conversions began a decade before (Baker, 2001). The Trans Canada Trail is not formed solely by railway conversion, but comprises different trail types: 'from wilderness pathways, rail trails, forested trails, rural tracks, historic canoe routes to paved urban walkways, downtown streets, country roads, logging roads, and secondary highways' (Trans Canada Trail, 2009). Its significance for the movement, however, comes from its length – 16,000 km – and the visibility the movement gained from such a large enterprise.

In Australia, rail trails are becoming important tourism attractions and are part of a broader effort to promote cycling tourism within the country (Faulks et al., 2007). An economic impact study of rail trails in Victoria presented promising results in terms of positive impacts of the trails on adjacent communities, especially regarding tourism-related revenue (Beeton, 2003). As of 2012, there were 127 rail trails in Australia, ranging in length from 0.5 km to more than 1000 km (RailTrails Australia, 2012). RailTrails Australia is the advocacy group that has been leading the campaign for rail trail development since 1994 (formerly named Australian Rails to Trails). It works to promote the rail trail idea and is one of the key actors in the establishment of the country's rail trail network.

Australia's state of Victoria, where the Australian rails-to-trails movement was initiated, presents the most comprehensive web of rail trails in the country, with 39 trails in total (RailTrails Australia, 2012). According to Irvine (2007), the factors that helped Victoria to lead the way in Australia were the combination of 'its potential, a politician's vision, organized lobbyists and community support'. However, despite Victoria's success, and due to a disparity in state regulations and political interests, there are sharp differences in rail trail networks between states, with some regions having only a couple of completed tracks. This situation shows how important political interest and momentum are for the successful establishment of what is frequently still a contested use of land (Bowman & Wright, 2008; Brown, 2008; Dowsett, 2008).

New Zealand has a recent, and still very limited, history of rails-to-trails development. Only three rail trails are currently in use in the country and only one allows for longer journeys. Recently, however, a public political development has involved the further provision of cycling opportunities in the country, targeting both local commuters and tourists. This proposal should foster rails-to-trails developments. These efforts aim to increase the impact of recreational/tourism products in rural communities, thereby contributing to rural tourism development (George et al., 2009).

New Zealand Rail Trails

New Zealand is still in the early development phase of constructing rail trails. At the time of writing (2012), there are two completed trails and one under development with a few sections already open to the public. The Rimutaka Rail Trail is located on New Zealand's North Island and is typically used by local residents. The Christchurch–Little River Rail Trail (under development) and the OCRT are on the South Island.

The Rimutaka Rail Trail has international heritage value as one of the 10 most significant railway heritage sites in the world (Department of Conservation, 2012). Its importance derives from the Rimutaka Incline, a steep section (with an average gradient of 1 in 15) constructed through the use of an 'innovative and bold engineering solution' – a Fell system – in the late 1870s (Department of Conservation, 2012). The trail also incorporates buildings and structures of historical significance, such as the Pakuratahi Tunnel and Bridge – the former being the first concrete block structure and the latter the first truss bridge in New Zealand. The railway ran using the Incline route until 1955, when a tunnel was built and the line was dismantled soon after that. In 1999 the rail trail was fully resurfaced from Kaitoke to Cross Creek and became available for walking and cycling recreation. With a rich history, the trail attracts more than 30,000 visitors each year (Greater Wellington Regional Council, 2012) and there are projects under way to reinstate and operate a state-of-the-art heritage railway at the site, which is expected to run as an added and connected product to the rail trail. It is hoped that this development will increase the potential of the rail trail to become a significant tourism product for the region. Until then, the trail serves mainly the population of the greater Wellington area, the second largest city in New Zealand, for recreation and educational activities.

The partially completed Christchurch–Little River Rail Trail has approximately 30 km of trail currently open to the public. It serves mostly commuters and locals from the greater Christchurch area. The overseeing RailTrail Trust was formed in 2003 'to transform the former railway route into a trail catering for walkers and cyclists wishing to view the region at close quarters, while avoiding the traffic on the busy road between Little River and Christchurch' (Christchurch–Little River Rail Trail Trust, 2012). The proposed rail trail will be 45 km long (Brown, 2008). If completed as proposed, the trail will link major residential and services areas to parks and recreational opportunities in the back-country, potentially increasing its appeal to domestic and international tourists. To date, however, there has not been a marked effort to market historical aspects of the trail, and the only natural attraction evoked by administrators and supporters is Te Waihora/Lake Ellesmere. For this reason, when the Christchurch–Little River Rail Trail is completed there may be potential to expand and develop a heritage tourism market.

Lastly, the OCRT was established in February 2000 through a cooperative effort between the Department of Conservation (DOC) and the Otago Central Rail Trail Trust. The 150 km recreational rail trail was built upon the historic railway foundations of the Central Otago region. As is commonly the case, the Otago Central Railway has an important and curious local and regional history contributing to its heritage value, which affords the current rail trail a more touristic appeal. It is this history and the current context in which the rail trail is now prospering that we discuss in the following section.

A Brief History of the Otago Central Railway

The social history of the Central Otago region where the OCRT is located involves a short and intense gold mining record followed by pastoral farming and development of a world-recognized wool industry. Today it is also known for its wine production. The Otago Central Railway was the selected route, out of six possibilities, to connect the gold rush districts of the Central Otago region to important trading destinations, such as Dunedin on the south-east coast of the South Island of New Zealand, and Invercargill, in the very south of the South Island (see Figure 7.1).

The Central Otago region is located in the south of New Zealand's South Island and comprises five major areas: Cromwell/Bannockburn, Alexandra/Clyde, Roxburgh, Manuherikia and Maniototo. In total, the region covers an area of 10,000 km^2, and has just over 16,500 permanent residents (Statistics New Zealand, 2006).

It took two years for the Otago Central Railway route to be fully surveyed, and then construction began in 1879. Twelve years, later in 1891,

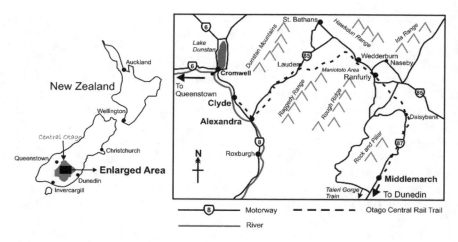

Figure 7.1 Otago Central Rail Trail, Central Otago, New Zealand
Source: This map has been previously published in Reis, A.C. and Jellum, C. (2012) Rail trails development: A conceptual model for sustainable tourism. *Tourism Planning and Development* 9 (2), 133–148 (p. 140)

the first section of the railway opened. The line was completed in 1918 (Hurst, 1990). The Otago Central Railway, the economic lifeline for over 83 years for one of the most isolated regions in New Zealand, served freight and passenger traffic with fluctuating levels of demand throughout its history. Originally the railway transported gold until the end of the rush in the 1920s and then switched to transporting wool bales and rabbit skins, while bringing supplies to the residents of Central Otago; it subsequently took fruit and construction equipment for other development projects across the region. However, with advancing automobile corridors the railway could not withstand the competition and entered an irreversible decline in the 1970s. The decommissioning of the railway began in 1980, when the stretch between Clyde and Cromwell was completely deactivated and subsequently flooded by the damming of the Clutha River. In 1990, the remaining sections from Clyde to Middlemarch closed when the railway system was no longer needed to transport material for the construction of Clyde Dam.

One section of the Otago Central Railway was, however, a popular tourism venture some time before the final closure of the line in 1990. In the late 1960s, the Otago Branch of the New Zealand Railway and Locomotive Society started running passenger trains through the Taieri Gorge, with unexpected success. The popularity of the route led to the establishment of regular excursions and in 1979 a trust was formed to acquire suitable carriages for the enterprise. To prevent this already popular tourism attraction ending, Dunedin City Council bought the land and track from Wingatui to Middlemarch, the first 64 km of the former Otago Central Railway (Hurst, 1990). Today, the Taieri Gorge Railway (TGR) runs daily tourist train trips and is one of the main tourism attractions of the greater Dunedin area.

In 1993, DOC purchased the remainder of the railway route as a recreational reserve. This 150 km section, between Middlemarch and Clyde, was considered of high amenity value and a historical asset (Department of Conservation, 1994). The Otago Central Rail Trail Trust was then formed and became DOC's main ally in the task of transforming the old railway into a multi-use rail trail. Construction work began in 1994 and in 2000 the whole OCRT was officially opened to the public. During the six years of intensive work, NZ$850,000 was spent to provide appropriate surfacing along the trail, as well as to enhance 68 bridges and several tunnels and viaducts, to accommodate safe recreational use (Graham, 2004).

Although the official launch occurred in 2000, visitors, mostly domestic, were using the trail soon after the purchase. Two sections – between Middlemarch and Daisybank, and between Lauder Station and Clyde – were completed in the first three years of DOC ownership and quickly attracted visitor numbers beyond initial expectations (Dowsett, 2008; Ross, 1996).

A trip along the entire 150 km length of the OCRT can begin at either end of the trail, at Clyde or Middlemarch, and is cycled in approximately four days, walked in approximately six days, or experienced by any number of shorter station-to-station trips. The OCRT's highest point is near the township of Wedderburn, 618 m above sea level, with gentle descents in either direction. Whether engaged in a multi-day excursion or a one-day trip, a selection of accommodation providers, restaurants and other businesses service rail trail visitors both in communities adjacent to the rail trail and at nearby off-trail locations.

Structural remnants of the Otago Central Railway can still be found in the OCRT (Figure 7.2). Such remnants are common in rail trails around the world, providing them with extra character: old stone, iron and/or wooden bridges, tunnels of different styles, high viaducts through gorges, and old distance markers and signals. An added attribute of the OCRT regarding its physical heritage, which contributes to its placement as a tourism product, is the conservation of old gangers' (maintenance workers) sheds: corrugated iron sheds spaced along the line where gangers sheltered, and alongside which they parked their jiggers (railway cars). Today, these sheds contain interpretive panels (with maps, colourful photographs and educational material) that help preserve and disseminate the heritage of the old railway

Figure 7.2 Structural remnants of the Otago Central Railway

Figure 7.3 Educational material on the Otago Central Railway

Figure 7.4 Converted old train station on the Otago Central Railway

line to visitors and the new generation of locals (Figure 7.3). Moreover, some of the old train stations have been preserved and contain museums for visitors, telling more of the history of the region and of the railway line (Figure 7.4).

Regarding the heritage aspect of the OCRT experience, the cultural history of the old railway line is a major highlight of the product today. Not only has the trail itself had an interesting, locally and nationally relevant history (Hurst, 1990), but the whole of the Central Otago area is imbued with a rich cultural heritage. The gold mining era and the stories of hundreds of immigrants overcoming or succumbing to the harshness of the Central Otago landscape and climate provides for a full cultural experience. In fact, several products related to this heritage are promoted in the area, and there is current regional political interest in developing the product further. This would only benefit the rail trail product.

The Perceptions of Businesses and Users

While few studies have been conducted so far on the OCRT to measure its impacts on adjacent communities (Blackwell, 2002; Central Otago District Council, 2009, 2011; Dowsett, 2008; Jellum & Reis, 2008; Otago

Central Rail Trail Trust, 2005) as well as to assess tourism developments of the trail (Reis *et al.*, 2010; Ross, 1996), those that have been undertaken continually identify its significance to the local community, with evidence highlighting the rail trail as a community asset and tourism product with a strong heritage component.

Jellum and Reis (2008) assessed the economic impact of the OCRT on businesses along the rail trail, as a follow-up to a study conducted by the Otago Central Rail Trail Trust (2005). The results of the two studies were very similar, with both indicating that businesses considered the OCRT an important asset to the region, providing business opportunities and increased tourism to their communities. In 2008, Jellum and Reis found that nearly a third of respondents (29.7%) considered the OCRT as very important in their decision to buy or start their business. Participants indicated also that the OCRT had positively affected their communities, with greater community pride and more services and facilities available being ranked as the most important effects. Comments such as 'the rail trail is a great resource', 'the OCRT is a wonderful asset' and 'what a wonderful positive creation the Rail Trail is, well done indeed' show the significance of this product to the local (business) community. Moreover, when asked what improvements could be made to enhance the OCRT experience, 'more information panels pointing out areas of interest' and 'greater use [of the OCRT] as an educational resource' were among the top five rated improvements, which shows that the business community perceived positively the heritage associated with the trail and wanted to highlight this aspect.

A year later, as part of a destination management plan, the Central Otago District Council conducted a visitor survey to identify the needs and expectations of visitors to the rail trail, their profile and their economic impact on the community, in order to help direct actions by the Council and by the local (business) community. The study was repeated in 2011 and, similarly to the surveys conducted or funded by the Otago Central Rail Trail Trust (Jellum & Reis, 2008; Otago Central Rail Trail Trust, 2005), the results were consistent across the two years, with the main difference being the perceived increase in the number of visitors using the rail trail and the rise in its percentage contribution to the local economy (from 0.5–1% to 1–2%) (Central Otago District Council, 2009, 2011).

The heritage aspect of the rail trail experience was measured in the two surveys by asking participants how they rated the interpretation panels provided along the rail trail; in both surveys the average rating was 9.7 out of 10. Also, the activity most cited in the 2010/11 survey as extra to their rail trail experience was using the TGR, which again shows the strength of the heritage aspect of this successful railway-based (combined) tourism product. Visiting the gold mining towns, which are a significant part of the heritage associated with Central Otago and the historic railway line, was rated first in 2008/09 and third in 2010/11 (Central Otago District Council, 2009, 2011).

The study conducted by Reis *et al.* (2010) also highlights the significance of the heritage component of the rail trail experience – one which is often ignored in some rail trail developments where the focus becomes the recreational (physical) activity and not the heritage of these trails – which can be successfully used to enhance the visitor experience, a strategy that has proved extremely successful in the OCRT. Reis *et al.*'s (2010) study measured the demand for an improved link between the TGR and the OCRT and the constraints associated with the development of an expanded transportation option for rail trail users (i.e. more frequent train trips to the beginning of the rail trail, in Middlemarch). The study concluded that all individuals and groups directly involved with either the OCRT or the TGR agreed that there was enough demand for an expanded train service to Middlemarch. All participants agreed also that the association between the OCRT and the TGR was greatly beneficial for all those involved with tourism in the region and should be fostered and further strengthened to increase the benefits of such a strong combined product. In addition, in general, tourists who were combining the two railway-related tourism products were extremely satisfied, which again highlights the value of heritage to rail trail tourists using the OCRT.

Conclusion

This chapter provides an overview of the development of disused railway infrastructure as tourism attractions. The focus has been on rail trails, their historical development and their significance as tourism and recreational assets that have the potential to provide experiences that combine heritage with other aspects of tourism/recreation. In fact, our case study, the OCRT, has shown how a rail trail can maintain its historical artifacts and infrastructure to provide for a 'more complete' tourism experience.

Another important aspect of rail trails around the world is their often rural location. This characteristic certainly poses some difficulties in the development of a tourism product that is provided with all of the basic infrastructure needed to host visitors to the area, but it also poses some very interesting new possibilities, as rail trails have the potential to link communities along the corridor of the disused railway line. This link is not only physical, through a connecting route that has been dismantled but that can be restored, but also social, when communities work together to offer a tourism product that will benefit all those along the corridor (Reis & Jellum, 2012). This has certainly been the case in New Zealand, and more specifically in Central Otago, as the research presented attests. Businesses and individuals in the community have formed organizations and interest groups that manage, promote and develop the rail trail product to different markets, which shows that transforming abandoned railway lines into a tourism product (i.e. a rail trail) can be not only profitable but also a sustainable resource fostering economic, social and environmental development.

References

Bahntrassenradeln (2009) A European rail-trail directory. At http://www.achim-bartoschek.de/bahn_rail-trails.htm (accessed January 2014).

Baker, T.R. (2001) A method to assess the potential value of railway corridors as recreation trails: A case study of three Nova Scotia rail-trails. Unpublished masters thesis in urban and regional planning, Queen's University, Kingston, Ontario, Canada.

Beeton, S. (2003) *An Economic Analysis of Rail Trails in Victoria, Australia.* Bendigo: La Trobe University.

Betz, C.J., Bergstrom, J.C. and Bowker, J.M. (2003) A contingent trip model for estimating rail-trail demand. *Journal of Environmental Planning and Management* 46 (1), 79–96.

Blackwell, D. (2002) Community and visitor benefits of the Otago Central Rail Trail, New Zealand. Unpublished dissertation, master's in tourism, Lincoln University, Lincoln, New Zealand.

Bowker, J.M., Bergstrom, J.C. and Gill, J. (2007) Estimating the economic value and impacts of recreational trails: A case study of the Virginia Creeper Rail Trail. *Tourism Economics* 13 (2), 241–260.

Bowman, S.A. and Wright, D.C. (2008) Charitable deductions for rail-trail conversions: Reconciling the partial interest rule and the National Trails System Act. *William and Mary Environmental Law and Policy Review* 32 (1), 581–634.

Brown, S.E. (2008) Bikes, trains and problem frames: Framing the Little River Rail Trail. Unpublished masters dissertation in applied sciences, Lincoln University, Lincoln, New Zealand.

Central Otago District Council (2009) Otago Central Rail Trail: User survey 2008/2009. Unpublished report, Central Otago District Council, Alexandra.

Central Otago District Council (2011) Otago Central Rail Trail: User survey 2010/2011. Unpublished report, Central Otago District Council, Alexandra.

Christchurch–Little River Rail Trail Trust (2012) Christchurch–Little River Rail Trail. At http://www.littleriverrailtrail.co.nz/fastpage/fpengine.php/templateid/1 (accessed January 2014).

Department of Conservation (DOC) (1994) *Otago Central Rail Trail: Interim Policies and Development Plan.* Dunedin: Department of Conservation Otago Conservancy.

Department of Conservation (DOC) (2012) Historic Rimutaka Incline. At http://www.doc.govt.nz/conservation/historic/by-region/wairarapa/rimutaka-incline (accessed January 2014).

Dowsett, O. (2008) Rural restructuring: A multi-scalar analysis of the Otago Central Rail Trail. Unpublished masters thesis in social sciences, Lincoln University, Lincoln, New Zealand.

European Greenways Association (2012a) Greenways: Definition of greenways. At http://www.aevv-egwa.org/site/1Template1.asp?DocID=144&v1ID=&RevID=&namePage=&pageParent= (accessed January 2014).

European Greenways Association (2012b) Presentation: The EGWA. At http://www.aevv-egwa.org/site/1Template1.asp?DocID=176&v1ID=&RevID=&namePage=&pageParent= (accessed January 2014).

Fábos, J.G. (2004) Greenway planning in the United States: Its origins and recent case studies. *Landscape and Urban Planning* 68, 321–342.

Faulks, P., Ritchie, B. and Fluker, M. (2007) *Cycle Tourism in Australia: An Investigation into Its Size and Scope*. Gold Coast: Sustainable Tourism Cooperative Research Centre.

Fletcher, K. (2006) A trip down memory trail: 20 years of RTC. *Rails to Trails Magazine* spring, 16–19.

George, E.W., Mair, H. and Reid, D.G. (2009) *Rural Tourism Development: Localism and Cultural Change*. Bristol: Channel View Publications.

Graham, O. (2004) *Otago Central Rail Trail: From Steam Trains to Pedal Power: The Story of the Otago Central Rail Trail*. Dunedin: Otago Central Rail Trail Trust.

Greater Wellington Regional Council (2012) Rimutaka Rail Trail. At http://www.gw.govt.nz/Rimutaka-Rail-Trail (accessed January 2014).

Hawthorne, T., Krygier J. and Kwan, M.-P. (2008) Mapping ambivalence: Exploring the geographies of community change and rails-to-trails development using photo-based Q method and PPGIS. *Geoforum* 39, 1058–1078.

Hurst, T. (1990) *The Otago Central Railway 1879–1990: A Tribute*. Wellington: IPL Books.

Irvine, N. (2007) Rail trails: Back to the future. At http://www.australiancyclist.com.au/article.aspx?aeid=2167 (accessed March 2012).

Jaffe, H. (2006) Peter Harnik: RTC first responder. *Rails to Trails Magazine* spring, 14–15.

Jellum, C. and Reis, A. (2008) Otago Central Rail Trail economic impact and trends survey 2008. Unpublished report, Otago Central Rail Trail Trust, Dunedin.

Moore, R.L. and Graefe, A.R. (1994) Attachments to recreation settings: The case of rail-trail users. *Leisure Sciences* 16 (1), 17.

Moore, R.L., Gitelson R.J. and Graefe, A.R. (1994a) The economic impact of rail-trails. *Journal of Park and Recreation Administration* 12 (2), 63–72.

Moore, R.L., Graefe, A.R. and Gitelson, R.J. (1994b) Living near greenways: Neighboring landowners' experiences with and attitudes toward rail-trails. *Journal of Park and Recreation Administration* 12 (1), 79–93.

Mundet, L. and Coenders, G. (2010) Greenways: A sustainable leisure experience concept for both communities and tourists. *Journal of Sustainable Tourism* 18 (5), 657–674.

Otago Central Rail Trail Trust (2005) The Otago Central Rail Trail means business. Unpublished report, Otago Central Rail Trail Trust, Dunedin.

Rails-to-Trails Conservancy (2012) Rails-to-Trails Conservancy. At http://www.railstotrails.org (accessed January 2014).

RailTrails Australia (2012) RailTrails Australia. At http://www.railtrails.org.au (accessed January 2014).

Reis, A.C. and Jellum, C. (2012) Rail trail development: A conceptual model for sustainable tourism. *Tourism Planning and Development* 9 (2), 133–147.

Reis, A., Jellum, C. and Lovelock, B. (2010) Linking the Taieri Gorge Railway and the Otago Central Rail Trail: A survey of users' demands. Unpublished report, Centre for Recreation Research, Dunedin.

Ross, N. (1996) Otago Central Rail Trail: Who's using it? Unpublished diploma dissertation in tourism, University of Otago, New Zealand.

Siderelis, C. and Moore, R.L. (1995) Outdoor recreation net benefits of rail-trails. *Journal of Leisure Research* 27 (4), 344–359.

Statistics New Zealand (2006) 2006 census of population and dwellings. At http://www.stats.govt.nz/Census/2006CensusHomePage.aspx (accessed March 2014).

Tiedt, G.F. (1980) From rails to trails and back again: A look at the conversion program. *Parks and Recreation* 15 (4), 43–47, 69, 81.

Trans Canada Trail (2009) Trans Canada trail greenways: Vision and core principles. At http://www.tctrail.ca/blog/?p=1334&language=en (accessed January 2014).

8 The Dining Car's Contribution to Railroad Heritage Tourism

James D. Porterfield

Introduction

The roots of this account of the origin, evolution and operation of dinner trains can be traced back to 1992 and a simple act of self-promotion. My first railroad book, *Dining by Rail: The History and Recipes of America's Golden Age of Railroad Cuisine*, was published in 1992. In an effort to call attention to the book within one of its primary markets, people who love trains, I contacted the late Jim Boyd, legendary curmudgeonly editor of *Railfan and Railroad* magazine, and pitched a monthly column – 'On the Menu' – devoted to aspects of rail dining today. My thought (and expectation) was to cover dinner trains and old stations converted into restaurants during the first year or two the book was in print. Little did I know that the column would not only run for over 20 years, but that it would result in a second railroad cookbook, *From the Dining Car: The Recipes and Stories Behind Today's Greatest Rail Dining Experiences*, published in 2004, and the opportunity to serve as a lecturer on a private luxury train, the American Orient Express. These experiences, plus the opportunities they provided to meet with Amtrak staff and other railroad officials, dinner train operators and chefs, private car owners and other fans of railroad dining cars and cuisine, as well as the numerous exchanges my travels facilitated with those who patronize dinner trains, form the basis of the personal essay that follows.

As an outgrowth of 'On the Menu', in 1996 I began compiling an annual guide to North American dinner trains for the June issue of *Railfan and Railroad*. While by no means exhaustive – train operators to this day often surface after the June issue is published to note that they were missed – this guide nonetheless provides a snapshot of the industry. And as with many snapshots, taken together over the years, the guides reveal the evolution of the industry.

Here, then, we briefly trace the growth and evolution of the practice of simulating key aspects of the rail dining experience, detail the forms today's simulations take, and comment on several current practices that are expanding the concept further. This is followed by a discussion of the benefits this unique historic re-enactment and fund-raising event can present to the railway heritage preservation community. Finally, drawing on 20 years of experience reporting on dinner train operations, we offer lessons to be drawn from both the successes and the failures of such trains.

An Informal History of Dinner Trains

Railroad dining cars have long held the attention and occupied the memories of people old enough to have traveled by train in the days when numerous first-class intercity trains traversed the country. The operators of those trains found it necessary to offer food services in an attempt to gain competitive advantage on routes between cities served by more than one carrier. Further, competition for shippers stimulated an effort by the railroads to outdo each other in showcasing the products of the food vendors who used their routes. The result was that, by the 1920s, many of the nation's top chefs worked in service to the railroads, creating menu items, providing instruction in their duplication and overseeing onboard operations.

Savvy railway heritage tourism administrators have taken advantage of the traveling public's memory, plus the growing popularity of dining as a social activity, and the desire of people of all ages to find unique and pleasant settings in which to dine or to celebrate special events, to build awareness, attendance and revenue for their sites. Today, passengers can still partake of a meal on the train, but they are just as likely to do that on an excursion railroad, in a private railroad car, or on a luxury train, as they are to dine on Amtrak or VIA Rail Canada.

When Amtrak was created out of what remained of long-distance passenger trains in the United States on 1 May 1971, Charles Crocker, a fourth-generation descendant of the Charles Crocker who, as one of the 'Big Four', built the transcontinental Central Pacific Railroad, saw an opportunity for a new type of restaurant, the dinner train. Crocker owned the Sierra Railroad Company, which operated 90 miles east of San Francisco. In 1972 Crocker granted the concession business on his railroad to one Richard R. ('Dick') Reynolds, who then launched the first dinner train. Reynolds promoted the train with a catchy name – the 'Supper Chief', a takeoff on the famous Chicago–Los Angeles first-class 'Super Chief' operated by the Atchison, Topeka & Santa Fe Railway. He ran a mixed fleet of food service cars that could feed as many as 240 people out of Jamestown, California, to

Oakdale on Saturday nights. There were two seatings on each run (diners out became passengers back and visa versa). The first year saw six trains operate April to September. The concept's success is apparent in that 10 Supper Chiefs ran in 1973, and in the growth that continued throughout the train's brief history. The end came in 1979, before most of today's dinner trains even started, when ownership and the priorities of the Sierra Railroad Company changed. In that last year, 29 Supper Chiefs ran.

Reynolds also innovated by introducing the 'ride-'n'-dine' concept, reminiscent of a practice railroads had begun using in the 1850s to feed passengers. Here, the train made a scheduled stop that allowed passengers to detrain and partake of a meal in the station dining room before re-boarding to continue their trip. Reynolds named his train the Twilight Limited, and it ran from Jamestown to Cooperstown and back from 1973 to 1979. Passengers were served drinks and hors d'oeuvres onboard; then, when the train returned to Jamestown, were greeted by a roast beef dinner. At the time of writing, the Sierra Railroad again operates dinner trains, including the Sierra Railroad Dinner Train, the Sacramento RiverTrain and, on the Skunk Train, a ride-'n'-dine experience.

The early Crocker/Reynolds success did not go unnoticed. In 1984, Jack Haley, who had been a railroad man in the 1950s, before serving in the Air Force, acquired the Cedar Valley Railroad, a 105-mile line that operated between Waterloo, Iowa and Albert Lea, Minnesota. In 1985, he partnered with Walt Vining, a local restaurateur, to create the Star Clipper Dinner Train running out of Osage, Iowa. The train made a splash sufficient to earn it an article in *People* magazine. And while Haley's railroad career was short-lived, the Star Clipper concept was eventually replicated in Michigan and Florida, as well as in Newport, Rhode Island, where the descendant of the Newport Star Clipper, today's Newport Dinner Train, continues in operation. Shortly after Haley's ventures, what is perhaps the best-known dinner train in the country, the Napa Valley Wine Train, went into service, when in 1987 a group of citizens bought a portion of a Southern Pacific route that bisects the Napa Valley and launched the train in 1989. Noted for its award-winning chefs and high cuisine, stylishly restored passenger cars and cross-promotions with the Valley's vintners, not to mention the pedigree and depth of its financial backing, the Napa Valley Wine Train continues to represent the high end of the casual rail dining experience.

Form and Function

From these early origins and handful of operations, nearly 100 separate and independent services have emerged, ranging from those that run just several days a year, often in conjunction with other local events, to the dozen or so that operate regularly on a year-round schedule. A diverse array of practices has evolved over the years as well, and falls into two broad categories: the ride-'n'-dine experience, and food served on the train.

Ride-'n'-dine operations consist of some combination of a train ride and food service off the train. It can take several forms. At the lowest-maintenance end, excursion operators who have more than one scheduled run each day between two or more points along their route, or who have a long layover at a destination (perhaps one tied to other tourist activities), can promote the layover(s) as a ride-'n'-dine opportunity. Food service takes the form of *à la carte* dining opportunities offered in cooperation with one or more local establishments in the destination city. A customized handout to passengers, with suggestions on where to eat, can assist them in making a favorable choice, and gains support from local eateries. This practice most closely replicates the scheduled '20 minutes for refreshments' at selected station stops, as practiced by many railroads beginning in the 1840s, long before there were dining cars.

More typically, a ride-'n'-dine excursion operator might run to a locale where there is a restaurant that is either within walking distance of (the average age of one's ridership will determine what this is) or just a short chartered-coach or a school bus-ride away from a point of debarkation. Or, the excursion might originate in a city with a cooperating restaurant, and as a result passengers partake of drinks and hors d'oeuvres on the excursion and return to the city of origin to complete the meal. Other practices have included providing beverages and appetizers going out, a meal at the destination, and dessert on the train coming back; picnic trains, where the train stops at a scenic high-point and passengers are greeted by a catered meal of anything from a barbecue buffet to a four-course sit-down meal; and a meal first, then the train ride, perhaps with after-dinner cocktails or dessert. In some cases these events are accompanied by live entertainment, either on the train or at the food service site, with music being the most common. Others have entertained with a magician, a dance revue or skit comedy, or even the re-enactment of a famous shoot-out. And they need not always be dinners. Excursions that run to or through spectacular daytime scenery often offer mid-day trips of this type.

The second, generally more elaborate rail dining option is to serve food on a moving train. This can be done in two ways: with catering or by cooking onboard.

Catering can take several forms. It can be an internal function of the railroad, wherein a prep kitchen is located adjacent to the departure point, and the food is prepared in advance by employees of either the railroad or a caterer, then moved onboard prior to departure. With recent advances in catering technology, cold menu items, like appetizers or salads, can be served chilled, while entrées and their sides can be served hot. On some dinner trains the dishes are fully prepared and plated prior to departure and kept at temperature onboard, while on others the food is prepared before boarding and the dishes 'finished' – assembled – onboard just prior to service.

More commonly, one or more local restaurants, or caterers that special-ize in banquets, provide food service. Menus are created in consultation between the railroad and the service, as are decisions on how to handle table service. Applications of this concept are numerous and varied, with examples ranging from pizza trains offered as a 'family fun night' to high cuisine offered as 'Celebrity Chef' celebrations with one or more restaura-teurs taking center stage over a season. One advantage of the latter practice is the opportunity it presents to cross-promote both the dinner train and the restaurant to each other's patrons.

At least one veteran of catered dinner train operations recommends the use of an upscale supermarket chain's catering service to reduce the likeli-hood of friction developing between the railroad and the caterer. This same operator turns for the pizzas on his family pizza night trains to a national chain, but with the provision that plain boxes and an unmarked vehicle be used to deliver the pizzas to the train, so his patrons don't know where they come from.

In all of these practices one sees similarities to chain restaurants and large-scale land-based caterers, such as those found in hotels and country clubs. In more than one case, dinner train operators compare their service to catering, not to operating a restaurant.

That said, however, onboard preparation strategies come closest to rep-licating dining car service as it was practiced by railroads during the golden age, generally thought of as the 1920s through to the 1950s. Such dinner trains, of course, have one or more dining cars or kitchen cars. Other service cars can include table cars, lounge and/or bar cars, cars adapted for enter-tainment. It is worth noting that while some trains include a gift shop, the up-scale operators are more likely to have arriving guests await boarding in a gift shop that is re-opened on the return of the train, at the end of its run. The preparation of food off the train, meanwhile, is kept to a minimum, limited perhaps to slicing or dicing ingredients for use in a recipe, preparing specialty sauces and dressings, or marinating meats prior to cooking. Menus consist of a three-, four- or five-course meal, often preceded by a cocktail hour as part of the boarding experience.

With the transition of today's dining public away from those old enough to remember the golden age, and to generations who view dining as a social or recreational activity, onboard preparation and service are more likely to be looked upon as a unique dining event, not as a nostalgia experience. Dinner trains offering onboard dining are to be thought of as restaurants first, trains second. As a result, they often showcase a specific chef's creativity, celebrate a particular cuisine, such as food inspired by and paired with wine, employ unique local ingredients or preparation techniques, or offer food that is meant to provide a pleasant accompaniment to passengers celebrating an important event or taking in spectacular scenery.

In addition to the food, onboard entertainment has proved a popular add-on. This includes variety shows themed on the USO (United Service Organizations) and other musical performances, murder mysteries and comedy club routines. And, as the number of wineries has grown and spread to previously untapped locales, the wine tasting experience is also growing in popularity and use. Some operators have taken to offering an after-work cocktail train with an open bar and appetizers. Several operators, including some with restored sleeping cars and others whose point of departure adjoins an inn or hotel, offer a bed-and-breakfast experience that might include the dinner train, followed by an overnight stay and a cooked or continental breakfast in the morning.

Among recent innovations, several private car owners have begun offering variations on these operations. In one case, a ride-'n'-dine service originates in Los Angeles, wherein a private car is hauled by Amtrak to Santa Barbara, where it is switched out of the train and picked up later that day for the return to Los Angeles. Passengers can either spend the day on their own agenda, or are offered a walking tour that includes wine tasting. In another case, a dining car departs New York's Penn Station, en route to Vermont, and in three segments serves meals to passengers whose fare includes a return to their point of departure on another Amtrak train. Several operators have experimented with excursions to and from a popular destination – a national park perhaps, or a casino – with the train offering overnight accommodations. In 2012, a 'green' dinner train was due to offer FLOSS (Fresh, Local, Organic, Seasonal, Sustainable) ingredients in cooperation with a local restaurant and three local farms.

In all of their forms, dinner trains offer the opportunity to customize – even operate exclusively in conjunction with – local tourist destinations or celebrations. Consider these examples: Octoberfest, Brewfest, or similarly named trains, perhaps sponsored by one or more local microbreweries; a chocolate train, offering candies and/or pastries, especially popular at Valentine's day; dessert trains, often popular with those operations with a limited right of way; holiday-themed trains, tied to such celebrations as Mother's Day (one operator pointed out that if there is ever a day to have a dinner train, it is Mother's Day, when more people eat out than on any other day of the year), Father's Day, 4th of July, Thanksgiving, Christmas and New Year's Eve. In some cases, local celebrations, such as Pioneer Days, Founders Days, Thresher Days and the like, are the only days on which a dinner train will operate. Most, except those in regions that experience a moderate climate, operate trains seasonally.

None of these efforts, it should be noted, is undertaken as an attempt to replicate a specific railroad's dining car operation in style, substance and pace. In North America, to enjoy a meal in a dining car traveling at speed on a main line, one has to travel on a long-distance train operated by Amtrak or VIA Rail Canada.

And lest you think all rail dining experiences have to lean toward the up-scale, know of one operator who, during normal excursion operations, offers hot dogs cooked on a grill set up on a flatcar that has been modified to offer outdoor seating as well.

Whatever form is employed, offering a rail dining experience has enabled many railway heritage operations, large and small, to capitalize on the popularity of both railway heritage and social dining. However, it has also proved a daunting and at times disappointing experience for those who undertake it without thinking through all of the implications the practice has for their operation.

The Benefits

Today's rail dining operations, as practiced in the railway heritage and tourism community, are seldom, if ever, attempts at historic preservation and authentic re-enactment. Rather, they are intended to tap into a fondness some people have for this history, or to capitalize on a popular contemporary pastime – social dining in interesting and unusual places. What can be gained by this effort? Several things, all of them conditional on the operator providing an experience that is consistent, enjoyable, safe and wholesome:

- The operation will attract an expanded audience, one that differs from those who typically attend a railway excursion operation, or may increase the draw to events the dinner train is associated with.
- Unique attendees, in turn, experience a greater awareness of the community around the railroad, and of others the train travels through, including businesses, other activities, historic sites and recreational facilities.
- It provides found revenue, to the railroad as well as to the community,

in the form of added tourist dollars, sales and service taxes, and income for those working on the train.

- By broadening the operator's revenue stream, it spreads the financial risk of an excursion operation to a larger base. This is especially true of those operations that are added to the schedule during non-peak hours, such as evenings.
- Done right, rail dining operations make money. One operator, whose primary business is running a freight short line, said recently that his year-around dinner train, running on a frequent schedule, clears 'only' $300,000. When asked why he put all of that effort into an excursion that delivered so comparatively little to his bottom line, he replied, 'Because it is $300,000'.

Challenges and Opportunities

Compiling the annual guide to dinner trains for *Railfan and Railroad* over the past 16 years has provided a front-row seat on the growth of this industry. That growth was, for a number of years, slow but steady, from about 50 operations to level off at 91 in 2005. The same number operated in 2012, running in 39 states, four provinces in Canada and in Mexico. Surprisingly, even the 2008–12 economic slump had little impact on the total. What has changed in the past eight years, though, is the make-up of the list. Each year uncovers a handful of operations that have ceased and a similar number that have launched. But even that dynamic holds a surprise: there is no clear single reason to account for the turnover. Instead, several factors appear to be at work at all times, and combine to produce the turnover.

- Fatigue sets in on those operating the train, those staffing the operation and/or the community supporting the railroad. A corollary phenomenon may simply be a loss of interest. These problems are especially prevalent where volunteers staff the train and operate the food service, and tend to occur after several years of operation, when the novelty and excitement wear off.
- Disputes arise between the operator and one or more of the regulatory agencies or community governments involved in overseeing the operation. Passenger and food safety is an ongoing and evolving responsibility. Operators not only have to remain compliant as a railroad, but also as a food vendor.
- Disagreements occur between the railroad operation and the food vendor and/or supplier, over the menu, the level or frequency of service, sharing rising costs, or assessing the relative importance of all parties to the success – or decline – of the operation.

- Record-keeping becomes onerous. The first session of the first informal conference of dinner train operators in the late 1990s did not even get through introductions before a discussion broke out concerning how to allocate ticket revenue to operating the train, paying for the meal, accounting for the sale of alcoholic beverages if offered, tipping the staff and separating the taxes on each activity.
- The equipment, if not owned by the operator, may be sold out from under the dinner train, or may be put to a different use by its owner(s). Beyond that are questions to be resolved about maintaining and upgrading the cars, kitchens, ticketing and boarding locations, and related recreation facilities.
- More than one operation has had to deal with citizen complaints over train noise that occurs when running from and returning to a point of origin at night, having, as it does, to whistle through crossings, or when switching is required at the end of a run in a residential neighborhood. Other complaints may derive from the consumption of community resources, whether water or parking spaces, or from the disposal of trash and sewage. Dinner train operators may want to shun such disputes with their host communities because the problems are complex or legitimately irresolvable, or the railroad has other business interests in the community, or it has a bigger stake in continuing in business with other forms of railway heritage preservation and tourism.

Nevertheless, practices have evolved over the years that provide many opportunities to employ some manner of rail dining experience to raise money and increase awareness and expand one's reach into the community. Whether it is an annual fund-raising and/or awards banquet that promises an authentic and historic dining car meal, one of the various types of rail dining operations outlined here, or the compilation and publication of an authentic dining car cookbook reflecting a class 1 railroad that once operated in a region of the country, rail dining is an approach to railway heritage that resonates with a broad spectrum of the public. It will generate, with the proviso that it be done with planning and sound execution, media attention and attendance beyond the typical circle of influence occupied by railway heritage venues.

Lessons Learned

In closing, consider two important lessons 20 years of reporting on dinner train operations has provided about success and failure when offering some type of rail dining experience:

First, understand that for this aspect of your operation you are no longer viewed by passengers – or by local, state and, if your operation crosses a state line, national authorities – as a railroad. Rather, you are now a restaurant. And restaurants are evaluated on food service. It must be perceived as being both of quality and value. It does not have to be a five-course, five-star experience, unless that is what you are promising, but it does have to be wholesome and tasty, as appropriate for your price. It is also worth noting that if you partner with a caterer or a restaurant for the food service, much of the regulatory burden may fall on your partner. Be sure to check into this situation thoroughly with your attorney and/or local authorities.

About trains as restaurants, one operator, with experience on more than one operation, sums it up this way:

> Because of the cost, many people try it once for the experience, but do not repeat. But, like restaurants everywhere, a dinner train needs to find ways to attract repeat customers. Meanwhile, running a restaurant is one of the hardest businesses to be in. The hours are brutal, something can always go wrong, and finding and retaining competent help is a challenge. Now, add the complication of having to do all of this on a moving train. And if you plan a regular operation, don't rely too heavily on volunteers. It may be difficult to always find the people you need, and among those who do try to help regularly, burnout is a real possibility.

Second, what appears to be the quickest and surest route to success is when a working short-line operation – one with motive power, rolling stock, right of way, and operating and maintenance crews – undertakes the launch of a dinner train as a means of increasing revenue during off-peak hours. It reminds one of the days when railroads built amusement parks at some distant location and then scheduled passenger trains to haul people to them on the weekends. And while it is by no means the only route to success, it strikes this writer as the lowest-risk, most-likely-to-succeed path to follow.

References

Porterfield, J.D. (1992) *Dining by Rail: The History and Recipes of America's Golden Age of Railroad Cuisine*. New York: St Martin's Press.
Porterfield, J.D. (2004) *From the Dining Car: The Recipes and Stories Behind Today's Greatest Rail Dining Experiences*. New York: St Martin's Press.

9 Revitalizing Community Values Through Railway Regeneration in the Asia Pacific Region: A Tourism Research and Education Approach

Ian Chaplin

Introduction

This chapter discusses a tourism research and education approach for the optimization of social capital invested in community action in support of railway tourism in the Asia Pacific region. The main hypothesis of the research is that railway restoration and regeneration, facilitating sustainable mobility, will revitalize local communities and ensure that sustainable tourism planning overcomes the problems of exclusion and inequitable distribution of the benefits of tourism development. The approach is based on studies of the economic and social value of railway heritage preservation, restoration and regeneration for marginal destinations. It aims to demonstrate that investment in rail transport infrastructure and services can enhance opportunities for employment in tourism and hospitality enterprises. A case study on plans for the regeneration of the railways in the Philippines provides an example of the potential for tourism planning to ensure sustainable mobility and derive optimum value from social capital invested in railway tourism.

The research aims to address concerns raised by many tourism researchers that there should be a stronger role for communities in tourism development. As Pearce *et al.* (1996: 212) have observed, 'Despite these sentiments there is little evidence to suggest that such research has contributed to the planning and management of tourism'. In this study, a key role for communities is identified as involvement in the preservation, restoration and regeneration of railway systems and heritage to optimize the economic and social value of railway transportation. It is argued that railway tourism will ensure sustainable mobility (Black, 2004) within tourism environments and will revitalize communities through investment in the development of railway heritage products and services. The approach presented here aims to provide a paradigm for research and education that will help to achieve the necessary coordination between transport planning and tourism planning and policy-making to improve the quality of life for host communities and the quality of the visitor experience.

In his research on the urban transportation crisis affecting developing countries, Vasconcellos (2003) analyzes eight key sets of issues exacerbating the problems of a values-based approach to transport planning: political, institutional, social, technological, technical, economic, operational and environmental. While his analysis is mainly concerned with how transport operations and management are crucial to quality of life in cities, it is also applicable to the situation facing many urban and rural tourism destinations shared by host communities in both developed and developing economies. For Vasconcellos, political issues derive from the failure of political systems to recognize the value of ensuring democratic representation of the conflicting interests of social groups and classes in the formulation and implementation of transportation and traffic policies. Institutional issues relate to the power invested in the command and control of transportation and traffic policies, and to the level of decentralization that would achieve the best results. Social issues relate to several inequities in transportation and traffic conditions. The first kind of inequity is unequal access to transportation. Most inequity problems derive from different approaches to the supply of both transportation infrastructure and means, most notably the situation where lower-income groups have to rely on public transport because they do not have the means to buy their own motorized vehicles. In this respect, the technological issues relate to the commitment to an automotive development model that militates against non-motorized and public transport systems. Traditional means of transportation have been constantly neglected and even banned (Banjo & Dimitrio, 1990) and railroads have been dismantled (Barat, 1985). The technical issues relate to the commitment to apply traditional values borrowed from developed countries without proper adjustment to conditions in the developing world. Economic issues continue to prevail because of the fiscal crisis of the state, which hinders support for efficient public transportation systems and distributive social policies.

Large transportation infrastructures, which rely on public investments, are becoming less feasible and subsidies to special groups are subjected to mounting opposition. This same crisis helps keep most of the population in poverty, which prevents people from having access to convenient public transportation. The inefficient and negligent operation of public transportation services, especially by large public operators subject to weak public controls, generates persistent economic deficits. Problems are exacerbated by irregular provision of transportation services and erratic traffic conditions. Failure to address these issues leads to the steady degradation of the quality of urban life, represented by high traffic accident rates, increasingly intolerable air pollution and disruption of residential and living spaces by undue motorized traffic. All effects impact on the adaptation of space for the automobile within a context of deep social, political and economic differences among social classes and groups. Vasconcellos argues for more attention to be paid to the rights of citizens and the role that public transport should play in restoring the values that underpin society, most notably equity and productivity:

> The right to public transportation should be seen as the right to participate in the social, economic, political and cultural activities that are essential to living. Thus the prevailing market paradigm must be replaced by a social paradigm, in which transportation is an essential tool for ensuring the right to access and the achievement of broader social goals. This may entail the subsidization of public transportation services whenever necessary to ensure equitable access, provided they reach the targeted groups and are not used to support inefficiency. (Vasconcellos, 2003: 197)

This analysis has implications for tourism transport planning and policy-making affecting the quality of life and livelihood of host communities. It raises a series of questions such as:

- What are the most democratic ways of making tourism transport and traffic policies?
- What are the best instruments to support tourism transport and traffic policies?
- How is the tourism transport environment organized?
- Who can use it and under which conditions?
- What are the main differences in access to public transport and space?
- How can we eliminate or minimize these differences?
- What are the most efficient, environmentally friendly and sustainable means of ensuring the equitable appropriation of space?

The value of transportation as an asset and attraction in itself is a relatively neglected field of research, yet for many destinations it is a vital component of the tourism experience. As Robbins (2003: 87) contends: 'Transport impinges on the visitor attraction sector at four different, but not mutually exclusive levels'. The first level is accessibility. Since visitors need to be able to get to visitor attractions, transport services are an essential component of the overall product offer. In many cases the journey to an attraction may be a pleasurable experience in its own right and may be a reason to visit a particular attraction. The second level is where transport itself is the central focus of the visitor attraction. The third level is where the vehicle has become a visitor attraction and yet retains the function of providing transport services, often to the local population more than to visitors. The final level, according to Robbins (2003: 87), is 'where the journey itself has become the visitor attraction and transport is principally undertaken for its own sake'. These four levels comprise the underlying conceptual framework on which this research on the potential for railway transport to revitalize communities through tourism is conducted.

A Tourism Research and Education Approach

The tourism research and education approach advocated in this chapter, aiming to optimize the value of rail transportation as a community asset and tourism attraction, incorporates the following objectives:

- analyzing the significance of the historical development of railway transportation and railway communities for implementing sustainable practices in tourism;
- identifying community values engendered by involvement in railway transportation and analyzing their importance for sustainable tourism development planning;
- analyzing the reasons for the decline of railway transportation and associated community values (also, assessing the impact of this decline on prospects for sustainable tourism development);
- identifying and assessing the contribution of tourism transportation to sustaining mobility, demand for rail travel and stakeholder support for railway regeneration;
- examining the phenomenon of investment in railway restoration and regeneration in developed and developing economies and the implications for tourism planning;
- analyzing the success of community rail initiatives and the implications for tourism planning;
- devising strategies for revitalizing community values through investment in community rail and railway tourism;

- formulating education and training policies for the revitalization of community values through railway regeneration;
- setting up a research and teaching network comprising academic and professional advisors for the conceptualization, design and coordination of teaching and research on railway tourism planning and development.

The selection of research instruments is contingent on destination-specific factors, taking into account national, regional and local strategies for economic development. For each objective, research instruments include one or a combination of the following:

- survey techniques – interviews and questionnaires conducted with an appropriate sample of respondents;
- focus groups involving different sections of the community;
- informal discussion groups held with interested participants from the community;
- photographic documentation and collection of data from private and public organizations and associations;
- participant observation and field research;
- projects undertaken by educational institutions in the community.

This research is intended to complement descriptive and prescriptive approaches to evaluating tourism transport development, community-oriented tourism planning and policy-making, tourism destination planning and management, and railway tourism marketing for developing economies. In addition to the methods employed in examining the strategic tourism planning process, the research involves approaches and methods used in tourism anthropology, geography and history, as well as disciplines relevant to the study of rail transportation: economics, engineering, logistics. In particular, it is hoped that by drawing upon the growing body of literature on community rail development, methods specific to the research problem will be devised. The research seeks to identify the reasons for the historical decline of railway transportation systems with reference to the impacts of line closures and lack of investment affecting communities in Europe, North America, South America and Africa. The literature on railway transportation in the Asia Pacific region is studied to compare public perceptions of the value of railway restoration and regeneration.

Data are obtained from the literature on railway planning, national policy-making and project implementation to analyze the historical significance of economic and social development for communities in destinations in the Asia Pacific region. Empirical studies are conducted on the current operation and state of preservation of systems, infrastructure, rolling stock and services involving the local community. The potential for tourism destination planning and tourism product development is assessed through an inventory of assets and attractions. These include tangible cultural assets – namely rolling stock and installations, built heritage in the form of railway stations, workshops, railway hotels and properties converted for adaptive re-use as hospitality amenities – as well as the intangible cultural assets evident in the community – in particular, the initiatives taken to communicate pride in railway heritage through cultural interpretation provided in museums, galleries, shops and visitor centers.

Empirical studies are conducted on the impact of rail transport development on the communities affected by national planning and project implementation. Studies focus on community initiatives in the Asia Pacific region to revive the 'railway family ethos'. Interviews are conducted with representatives within the community who are working to optimize abandoned or disused railway assets, especially for tourism development, through initiatives such as community rail schemes, railway preservation societies, theme park design and management, event design and management, and various modes of cultural interpretation – for example through print publishing and website design. Government planning strategies for community revitalization through rail transport development compared with those envisioned by non-governmental organizations (NGOs) and community-based organizations will be examined using data from sources, interviews and questionnaires (see Cooper, 2008).

Quantitative and qualitative research methods are used to examine the historical and contemporary contribution of the tourism industry to sustaining the demand for rail travel. The research concentrates on the use of railway transportation for domestic and international tourism and the conditions engendering stakeholder support at national, regional and local levels for community-oriented tourism development. Comparative studies are conducted on the use, viability and sustainability of other modes of transportation, focusing on the potential for integration of railway systems in tourism infrastructure planning.

Of central significance to this research is the growing body of literature on community rail development, as both public and private sectors recognize the importance of railways for sustainable urban planning and the revitalization of rural communities. The literature is examined to analyze the significance of community rail for tourism planning and development. Empirical studies are conducted to document and describe initiatives taken by communities to devise strategies for tourism product development allied with community rail services. These initiatives are analyzed to identify the values which have been instrumental in motivating individuals to form preservation and operational management groups – in many cases with the support of active stakeholders and volunteers. Investment opportunities in community rail and railway tourism for national, regional and local tourism destination development are identified. Strategies for revitalizing communities will be proposed based on data obtained through surveys to ascertain the level of interest among stakeholders, especially small and medium-sized business enterprises. A survey of tangible and intangible economic and cultural assets will be conducted to provide data for potential investors. Recommendations will be made for human resources training and education for tourism and hospitality product and service development.

The case study approach to the potential for rail transport to revitalize communities through tourism and hospitality employment opportunities is formatively based on an inquiry conducted by the UK Department of Transport (DOT) into the factors that contribute to social exclusion in the transport planning and policy-making process. Findings revealed that there appear to be clear connections between transport and social exclusion. This is particularly marked among unemployed people, families with young children, young people, older people and all those on low (benefit-level) incomes. While socially excluded people are not found in dense numbers in rural areas, public transport is especially important to those small-town or village dwellers who do not have access to a private car. The DOT considers transport as a part of the livelihood of communities, integral to work, health, social services, shops, education, leisure and so on. If high costs are incurred in transportation, exclusion prevails.

In the context of employment in tourism and hospitality facilities, availability and accessibility are key issues. There is a need to try to define what is an acceptable basic minimum mobility/access provision. There is also a need to define how much travel an individual should be prepared to undertake to access work. Improvement of travel possibilities might make areas more desirable to work and live in. However, while it could enhance the lives of many engaged in the tourism and hospitality industries, it could also accelerate the loss of facilities from the tourism area unless care is taken to cater for employees and local residents.

The DOT also conducted a review of its Community Rail Development Strategy of special relevance for this research. The main objective of the strategy was to increase community involvement in local railways and provide evidence of successful initiatives to revitalize community values. The measures of success to be determined in this area include (Department of Transport, n.d.):

- the existence of an active community rail partnership;
- evidence of links to schools and the wider community;
- local initiation of enhancements to stations and rail facilities;
- changes in the way that the railway is run to match local aspirations.

In a consultation paper on a strategy for community railways, Butcher (2012) provides a strong case for the value of community-oriented tourism planning and development through community rail partnerships:

> Increasing sales volume and income while managing unit costs downwards would be admirable objectives for most businesses, and that includes the rest of the railway system. Involving the local community more closely is desirable, but may bring its own problems. That there may be disagreements between different elements of the local communities is at least a possibility, and the formal Community Rail Partnerships will have to do their best to resolve them.

Case Study of Railway Restoration and Regeneration in the Philippines

The following brief outline of a case study of railways in the Philippines concerns the historical development of transport by rail and current initiatives for the regeneration of lines and networks on the island of Luzon and further expansion to islands in the south. The case study focuses on the economic, political and socio-cultural issues affecting planning, policy-making and stakeholder consultation. The analysis is derived from application of the research objectives. The study incorporates data from secondary sources on railway construction initiated during the Spanish and American colonial periods from 1875 to 1935, and from empirical studies of the assets still extant but dispersed through the islands. A key reference for this research is a detailed account by Arturo G. Corpuz (1999) of the work undertaken under the auspices of the Manila Railway Company (MRC), in which he reminds us:

> The Manila–Dagupan railroad was the single most important infrastructure built in the Philippines during the Spanish colonial period that was not initiated by the Church. It was constructed and operated by a London-based company in the late 19th century, starting in 1887, sixty-two years after the first railroad was built in England. Open to

public traffic in 1892, the railroad was part of a worldwide trend of technological advances in transportation and communication that led to unprecedented trade expansion and urban development. (Corpuz, 1999: 1)

This statement would add weight to any proposal for World Heritage designation and the potential that this would afford for tourism destination branding and positioning. Unfortunately, the tangible and intangible heritage assets of the railway systems and stock in the Philippines have not been well preserved.

Limited data are available on the impact on communities of railway operations and management since the initial effects were examined after the opening of the Manila–Dagupan line. According to Corpuz, these effects can be summarized as follows:

The opening of the Manila–Dagupan line has been credited with beneficial development to surrounding regions and to the country as a whole. The most often-mentioned benefits and symptoms of development include: (a) increased real estate values; (b) renewed development in old towns and the rise of new ones near railroad junctions and stations; (c) the stimulation of the consumption of import goods especially in the rural areas; (d) increased production and flow of export crops from provincial haciendas to the international port of Manila; (e) increased labor mobility, and (f) new employment opportunities in the railroad company itself and in other related services and concessions. (Corpuz, 1999: 32)

In terms of effects on railway communities, Corpuz observes that although the opening of the Manila–Dagupan railroad had an overall positive impact on the region it served, its effects on specific towns were mixed. Many towns accessed directly through the railroad benefited and experienced population increases as a result. One town in particular, Tarlac, known as the 'melting pot province' (Corpuz, 1999: 378), was created only in 1873 and grew at a much faster pace than any other locality. The railroad was the key to opening up this town, along with other parts of landlocked Luzon, to the Manila-centered colonial economy. Some railroad station towns, however, did not appear to have been significantly affected. These towns experienced a surge in their respective shares of the provincial population, presumably corresponding to a similar increase in economic activity, but these eventually stabilized to their previous levels. This pattern suggests that, for these towns, the opening of the Manila–Dagupan railroad provided an initial access advantage that was not sustained or optimized for increased production relative to other towns.

Under the American colonial administration there were various plans for the extension of railways from Manila north of Luzon as far as Baguio and to the south through to the islands of Negros, Cebu, Leyte and Samar. Although there were some US companies bidding for construction and operation contracts, even involving cooperation among prospective bidders, uncertainties regarding the future of the Philippine islands curtailed future expansion. According to the US President of the time, William H. Taft, lack of commitment was attributable to:

> The reported depression in business in the islands, the uncertainty which still exists as to the disposition which the U.S. will make of the islands, the doubt whether a native government may come in, and the great opportunity for profitable investment by any except those who have a present interest in the islands' (Corpuz, 1999: 53)

Had there been an interest in tourism development at the time, the opportunities for passenger traffic as well as freight transportation may have encouraged the necessary investment from overseas as well as support from the national government.

During World War II there was considerable destruction of the rail network. Of the more than 1000 km of railroad before the war, only 452 km were operational after it. On 1 February 1946, the US Army restored the control of the railway to the Commonwealth Government and work was undertaken on what could be salvaged of the railroad system. Despite the post-war challenges, the Philippine railroad entered into the modern age. From 1954 to 1956, the Manila Railroad Company converted its fleet of trains from steam to diesel engines. After the company was given a new charter under Republic Act No. 4156, its name was changed to Philippine National Railways (PNR). It became the wealthiest among government agencies in terms of assets, with such diversified investments and properties such as hotels, bus lines and freight services.

Philippine National Railways contends in its mission statement that it provides railway services within the integrated national transport system in order to serve as a socio-economic development tool while ensuring the viability of operations for optimum service at minimum cost. It aims to operate an economical, safe and efficient railway network throughout the province of Luzon, including Batangas, Cagayan Valley in Maralilaque, and in Mindanao, Panay and other islands in the Visayas. In corporate terms, it seeks to ensure maximum utilization of resources, to ensure financial viability, to provide for continuous progressive growth through an accelerated improvement of all its facilities, and to professionalize and improve long-range training programs to upgrade its manpower, and to promote and enhance employees' welfare.

According to Brad Peadon (2008) of Philippine Railways Special Interest Group (PRSIG): 'the story of the Philippine National Railways has been one of reduction over many years'. What was once a massive operation spreading north and south of the capital city, Manila, has now been reduced to a short irregular commuter-type service on the remaining open section of the south line. Into the new millennium, services still extended the length of the south line down to Legaspi and on the sole remaining branch to Carmona (just south of the Manila area) until a particularly bad typhoon struck these regions, causing much damage to these lines and resulting in the suspension of services beyond Binan. With so few passenger operations and virtually non-existent freight activity, the PNR was left with a fleet far larger than required.

As has been the case with many railway companies in other countries, including government-owned entities, the Manila Railway Company's ownership and optimization of its assets were neglected in favour of opportunities afforded by the growing demand for road transportation. Ironically, as Corpuz (1999: 81) points out:

> Abandoning unprofitable lines was an important component of MRC's overall response to motor vehicle competition. The company reduced expenses and allowed resources to be channeled into more profitable investments, including the establishment of express, rail, motor car, motor vehicle, and steamer services.

He added that, by 1933, the only division in the railroad company which experienced a steady increase in personnel and operating capital at that time was the MRC's Bus Services Division.

Research for this case study sought to examine recent projects to restore, regenerate and extend the network, financed by foreign investment ostensibly aimed at exploiting the islands' resources. Since the turn of the 21st century, PNR was supported by the government in its efforts to rehabilitate and expand the rail network to reduce the burden on the Philippine road network, cut down on traffic congestion, reduce travel times between key urban centers and spur economic growth. Initial revitalization efforts involved the total reconstruction of rail bridges on the North Rail and South Rail as well as the replacement of rail track. Stations were also set to be remodeled as part of the rehabilitation process. The first phase, regenerating the entire Metro Manila portion of North Rail and South Rail, aimed for completion in 2009.

Foreign investment was seen as the key to restoration and modernization, with South Korea offering to assist with the modernization of the South Rail. The US$70–100 million Korean-funded portion was to cover the section of South Rail from Manila to Calamba. The section from Calamba to Legazpi and further on to Matnog and Sorsogon would be funded by Chinese investment, as well as the section from Manila to Malolos City in Bulacan and further on to Angeles city and the Clark Special Economic Zone. The cost of the latter section was estimated to be around US$500 million, with China providing some US$400 million in concessionary financing. Congress also passed a bill to restore and modernize old existing lines and extend lines northwards to Tuguegarao City in Cagayan and on to Laoag City in Illocos Norte, and southwards as far as Matnog in Sorsogon, which was covered by the China-funded South Rail project. The bill was also intended to provide for the construction of a new four-line railway on the southern-most island of Mindanao, with projected investment from Thailand.

Construction began in early November 2006 and the aim was for the line to become operational by 2010. Due to delays in the construction work, the project was suspended while subject to renegotiation with the Chinese government. Construction temporarily continued in January 2009 with the support of the North Luzon Railways Corporation. The project was cancelled again in March 2011 following delays, work stoppages and further controversy. This implicated former President Arroyo in funding irregularities with the construction company Sinomach. As a result, in December 2011 President Benigno Aquino III canceled North Rail's Sinomach involvement. The continuation of the project then rested on the ability to find alternative foreign investment.

Despite setbacks to the major schemes for revitalization, there have been improvements in the services operated by PNR. New air-conditioned commuter trains have been introduced on the line up to Sucat, Paranaque. These trains travel from Tutuban to Bicutan, passing through stations in Blumentritt, Laong-Laan, España, Sta. Mesa, Pandacan, Paco, Vito Cruz, Buendia, Pasay Road, EDSA, FTI and Bicutan. In 2011 the operation of the Bicol Express was revived to give the riding public an alternative means to reach provincial destinations in southern Luzon and have better access to the region around Mount Mayon. PNR decided to field the additional services because of the increasing demand for rail destinations and also in anticipation of the heavy influx of travelers during Holy Week. Holy Week is one of numerous important festivals celebrated throughout the Philippines and a vital asset to the domestic tourism industry. As is the case with the New Year celebrations in China, all forms of transportation experience demands that it is impossible to meet.

Realizing the Potential for Railway Tourism in the Philippines

Interviews with advocates of railway regeneration in the Philippines reveal the potential for the revitalization, through tourism, of communities in the regions served by the existing network. The general manager of PNR, Junio M. Ragragio (2012), contends that:

> The PNR played an important role that shaped our nation to what it is today. It is very rich in history, and giving due recognition on its historical significance should be part of our tourist attraction. Having a revitalized railway system that would take passengers towards the Bicol region will promote tourism and spur economic activities.

Bicol has been described as the poorest region in the country, with about half of the families living below the national poverty threshold of P10,378 per annum in cash and non-cash income (approximately US$200 per year). Best known for the location of the active Mayon volcano, it has great potential for tourism, with its historical significance and cultural assets. Improvements to the rail network would help promote the region and generate employment opportunities, especially in the hospitality sector. Figures for 2008 showed that tourist arrivals in Bicol grew by 8% that year, to 974,000, with tourism receipts projected at P481.3 million. In the first quarter of that year, 256,746 tourists arrived in Bicol, 35,258 of whom were foreign travelers.

According to Rico Laxas (personal communication), general manager of the Philippine National Housing Authority, the revitalization of the railway system could mean millions of local and foreign tourists exploring the less accessible corners of the island of Luzon, bringing colleagues, friends and family to enjoy local hospitality and appreciate the heritage and culture of local communities. Laxas envisages a Luzon-wide railway system with quality tourist facilities at every stop, such as those found on Japan Railways (JNR), along Eurorail connecting stations and at Amtrax 'whistle stops'. Facilities would include tourist information centers at major train stations for backpackers as well as first-class travelers. Laxas believes every train ride should be visually challenging; with track-side views like those of the European and Japanese countryside in springtime, when 'flowers bloom and the sun through the carriage windows is neither mercilessly hot nor numbingly cold'.

One vision of railway tourism presented in an itinerary offered to local and foreign travelers focuses on railway heritage. An introduction to the tour highlights this appeal:

The Philippines still has some very nice narrow gauge railways. The once extensive network of sugar cane railways has been reduced step by step and now most of the sugar mills have stopped using railway transport completely. Before the last tracks have been filled, we want to visit three of the railways. On two lines it is still possible to bring the beautiful steam locomotives back to life. We will charter these more than 80-year-old veterans.

The tour itinerary was described by Peadon (2008) as follows:

- Flight from Europe to Manila.
- Visit depots and the workshop of the Philippine National Railways in Manila. Afternoon flight to Dumaguete City.
- Visit to the narrow gauge railway of the sugar mill Bais. About a dozen of three-coupled Plymouth diesels are active on a 90-km long system. Visit to the depot in the sugar mill.
- Fly to Negros to witnesses the island's great narrow gauge past. First visit: closed sugar mill San Carlos with some dumped Henschel and Baldwin steam locomotives. Continue to Sagay (one plinthed loco left), and Lopez, where two Shay geared articulated locomotives are still present. Continue to Victoria mill which recently stopped all railway activities. One steam loco is still on display in Manapla. Evening arrival in Bacolod.
- Visit Hawaiian Philippine sugar mill, 22 km north of Bacolod. Ride on scheduled trains in the fields which are operated with diesel loco-motives.
- Travel 37 km south to reach the sugar mill La Carlota. View regular traffic with diesel locomotives. Visit the mill to see the milling process to get an impression how sugar cane becomes refined, white sugar.
- Train ride with 20 empties behind a steam locomotive to Ana Maria. Watch local fire brigade fill the tender of our loco.
- Continue to the exciting mountain line, Velez Malaga (maximum eight empty cane trucks allowed). Return with the locomotive (light engine) to the sugar mill. Here we'll turn the loco, serve it with water and fuel and return into the fields to pick up a train of loaded wagons.

Around 15 hrs our charter train, loaded up to the brim, will start to the mill. In the evening we'll continue by charter bus to Binalbagan.
- Visit to the sugar mill BISCOM in Binalbagan. View small operation with one or two diesels. Return to Bacolod and visit two plinthed steam locomotives there. Hotel in Bacolod.
- Fly back to Manila. Sightseeing tour through Manila and visit to the two plinthed steam locomotives in the city.
- Evening return flight to Europe.

Conclusions

Steadfast support for the Philippines railway regeneration projects was provided by the broadsheet newspaper the *Manila Standard Today*, with the fourth-largest circulation in the Philippines. It published an article on 15 December 2005 heralding the opportunities that this investment would provide.

The two projects will inject a total of $500 million (about P27 billion) into the country's economy. Imagine the benefits that this huge amount will generate in terms of the thousands of jobs not only during the rehabilitation of the rail system, but also in the actual operation phase, in the sale of construction supplies and materials, taxes and increased demands for goods and services along the length of the railway. Think of how easily and speedily the railway system will transport people, agricultural products and manufactured goods and how it will perk business and economic activity in the Calabarzon area and in Central Luzon.

The benefits outlined here affirm the government's plans, policies and intentions to stimulate the economy and revitalize communities through the regeneration of the rail network. An ongoing debate, however, concerned the benefits to be accrued through these projects being primarily for the foreign investors, rather than the local population. Although regeneration was expected to open wider the Philippine trading doors to China and South Korea, the priorities for the optimization of resources, including human resources, need to be the subject of consultation at the community level.

As is the case with many transportation networks in Asia, railways are home to impoverished communities living in close proximity to the tracks. These encroaching settlers eek out a tenuous living and have poor prospects of finding employment in the wider community. Nevertheless, as citizens these settlers have rights which the government is at pains to recognize. The regeneration of the Philippine railway system on the mainline South Rail, for example, requires the eviction and relocation of some 30,000 families on both sides of the track. This situation is being tackled by the Community Organization of the Philippines Enterprise (COPE), which seeks to provide relocation sites with basic infrastructure and services with P17.3 billion allocated for the 15-meter clearance on both sides of the track. It is a contentious issue, since relocation will not solve the problem of individual employability or address community needs. The regeneration of the railway system should incorporate projects for community development, allowing for more permanent settlements along the routes. Historically, this has been one of the attractive features of rail travel, especially for tourism, where the journey provides glimpses of urban and rural life, including architectural and cultural heritage.

The initial conclusions from this case study are that while the projects endorsed by the Philippine government may help to achieve the goals of economic development through encouraging foreign investment in accessing extractive and manufacturing industries, the goal of providing a viable solution to the problems faced by the potentially more sustainable service industries, particularly the tourism sector, needs to factor into plans for the regeneration and expansion of the railway system. This research is based on the premise that tourists traveling by rail would have greater access to the abundant natural and cultural heritage of the Philippine islands, as the Bicol case illustrates. The tourism industry as well as its market would not have to contend with the congested roads along which ply various modes of motorized passenger and freight transport. While container trucks would continue to monopolize the road networks, rail passengers could enjoy unhindered progress to their destinations along routes through rural as well as urban communities. In addition to providing express services facilitating the rapid movement of goods and commuters, more opportunities could be availed for community rail initiatives providing tourism and hospitality attractions and services, including stations with restaurants, museums, visitor centers and retail outlets showcasing the heritage of different regions, perhaps with new lines modeled on the Philippines' railway heritage.

This case reveals the imperative for alternative proposals to be considered, which will ensure that the regeneration of the railway system will benefit local communities and secure the sustainability of the resources on which they depend. With respect to this recommendation, reference is made in this research to studies of urban regional planning and development in the Philippine islands aimed at poverty alleviation. According to Shatkin (2007: 20), globalization has generated unique social and political changes that have created pressures for decentralization and citizen participation in government in the Philippines, pressures which are largely a legacy of the

Marcos dictatorship (Karaos, 1995; Ruland, 1996; Siliman & Noble, 1998). Initial findings from this research support the contention that community action, through NGOs, is essential for the optimization of the economic and cultural values associated with the country's railway heritage assets.

This research approach aims to optimize the value of railway transportation planning and the achievements of communities involved in its implementation. While the research area comprises communities in the Asian region, especially China and India (Srinivasan *et al.*, 2006), reference to the history of the railway and its communities in Britain, the birthplace of the railway phenomenon, is essential to an understanding of its impact on communities which were once linked to the engine of British imperial power. In the case of railway transportation, this link may be argued as being for the better rather than the worse. The catalyst for the growth of the phenomenon through the world is encapsulated in an observation made by Simmons in his study of railway development in England and Wales:

> The spirit [of the times] was competitive through and through: it was commerce against agriculture, North against South, London against the provinces, the middle classes against the aristocracy – and behind it sits Britain in competition with the rest of the world. (Simmons, 1978: 15)

The colonial railway phenomenon was a form of globalization: connecting the world of economic processes and technological ideas; creating distribution channels for enterprises involved in the exploitation of raw materials; spreading industrialization as well as innovative agricultural methods for the production of foodstuffs; and opening up avenues for foreign investment. It is contended here that the significance and relevance of this heritage to the renaissance of globalization has not received the attention it warrants.

The sustainability and optimization of the value of this heritage for the future requires a reassessment of this historical legacy and research on heritage from a multidisciplinary perspective. Coulls (1999: 5) argues that while some lay work has achieved academic standards of scholarship supporting the designation of railway heritage as World Heritage, recognition of its value is impeded by often conflicting points of view over the merits of proposed sites. He points out that the role of the World Heritage Convention is to provide the basic tools for any study of the value of railway heritage so that consensus can be reached. One of the criteria for selection rests on the premise that 'the historical significance of any particular railway will only be gained by seeing it in the round; as both a product of, and an influence on, wider social circumstances'. There is, however, 'a real danger that important sites will be missed as our understanding of the international significance of these lines and their remnants is not, with one or two exceptions, as deep as it might be' (Coulls 1999: 5).

With respect to the above, the contention here is that the growing body of research on the significance of the identity of World Heritage communities has overlooked the role of railway heritage in community development, with the sense of cohesion and pride in national identity that this engenders. Railway tourism will draw attention to assets and attractions of cultural significance for revitalizing communities through tourism-related enterprises at the local level, supported by national strategies. The distinct advantage which railway heritage assets has over other forms of heritage is that the tourist can engage and interact with the community – whether it be sharing the experience of a visit to a railway museum or a ride in a carriage along a contemporary or historical route. Investment needs to be made in educating the community to be aware that visitors derive enjoyment from sharing their local transport – that even a short 'fun ride' to the city center by mass transit, light rail or tramway can be an exhilarating cultural experience. Facilitating community enterprise in the provision of this cultural experience will depend on government policy and planning for sustainable tourism development that addresses the problems of exclusion and inequitable distribution of the benefits from investment in transportation.

The research approach outlined in this chapter is intended as a conceptual framework for formulating empirical studies and education policies for national, regional and local implementation. Policies should be congruent with the tourism development goals of supporting and revitalizing community values through stimulating a spirit of enterprise and productivity. Interdisciplinary programs are needed that provide both academic and vocational education and training, facilitated by the establishment of a research network that comprises academic and professional advisors as well as stakeholders. Achieving the best education and training for tourism planning and development requires a commitment to optimizing the value of railway transportation and its associated community values. The author contends that the most important value is the sustainability of the natural, cultural and social environments, invigorating tourism destinations linked by rail throughout the Asia Pacific region.

References

Banjo, G.A. and Dimitriou, H.T. (eds) (1990) *Transport Planning for Third World Cities.* London: Routledge.

Barat, J. (1985) Integrated metropolitan transport – reconciling efficiency and environmental improvement. *Third World Planning Review* 7 (3), 242–261.

Black, W. (2004) Sustainable mobility and its implications for tourism. In L. Lumsdon and S.J. Page (eds) *Tourism and Transport: Issues and Agenda for the New Millennium* (pp. 57–68). London: Elsevier.

Butcher, L. (2012) Railways: Rural and community lines. London: House of Commons Library. Available at http://www.parliament.uk/briefing-papers/SN03285.pdf (accessed 14 September 2008).

Cooper, M. (2008) Brazilian railway culture. Unpublished PhD thesis, Institute of Railway Studies, University of York.

Corpuz, A.G. (1999) *The Colonial Horse: Railroads and Regional Development in the Philippines 1875–1935.* Quezon City: University of the Philippines Press.

Coulls, A. (1999) *Railways as World Heritage Sites.* Occasional Papers for the World Heritage Convention. Paris: International Council on Monuments and Sites (ICOMOS).

Department of Transport (n.d.) Review of Community Rail Development Strategy. At http://www.dft.gov.uk/pgr/rail/strategyfinance/strategy/community (accessed 18 April 2009) (archived at http://webarchive.nationalarchives.gov.uk/20091009111237/http:/www.dft.gov.uk/pgr/rail/strategyfinance/strategy/community/revcomrail).

Karaos, A. (1995) Manila's urban poor movement: The social construction of collective identities. Unpublished PhD dissertation, New School for Social Research, New York.

Peadon, B. (2008) Philippine Railways Special Interest Group. At http://www.geocities.com/steel-haven_ee/LocoShed.html (accessed 11 September 2008).

Pearce, P.L., Moscardo, G. and Ross, G.F. (1996) *Tourism Community Relationships*. Oxford: Pergamon.

Philippine Railways (n.d.) At http://www.philippinerailways.com (accessed 9 August 2007).

Philippine Railways Special Interest Group (n.d.) At http://www.geocities.com/steel-haven_ee/LocoShed.html (accessed 11 September 2008).

Ragragio, J.M. (2012) PNR at 119: Played important part in shaping nation. At http://www.pnr.gov.ph/pr_2012-01.htm (accessed 1 May 2012).

Robbins, D. (2003) Public transport as a visitor attraction. In A. Fyall, B. Garrod and A. Leask (eds) *Managing Visitor Attractions* (pp. 86–103). Oxford: Elsevier Butterworth Heinemann.

Ruland, J. (ed.) (1996) *The Dynamics of Metropolitan Management in Southeast Asia.* Singapore: Institute of Southeast Asian Studies.

Shatkin, G. (2007) *Collective Action and Urban Poverty Alleviation*. Aldershot: Ashgate.

Siliman, G. and Noble, L. (eds) (1998) *Organizing for Democracy: NGOs, Civil Society and the Philippine State.* Honolulu: University of Hawaii Press.

Simmons, J. (1978) *The Railway in England and Wales, 1830–1914.* Leicester: Leicester University Press.

Srinivasan, R., Tiwari, M. and Silas, S. (eds) (2006) *Our Indian Railway: Themes in India's Railway History.* Delhi: Foundation Books.

Vasconcellos, E. (2003) The urban transportation crisis in developing countries: Alternative policies for an equitable space. In J. Whitelegg and G. Haq (eds) *World Transport Policy and Practice* (pp. 189–198). London: Earthscan Publications.

Part 3

National and Regional Railway Heritage Tourism

10 Railroad Tourism in Brazil

Carla Conceição Lana Fraga,
Marcio Peixoto de Sequeira Santos and
Sergio de Castro Ribeiro

Introduction

Medium- and long-distance passenger train services in Brazil are scarce, mainly because after the privatization of the national railway system at the end of the 1990s the newly privatized operators focused on cargo. Nevertheless, cultural tourism involving railroads is growing in the country. There is an expanding supply of private trains catering to tourists, running on the tracks of freight carriers or over routes built or refurbished specifically for tourism. Among the attractions along these routes are visits to railroad museums, restored rail stations, historic towns, scenic regions and restored trains. There is also growing demand on the part of railroad enthusiasts, variously known as railfans, train buffs and so on.

The main objective of this chapter is to present the cultural tourism railroad market in Brazil and to discuss the experience provided by this type of tourism in the country. The chapter is divided into three parts, and is based on information obtained by consulting the relevant literature, websites and historic documents.

The first part sets the context – the interface between trains, culture and tourism – by presenting the significant milestones of the market and the public policies structuring this segment. It also analyzes the sustainability of trains for tourist and cultural purposes as an element for development not only of the segment itself, but also of the regions through which the trains run.

In the second part the focus is on the supply of trains for tourist and cultural purposes available in the country, the operators of these trains and the associated attractions, such as museums and historic towns.

The third section examines the profile of demand for these attractions, and summarizes some studies on the tourist train experience, tourists' perception of the trains and the use of virtual tools to whet the interest of people in taking tourist train outings.

This chapter on railroad cultural tourism in Brazil provides a snapshot of the current situation and a good understanding of the future prospects for this segment. As such, it makes an important contribution to a theme not often addressed in the literature on rail transportation, tourism or culture.

Trains, Culture and Tourism in Brazil

Brazil is the world's fifth largest country in area and the largest by far in South America, covering roughly 8.5 million km^2. It is officially subdivided into five regions: North, Northeast, Midwest, Southeast and South. Expansion of its transportation infrastructure, promotion of accessibility, sustainable management of mobility and diversification of tourist destinations are all important challenges facing public and private policy-makers. While there are many obstacles to overcome, there are also great opportunities, based on Brazil's position as one of the leading emerging economies in the world and its great variety of cultural and natural attractions.

Brazil's transportation system is mainly based on highways, although air travel in the past decade has made major strides, as fares have fallen significantly. Also, the liberalization of coastal shipping in the late 1990s, allowing foreign companies to compete on a more equal footing, has greatly boosted the number of cruise ships calling at Brazilian ports (Paolillo & Rejowski, 2002). Rail transport, for both freight and passengers, is also expanding, after a long history of ups and downs. The study by Suevo (2008), presented at an event in 2008 organized by the Movement for Railroad Preservation, depicts the history of railroads in Brazil, broken down into periods (Figure 10.1):

The initial part (14.5 km) of the first railroad in Brazil was launched in 1854, during the imperial period. The first kilometers connected the back of Guanabara Bay to Parada de Fragoso, both located in the state of Rio de Janeiro. The destination of that railroad was Petropolis (location of the emperor's summer palace), also located in the state of Rio de Janeiro (Schoppa, 2004). According to Suevo (2008), the greatest expansion of the nation's railroad network occurred in the period from 1957 to 1995 (Figure 10.1). This period was book-ended by the creation by the Brazilian government of Rede Ferroviária Federal S.A. (RFFSA, 'Federal Railway System Corporation'), unifying all the country's railroads (mainly lines that had been nationalized in previous years), and the decision to break it up and privatize the constituent lines.

The decision to privatize was part of a larger privatization program undertaken to attract private investment in the nation's economy. The

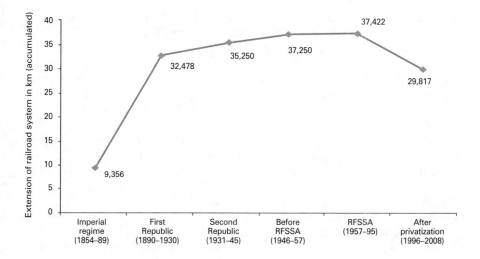

Figure 10.1 Advances and declines of railroad transportation in Brazil
Source: Prepared by the authors, based on Suevo (2008)

sell-off began in 1996 and was concluded in 1999. The process consisted of awarding, through a public tender, concession contracts lasting 20–30 years. Despite the new investments made by the private operators, nearly all of these outlays were aimed at increasing cargo capacity, to carry mineral and agricultural commodities. The extension of the system actually declined in recent years, as did the supply of passenger trains (Figure 10.1).

Despite the growing freight traffic, there is still a good deal of idle capacity. There are also incentives now in place to diversify by expanding the offer of tourist trains, relying heavily on the country's railway heritage (museums, stations, roundhouses, etc.), favoring the development of this segment of the cultural tourism market. This segment – railroads aimed at tourism and cultural activities – is gaining ground and becoming a separate field for analysis. Indeed, according to Fraga (2011), railway tourism can be seen as an independent segment from cultural tourism, with its own peculiarities, although the two are complementary, since cultural attractions are important magnets for tourist train customers.

The profile of tourist trains in Brazil is varied. Some mainly focus on the nostalgic experience of riding a restored train, while others mainly attract riders due to the scenery on the route or the attractions at the destination. Therefore, the segment is very complex, with specific products and services serving niches within it. To understand this complexity, it is important to consider that tourism did not originate from a theory, but rather the practice precedes the theory (Panosso Netto, 2005). Therefore, the formulation of specific public policies for the tourist sector should be based on both theoretical analysis of the phenomenon and the actual structure of the activity.

The Brazilian government created the Ministry of Tourism in 2003 and formulated a national tourism policy oriented by regionalization and diversification. Efforts to promote tourism, both internal and international, were intensified with the implementation of the National Tourism Plan (2003–07 and 2007–10). This was accompanied by enactment of Law 11,771 in 2008 (known as the General Tourism Law), which provides the basic framework for the regulation of the tourist railway market.

Other academic and marketing actions for the development of railway tourism deserve mention. In 2002 a study was published by the Transport Engineering Program at the request of the National Bank for Economic and Social Development (BNDES). Through a ranking method, the study indicated the main routes for the establishment of new regional trains in Brazil. One of the vectors for identifying these routes was tourism (Scharinger, 2002).

In 2004 the Brazilian Association of Touristic and Cultural Train Operators (ABOTTC) was formed. According to its statistics, there are currently over 20 trips offered in various regions of the country, as well as a series of projects to establish new trains running on freight routes with spare capacity.

Since 2007, the National Institute of Historic and Artistic Heritage (IPHAN) has been developing a Railway Heritage Inventory, and in 2008 it accordingly established the Technical Office for Railway Heritage. These are important developments for the structuring of railway cultural tourism in the country.

Train buffs and other people interested in Brazilian railway history and heritage have a virtual space available to them, called Clube Amantes da Ferrovia, http://www.amantesdaferrovia.com.br. In January 2012, the Club announced the site had over 5000 users. Further, according to information posted at the Club's site, the Brazilian market for touristic/cultural trains is growing by roughly 9% per year, based on information provided by the head of one of the main Brazilian tourist train operators.

As part of the government's efforts to encourage this expansion, in March 2010 the Ministry of Tourism established the Working Group on Railway Tourism. It is formed by representatives of the Ministry of Tourism, the Ministry of Transportation, IPHAN, the National Land Transportation Agency (ANTT), the National Department of Transportation Infrastructure (DNIT), the Federal Property Secretariat (SPU) and the Inventariança da Extinta Rede Ferroviária Federal S.A. (the entity set up to manage the remaining assets and liabilities of RFFSA after privatization of its component railroads), among others.

One of the first undertakings of the Working Group was to prepare a folder providing practical guidance and explaining the requirements for proposing projects to establish new tourist/cultural trains in the country. In January 2012 the Ministry of Tourism indicated on its website that the Working Group was analyzing in detail 50 projects proposed by municipal governments and private non-profit organizations to implement new tourist trains in the country, reflecting the growing interest in this activity.

An important academic work on the theme is the study by Fraga (2008) on the sustainable development of Brazilian tourist trains. Based on the use of the multicriteria analytic hierarchy process (MAHP) proposed by Saaty (1977), Fraga (2008) formulated a decision tree, after a literature review and consultation with specialists, to respond to the question 'Are tourist trains sustainable?' The tree incorporates environmental, social, cultural, economic, political-institutional, technical and spatial dimensions. The Brazilian tourist trains selected in the study were analyzed according to the criteria created for the tree, with weights assigned to each dimension.

The next section analyzes the varied management and operations of Brazilian tourist trains, railroad museums and stations and destinations to attract tourists.

The Supply of Tourist Trains in Brazil

The supply of tourist trains is directly related to the physical cultural heritage (trackage, buildings, bridges/trestles, etc.) and the intangible heritage (habits, customs and histories). For Allis (2006), railway tourism 'emerges from a refinement of the relationship between cultural heritage and tourism'. While the train trip itself is one of the central elements of the experience, attractions along the route or at the final destination also play an important role, such as museums, restored stations and natural and/or historic landmarks. These exist independently of the supply of train trips, but in many cases they spur the reactivation of a particular railway for tourism, in turn favoring the further development of tourism in the city or region, in a virtuous circle.

Railway outings

According to Suevo (2008), 3.9% of Brazil's current railway system (1162 km) is operated for tourism purposes. These tourist train services vary greatly, in terms of both management and operation:

- *management* – the railways may be managed by private enterprises, by non-governmental organizations (NGOs) or by government (federal, state, municipal), as well as by public–private partnerships.
- *operation* – the train services may be regularly scheduled, with departures every day or on particular days (e.g. weekends), or seasonal (only during the tourist high season or on dates of local commemorations and festivities).

Table 10.1 shows the geographic distribution, the name of the operators and the type of management of all Brazilian tourist train services that the authors could ascertain between 2010 and 2011, along with a brief description of their attractions; all but two ran regular schedules, as opposed to seasonal ones. The information presented in Table 10.1 is taken from Fraga (2011), the websites of the operators (see Table 10.2) and the websites of private and government organizations, such as the Brazilian Association of Touristic and Cultural Train Operators (ABOTTC) and the National Land Transportation Agency (ANTT). According to Table 10.1, the South and Southeast regions have 92% of the tourist trains and trolleys. In terms of management, NGOs, especially various state chapters of the Brazilian Association of Railway Preservation (ABPF), stand out among the operators, followed by Serra Verde Express, a private operator. (According to the ABPF site, it is a 'nonprofit civil association with historic, cultural and educational purposes, recognized by the Brazilian government as a Public Interest Social Organization [OSCIP]'.)

Regarding the fares charged, Coelho (2011) analyzed the prices of train outings in his study of railway cultural tourism. There was a wide range, the lowest being R$0.60 and the highest R$270.00, although most of the fares were below R$50.00. This price diversity is not surprising, since the outings differ greatly, from short trips on trolleys to all-day luxury excursions with onboard meals included.

The description of the outings shows the associations between interest in trains themselves and other tourist segments. For instance, ecotourism is the main attraction on the trip between Curitiba/Morretes and Paranaguá. This route runs through the Atlantic Forest and provides passengers with information on the environment as well as railroading (Fraga, 2011).

Table 10.1 Tourist trains and trolleys[a,b,c] (state and operator)

State (no. of trains in state)	Name	Operator	Management	Description
Rio Grande do Sul (1)	Trem do Vinho	Giordani Turismo	Private	Steam locomotive, wine tasting, shows of local folklore
Santa Catarina (4)	Trem da Serra do Mar	ABPF-SC	NGO	Steam locomotive; scenery and nature
	Trem do Contestado[a]	ABPF-SC	NGO	Commemorative, related to events
	Trem Rubi	Museu Ferroviário de Tubarão	NGO	Steam locomotive, historic interest
	Trem das Termas	ABPF-SC	NGO	Steam locomotive, scenery and nature
Paraná (2)	Serra do Mar Paranaense Train	Serra Verde Express	Private	Coastal scenery and ecological interest
	Great Brazil Express	Serra Verde Express	Private	Coastal scenery, luxury accommodation
São Paulo (7)	Trem dos Imigrantes	ABPF-SP	NGO	Steam locomotive, cultural, ethnic and historic elements associated with immigrant routes
	Viação Férrea Campinas Jaguariúna	ABPF-SP	NGO	Steam locomotive, educational experience, with a stop to explain the workings of the locomotive
	Trem dos Ingleses	ABPF-SP	NGO	Steam locomotive; outing associated with the historic interest of Vila de Paranapiacaba
	Expresso Mogi das Cruzes	CPTM	Government	Stainless-steel cars from the 1950s; historic and cultural interest
	Expresso Jundiaí	CPTM	Government	Stainless-steel cars from the 1950s; historic and cultural interest
	Expresso Paranapiacaba	CPTM	Government	Stainless-steel cars from the 1950s; historic and cultural interest
	Estrada de Ferro Campos do Jordão	São Paulo State Government	Government	Train, urban trolley; scenic and historic interest

Table continues over

Rio de Janeiro (4)	Trem do Corcovado	ESFECO Adm Ltda.	Private	Electric train, with historic, cultural and scenic interest; provides access to the Christ the Redeemer statue in Rio de Janeiro
	Trem Estrada Real[c]	Paraíba do Sul Municipal Government	Government	Steam locomotive; historic and cultural interest
	Maria Fumaça SESC	SESC Mineiro Grussai	Entity focused on providing social services	Steam locomotive; historic and cultural interest
	Bonde Santa Teresa[b,c]	Rio de Janeiro State Government	Government	Electric trolley; historic, cultural and ecological interest
Minas Gerais (4)	Trem das Águas	ABFP –MG	NGO	Steam locomotive; historic and cultural interest
	Trem da Serra da Mantiqueira	ABPF – MG	NGO	Steam locomotive; historic and cultural interest
	Maria Fumaça São João Del Rei Tiradentes	FCA-Vale	Private	Steam locomotive; historic and cultural interest
	Maria Fumaça Ouro Preto Mariana	FCA – Vale	Private	Steam locomotive; historic and cultural interest
Espírito Santo (1)	Trem das Montanhas Capixabas	Serra Verde Express	Private	Coastal scenery and historic, cultural and ecological interest
Mato Grosso do Sul (1)	Trem do Pantanal	Serra Verde Express	Private	Coastal scenery and historic, cultural and ecological interest
Pernambuco (1)	Trem do Forro[a]	Serrambi Turismo	Private	Diesel locomotive, decorated with seasonal motifs of the Feast of São João in Pernambuco

[a] All the trains operated regularly with the exception of the third listed, Trem do Contestado, and the last listed, Trem do Forro, which are seasonal operations.
[b] Trolleys (both over flat routes and those climbing steep inclines) are included.
[c] Temporarily deactivated.

Source: Prepared by the authors based on consultation of the work of Fraga (2011) and the websites of the operators and of ABOTTC and ANTT.

Another example is the Trem do Vinho ('Wine Train'), which circulates between cities settled by Italian immigrants – Bento Gonçalves, Carlos Barbosa and Garibaldi. Besides the nostalgia of the restored cars pulled by an original steam locomotive, the passengers have an opportunity to sample the local wine and food and learn of the region's culture. There are wine and cheese tastings at the stations and shows with traditional Italian music and dance, such as the Tarantella. Therefore, this operation combines interest in trains with culture and gastronomy (Fraga, 2011).

The tourist train experience in Brazil is not limited to outings. Attractions along the routes can also be important, such as restored rail stations, museums and other tourist attractions, all of which are important for development of the segment.

Stations, museums and tourist destinations with railway appeal

Some rail stations have become tourist attractions in their own right. The Estações Ferroviárias site (http://www.estacoesferroviarias.com.br) catalogs more than 3000 rail stations in Brazil. Many are visited for their historic, cultural and architectural value, independent of their use for rail transportation. Others are visited for their functionality, after being refurbished and transformed into libraries, museums, restaurants and so on. Finally, many are still used on a daily basis, especially those serving commuter traffic between central cities and outlying suburbs.

These structures are located virtually throughout the country. According to the keeper of the Estações Ferroviárias site, Ralph Geisbrecht, these stations were important to the foundation and growth of many cities and to progress in general in the country (Geisbrecht, n.d.). With the decline of long-distance railroad passenger services, only some of these stations have been converted to other uses. Many have fallen into neglect. In this respect, railroad tourism can play an important role in the preservation of these landmarks.

Other attractions are railroad museums, able to attract visitors independent of a train outing. The main such museums in Brazil are located in the Southeast and South regions, notably in the cities of São João de Rei and Juiz de Fora (Minas Gerais), Bauru and Jundiaí (São Paulo), Curitiba (Paraná), Vila Velha (Espírito Santo) and Rio de Janeiro (Rio de Janeiro).

Based on the notion of ecomuseum, in which the identity of the entire knowledge and activities of a local community is the object of attention, some places have become railway tourism destinations due to the great influence of the railroad in their development. In Brazil there are several cities that have a preserved railway ambience independent of the continuing existence of passenger rail transportation. A good example is the city of Juiz de Fora.

The leading destination for railroad fans and tourists in Brazil is Vila de Paranapiacaba, located in the municipality of Santo André in the state of São Paulo, in the region called Serra do Mar ('Seaside Range'). The average elevation in the region is 796 m and access is usually by the Via Anchieta highway. Visitors can, though, also reach it by train and there is a functioning train they can ride while there. The railroad was built in 1867. The restored historic site is divided into an upper and lower part and the railroad structures remain from two distinct phases, one from 1860 to 1946 and the second from 1946 onward (Oliveira, n.d.). According to Oliveira (n.d.), the first phase started with the establishment of a village to house the workers who constructed and later maintained the railroad (the São Paulo Railway, owned by British investors) and finished with the end of that company's 90-year concession. The second phase was marked by the decline of rail transport in the region in general, as highways were built in the 1950s, but there was a comeback that started in 1987, when the village was made an official landmark. Since then, many of the old houses and other facilities have been restored and visitors can see examples of original railcars and locomotives. There is still further potential for exploitation of the relationship between railroading and cultural tourism, according to a study by Allis (2002).

Demand for Railway Tourism in Brazil

Just as with the supply side, the demand for tourist trains in Brazil is fragmented and differentiated. There have been very few academic works on this subject.

One exception is Fraga (2004), who performed a study of riders' experience with the Corcovado Train, which takes visitors from the Cosme Velho district up to the Christ statute on top of Mount Corcovado in Rio de Janeiro. The Christ the Redeemer statue was elected the seventh wonder of the modern world in 2008 and is a major tourist attraction because of the stunning view of the city below. The train competes with toll road access to the site. The line, opened in 1884, was built exclusively to carry visitors up to the peak. It currently carries approximately 600,000 passengers a year. Of the 400 people interviewed (most of them foreign tourists), 89% stated they chose to use the train rather than road access (taxi or private car) due to a series of associated values, such as the ecology of Tijuca Forest, one of the world's largest urban forests, through which the train runs, the historical value of the train and the inclusion of the local community. In this respect, the Corcovado Train is similar to many others, in that both internal and external considerations prompt passengers to ride the train (Fraga, 2004).

Debenetti (2008) carried out a similar study of the perceptions of tourists riding the steam-powered train that runs through the towns of Bento Gonçalves, Garibaldi and Carlos Barbosa in the southern state of Rio Grande do Sul. She concluded that 'although some tourists made negative comments about the outing, in general those surveyed said it lived up to their expectations by providing diversion, interaction and culture' (Debenetti, 2008: 121). Her study also revealed the importance of cultural interest to attract and satisfy riders.

The internet is an important way to spread knowledge about strategies to offer services in this market segment and to gain the interest of tourists. This can occur through dedicated sites run by the train operators, institutional sites of government tourist bureaus or sites aimed at train buffs, in the last case through virtual bulletin boards, chat rooms, online communities, blogs and so on. Table 10.2 shows the various tourist railways in Brazil about which information can be obtained over the internet, either through dedicated sites or the other means delineated above (Fraga, 2011). In any event, the existence of search engines in recent years has opened a whole new channel for information to spread about railway tourism to entrepreneurs, academics and prospective passengers all over the world.

An analysis of the dedicated sites shows that all of the operators initially supplying historical information about the trains and other attractions, and then technical information about the services provided. More than half (52%) have a page for frequently asked questions, a link to a call center or online response service or an ombudsperson. The others provide only contact information. Only 41% enable visitors to book trips, while 47% have some type of tool to allow people to find social networks and 94% have links to other sites on railway tourism or railroading themes. This brief analysis shows that the operators are not taking full advantage of the tools provided by the internet to attract riders (Fraga, 2011).

In summary, based on the studies by Debenetti (2008) and Fraga (2004, 2011), it is possible to highlight some points for future reflection:

- the railway tourism experience is highly varied, depending on the values associated with each train, so players in the segment need to analyze potential market niches;
- gathering and interpreting data from consumers is essential in order to be competitive;
- investing in communication to attract interest is a strategy with much room to grow in the Brazilian railway tourism market.

Table 10.2 Tourist trains and trolleys with information available over the internet

Tourist train or trolley	Website
Trem do Vinho	http://www.mfumaca.com.br
Trem da Serra do Mar	http://www.abpfsc.com.br/
Trem do Contestado	http://www.abpfsc.com.br/
Trem Rubi	No dedicated site
Trem das Termas	http://www.abpfsc.com.br/
Serra Verde Express	http://www.serraverdeexpress.com.br
Great Brazil Express	http://www.greatbrazilexpress.com
Trem dos Imigrantes	http://www.abpfsp.com.br/
Bonde dos Imigrantes	http://www.abpfsp.com.br/
Viação Férrea Campinas Jaguariúna	No dedicated site
Trem dos Ingleses	http://www.abpfsp.com.br/
Expresso Mogi das Cruzes	http://www.cptm.sp.gov.br/
Expresso Jundiaí	http://www.cptm.sp.gov.br/
Estrada de Ferro Campos do Jordão	http://www.efcj.sp.gov.br/
Trem do Corcovado	http://www.tremdocorcovado.com.br/
Trem Estrada Real	No dedicated site
Maria Fumaça SESC	No dedicated site
Bonde Santa Teresa	No dedicated site
Trem das Águas	No dedicated site
Trem da Serra da Mantiqueira	No dedicated site
Maria Fumaça São João Del Rei Tiradentes	http://www.tremdavale.org/pt/trem-turistico/
Maria Fumaça Ouro Preto Mariana	http://www.tremdavale.org/pt/trem-turistico/
Trem das Montanhas Capixabas	http://serraverdeexpress.com.br/montanhas/destinos
Trem do Pantanal	http://serraverdeexpress.com.br/pantanal/destinos
Trem do Forró	http://www.tremdoforro.com.br/

Source: Fraga (2011).

Final Considerations

The railway tourism market in Brazil is expanding both in the number of trains and in demand. But there are still many challenges to overcome for the segment to reach its full potential; these will require various actions and plans, with the participation of public authorities, non-governmental organizations, academia and entrepreneurs.

The public sector, when not directly exploiting the rail lines, must create the proper incentives and formulate an effective legal framework to make investments in railway tourism attractive. Non-governmental organizations must work effectively with government to improve the management of existing lines and establish new ones. Researchers also have a key role, to shed light on the factors that can lead to the success of railway tourism. Finally, investments are necessary from the private sector to improve existing trains and establish new ones.

References

Allis, T. (2002) Ferrovia e turismo cultural – Alternativa para o futuro da vila de paranapiacaba (SP). *Turismo em Análise* 13 (2), 29–53.

Allis, T. (2006) Turismo, patrimônio cultural e transporte ferroviário. Um estudo sobre ferrovias turísticas no Brasil e na Argentina. Unpublished master's dissertation in Latin American integration, Universidade de São Paulo, Brazil.

Amantes da Ferrovia (n.d.) Trens turísticos voltam a agradar brasileiros. At http://amantes daferrovia.com.br/profiles/blogs/trens-turisticos-voltam-a-agradar-os-brasileiros (accessed January 2014).

Associação Brasileira das Operadoras de Trens Turísticos e Culturais (ABOTTC) (n.d.) At http://www.abottc.com.br (accessed January 2014).

Coelho, D.H.S. (2011) *Análise da oferta e da demanda turística no Brasil. Subprojeto do Projeto de Pesquisa Turismo Cultural Ferroviário*. Rio de Janeiro: Universidade Federal do Estado do Rio de Janeiro.

Debenetti, V.E.S. (2008) Passeio de Trem Maria-Fumaça: Um exemplo de turismo cultural e de lazer. Estudo das percepções dos turistas. *Revista de Cultura e Turismo* 2 (1), 120–136.

Fraga, C.C.L. (2004) Trem do Corcovado: Experiência funcional ou turística? Monograph for bachelor's degree in tourism, Universidade Federal de Juiz de Fora, Minas Gerais.

Fraga, C.C.L. (2008) Análise da sustentabilidade de trens turísticos no Brasil. Unpublished dissertation, Transport Engineering Program, COPPE/UFRJ.

Fraga, C.C.L. (2011) Contribuição metodológica para a implantação de trens turísticos no Brasil. Unpublished doctoral thesis, Programa de Engenharia de Transportes da COPPE, Universidade Federal do Rio de Janeiro.

Geisbrecht, R. (n.d.) Estação ferroviária. At http://www.estacoesferroviarias.com.br (accessed January 2014).

Instituto Brasileiro de Geografia e Estatística (IBGE) (n.d.) At http://teen.ibge.gov.br/censo/censo-2010 (accessed February 2014).

Instituto do Patrimônio Histórico e Artístico Nacional (IPHAN) (n.d.)

Patrimônio ferroviário. At http://portal.iphan.gov.br/portal/montarPaginaSecao.
   do?id=15825&retorno=paginaIphan (accessed January 2014).
Oliveira, A.C.C.M. (n.d.) Paranapiacaba. At http://www.paranapiacaba.ana.nom.br
   (accessed January 2014).
Panosso Netto, A. (2005) *Filosofia do turismo: teoria e epistemologia*. São Paulo: Aleph.
Paolillo, A.M. and Rejowski, M. (2002) *Transportes – Coleção ABC do turismo*. São Paulo:
   Aleph.
Saaty, T.L. (1977) A scaling method for priorities in hierarchical structures. *Journal of
   Mathematical Psychology* 15 (3), 234–281.
Scharinger, J.F. (2002) *Trens Regionais de Passageiros*. BNDES/Coppe UFRJ. Rio de Janeiro,
   RJ.
Serra Verde Express (n.d.) At http://www.serraverdeexpress.com.br (accessed January
   2014).
Schoppa, R.F. (2004) *150 anos do trem no Brasil*. Rio de Janeiro: Milograf.
Suevo, H. (2008) Paper presented at the Railway Cultural Tourism Seminar, Rio de Janeiro.
Trem do Corcovado. História (n.d.) At http://www.corcovado.com.br/portugues/
   historia.html (accessed March 2014).

11 Railway Tourism: An Opportunity to Diversify Tourism in Mexico

Blanca A. Camargo, C. Gabriela Garza and Marel Morales

Introduction

Mexico is one of the world's most visited countries. In 2011, despite challenges related to violence and internal drug wars that have affected the country's image, Mexico welcomed approximately 22.3 million international arrivals, a 4.4% increase from 2010. These visitors generated approximately US$11.8 billion in tourism revenue (United Nations World Tourism Organization, 2011). Mexico's most popular destinations are located in the Riviera Maya, the corridor of white sand, sparkling blue water, Caribbean beaches, all-inclusive resorts and tourist towns such as Cancun, Playa del Carmen, Tulum and the island of Cozumel, among others. These towns join other coastal areas in the Yucatan Peninsula and the Pacific coast as popular destinations. Tourism development in these sun–sand–sea (and sometimes sex) destinations in Mexico, however, has been highly criticized for following a neo-liberal agenda that has caused rapid and uncontrolled growth and brought environmental, social, economic and cultural problems to the local people and their resources (see Pi-Sunyer *et al.*, 2001; Torres, 2002; Torres & Momsen, 2005a, 2005b).

Numerous calls have been made to diversify Mexico's tourism offerings, to attract better and more specialized tourist segments and to develop tourism in a more sustainable way. In response, in 2011, the federal government decreed the Year of Tourism in Mexico and signed the National Agreement for Tourism, which sought to have 'all sectors related to this activity ... carry out actions that can allow more tourists to make Mexico their main travel destination' (Secretariat of Tourism of Mexico, 2011). The National Agreement, signed by the government and diverse tourism stakeholders, seeks to make Mexico one of the world's tourism leaders by diversifying tourism markets, products and destinations. To accomplish this, the government has been undertaking initiatives to promote medical, adventure, and meetings and convention tourism, as well as developing new cultural tourism products, such as gastronomic and historic routes. In 2010, for example, to celebrate the 200th anniversary of Mexican independence and the 100th anniversary of the Mexican Revolution, the Secretariat of Tourism of Mexico launched eight commemorative routes related to these historic events. Each one is named after a military leader of the Revolution (Secretariat of Tourism of Mexico, 2010).

In this chapter, we argue that, given its railway infrastructure and richly diverse cultural and natural heritage, Mexico should seize the opportunity to develop railway tourism. More specifically, the country should develop heritage railway journeys as an alternative tourism option that can help diversify the country's tourism products and attract a more educated, lucrative and responsible tourist segment. Dallen (2007) found that tourist train devotees tend to be married couples in the middle-age range, whose main motivations are to enjoy the ride and use the train because it is good for the environment. A survey of tourists and residents that explored interest in train excursions on Vancouver Island in Canada (IBI Group, 2010) found that potential tourist train users would be willing to pay between up to CAD\$60 for a half-day excursion and up to CAD\$120 for a full-day excursion.

Railway tourism has become an important alternative tourism product in many destinations around the world. Examples of popular railway journeys include the Darjeeling Himalayan Railway in India, the Blue Train Route in South Africa, the Harz Mountain Railway in Germany and the Cusco–Sacred Valley–Machu Picchu route in Peru, to name just a few. This type of tourism is gaining support in part because trains are less likely to negatively impact the environment compared with other forms of transportation. They also enjoy good safety records, demand less physical space and are generally low cost (Dickinson & Lumsdon, 2010). Moreover, Dickinson and Lumsdon (2010) argued that train tourism offers a better travel experience than other types of tourism and promotes the economic development of remote destinations. We extend this line of thought to argue that railway tourism can contribute to the economic and social development of remote areas in Mexico that are accessible through the national rail system.

In this chapter we next provide a brief literature review on railway tourism, which is followed by a case study that examines Mexico's railway infrastructure and current railway tourism development in the country. We then discuss key factors and issues that should be considered when planning and developing railway tourist journeys. As sustainable tourism scholars, we believe that participating in tourism decision-making and gaining the informed consent of local communities is critical for tourism development.

Local stakeholders' opinions and concerns, therefore, must be included early in the planning and development process.

Railway Tourism

Railway tourism is not a new phenomenon. Rail journeys date back to late 1800s, when train services were developed and expanded in many parts of the world. Although train infrastructure was not originally developed for leisure and tourism, regular journeys become tourist routes due to the uniqueness and beauty of the landscape, the elegance of train carts and the experience onboard. Rail transportation has been singled out as one of the main reasons for the leisure revolution in Victorian and Edwardian times, and the expansion and sophistication of train services contributed to tourist destinations being developed and popularized, especially coastal towns (Page & Ge, 2010). Railways built at the end of the 19th and beginning of the 20th century such as the Semmering railway in Austria, the Mountain railways of India and the Raethian railway in the Albula-Bermina landscape of the Swiss Alps (see Chapter 14) have become UNESCO World Heritage sites for their outstanding technological achievements when they were constructed, as well as for their socio-cultural and economic value. Today, the train continues to be an important mode of tourist transport, especially in European countries, Japan with its high-speed trains, China and India, where the train accounts for a large proportion of all domestic travel. In 2009, France and Germany alone transported the most national (78 and 77 million) and international (9.9 and 4.1 million) rail passengers (European Commission, 2011).

Despite its importance, research on railway tourism is scarce. The very few empirical studies available have focused mainly on segmenting rail passengers (Bichis-Lupas & Moisey, 2001; Dallen, 2007; Pas & Huber, 1992) or assessing traveler experience during the train route (Lyons et al., 2007; Su & Wall, 2009). In recent years, scholars have highlighted the advantages of the train as a *slow* and sustainable form of both transportation and tourism, based on its lower environmental impact compared with other forms of transport, including lower carbon dioxide emissions (Dickinson et al., 2011; Kosters, 1992) and the social inclusion of those who do not possess their own means of transportation (Dallen, 2007). Even fewer studies have empirically assessed the scale and nature of the economic, environmental, and social effects of this type of tourism. Fu (2009), for example, found that the opening of the Qinghai–Tibet railway had several impacts on the town of Lhasa in China. Specifically, the author reported growth in tourist arrivals, an increased number of tour operators, hotels and guest-houses, and more business investments. Additionally, the railway created jobs, improved living standards, provided opportunities for cultural exchange and promoted regional cooperation among stakeholders. On the other hand, tourism growth in Lhasa led to a higher cost of living, social problems, community conflict and hegemony of the Mandarin language (Fu, 2009).

Despite the dearth of academic studies, industry information is abundant. Tourist trains generate important revenue and economic benefits. The Orient Express Hotels Corporation, owner of luxurious tourist trains in Europe and Asia, reported US$58 million in revenue from its routes in 2009. The economic impact of visitors to the Bellarine Railway in Australia is also significant: it generates approximately 60 local jobs and AU$14.7 million in direct and indirect annual output (Nichol & More, 2010). In Canada, leisure travelers account for 50% of all riders on the VIA railway, whose economic impact could be approximately CA$1.5 million annually (IBIS Group, 2010).

Railway tourism is also generating attention, which government and private operators promote in several countries. In the United States in 2002, for example, Amtrak, in partnership with the National Park Service (NPS), developed the Trails and Rails program to 'provide rail passengers with educational opportunities that foster an appreciation of a selected region's natural and cultural heritage; it promotes National Park Service areas and provides a value-added service to encourage train ridership' (National Park Service, 2012: para. 1). This program operates 18 routes across major cities in the United States. In 2009, 401,600 passengers participated in this program (National Park Service, 2012). Latin America is experiencing a growing demand for train passenger services, due in part to the uniqueness and beauty of its landscapes and destinations. Among the most popular train tourist routes in Latin America are El Chepe in Mexico, Tren a las Nubes (Train to the Clouds) in Argentina, the Serra Verde Express in Brazil and the Cuzco-Macchu Picchu in Peru. Shorter heritage tourist rail lines are found throughout other Latin American countries as well.

Despite railway tourism's potential, tourism research has not adequately addressed the product planning and development, and criteria for developing railway tourism products particularly lacking (see Charlton, 1998). In the remainder of this chapter, we aim to open a discussion of the potential, issues and challenges in developing railway tourism. We illustrate our points with practical examples from around the world, but with a focus on Mexico. In the next section, we discuss current railway tourism projects in Mexico and explore the potential for expanding this type of tourism in order to accomplish the objectives of the 2011 National Agreement for Tourism.

Railway Tourism: An Alternative Tourism Product for Mexico

Mexico has 20,702 km of railroads, which are classified into three categories: long distance (class I), short-line (class II) and remnant roads (not in service). After the national railway company, Ferrocarriles Nacionales de Mexico, was privatized in 1998, 87% of all Mexican railroads began operating through private companies such Ferromex (with 8427 km of line, 41% of all railroads in the country), Kansas City Southern de Mexico (4283 km, 21%), Ferrosur (1955 km, 9.4%) and smaller operators that serve an additional 3112 km of railroad (Secretaria de Comunicaciones y Transportes, 2010).

Active railroads extend across the country (Figure 11.1), connect major cities and pass through thousands of kilometers of natural landscapes and small towns. With the exception of one passenger and one suburban train, however, they are used exclusively for freight; indeed, passenger services

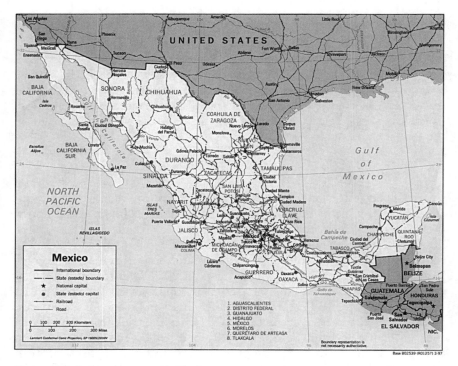

Figure 11.1 Railroad coverage in Mexico

Table 11.1 The main characteristics of each of the tourist trains operating in Mexico

	El Chepe	Tequila Express	Jose Cuervo Express
Start of operation	1961	1997	2012
Operator	Ferromex	Chamber of Commerce, Services and Tourism of Guadalajara in association with Ferromex	Private operator
Distance (km)	630	49	60
Duration of itinerary	16 hours	1 hour 45 minutes (total of 9 hours 30 minutes for all activities included in the itinerary)	9 hours for all activities included in the itinerary
Passenger capacity	64	340	395
Current approximate cost (US$)	$153 for complete itinerary	$83	$118

were suspended in 1997. In addition to the only passenger line, El Chepe, two tourist trains operate in Mexico, and they have become important tourism products in the country: the Tequila Express and the recently launched Jose Cuervo Express. Table 11.1 summarizes the main characteristics of each of the tourist trains operating in Mexico.

El Chepe

El Chepe is the only passenger train service in Mexico. This route (Figure 11.2), which started in 1961, extends along 630 km in the northwestern part of Mexico, passing over dozens of bridges and tunnels, as well as impressive natural landscapes such as the Sierra Tarahumara and Barrancas del Cobre (Copper Canyon). It is an important mode of transportation for local residents (serving 68,577 passengers in 2009) and tourists (134,000 in 2009) and is itself a tourist attraction (Grupo Mexico, 2009). With its carriages renovated in 1998, El Chepe offers first- and second-class services, as well as food and beverage options for the 16-hour ride from Chihuahua to Los Mochis. The train departs at 6.00 am, arrives at the route's last stop at 10 pm and makes 15-minute stops at points of interest where tourists can spend some time enjoying scenic views of the area (El Chepe, 2012). The

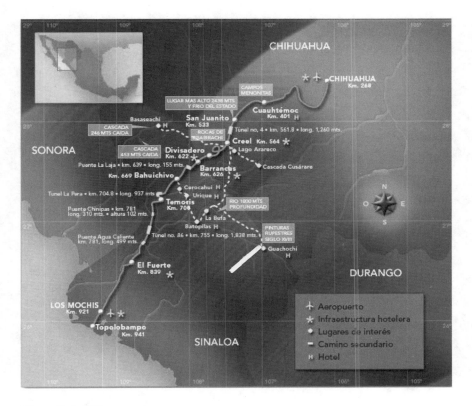

Figure 11.2 El Chepe route

cost for first-class service is US$153, with second class costing US$94 for the entire route. Passengers can, however, buy tickets for cities in between the start and end points of the itinerary. Discounts are available for children, students, teachers and senior citizens.

The Tequila Express

The Tequila Express was launched in 1997 with the goal of promoting the three pillars of Mexican identity: tequila, mariachi and *charrería* (Mexican rodeo), while also reviving interest in and nostalgia for passenger trains (Tequila Express, 2009). The train connects the cities of Guadalajara, the country's second most important city, and Amatitán in the state of

Jalisco; the 49 km journey takes 1 hour 45 minutes. This region is known for its rich culture and agave plantations, which were declared UNESCO World Heritage sites in 2000. The Tequila Express, which operates only on weekends, operates four refurbished train carriages and offers live mariachi music and tequila sampling onboard. Along the route, the train stops at haciendas where tourists can learn the process of distilling tequila and participate in music and dance performances. It is currently operated by the Chamber of Commerce, Services and Tourism of Guadalajara, and in 2009 it hosted 27,534 passengers (Velazco, 2011). The itinerary is priced at US$83, with discounts available for children and senior citizens.

Jose Cuervo Express

The Jose Cuervo Express, the newest and more upscale tourist train in Mexico, was launched in 2012 and also operates in the Tequila region. It has a capacity of 395 passengers, accommodated in seven newly renovated carriages. The train operates Fridays, Saturdays and Sundays between Guadalajara and Tequila, in the state of Jalisco, and offers a 60 km itinerary through the agave plantations, a visit to the oldest distillery in Latin America and live mariachi music. The itinerary is priced at US$118, with discounts available for children, young adults and senior citizens. During its first months of operations, it transported between 200 and 250 passenger per journey. It was estimated that the train will serve around 40,000 passengers by the end of 2012.

Prospective new tourist railways

With thousands of kilometers of railway infrastructure and its unique natural resources, landscapes and cultural heritage, Mexico should be able to expand its railway tourism offerings to diversify its tourism supply and promote economic and social development in many rural communities and destinations that are off the beaten track. With this in mind, several railway products have been proposed. Among them is the Teotihuacan Express, which would link Mexico City and the archeological site of Teotihuacan, and the Sierra Madre Express in the north-west of the country. These efforts have not materialized to date, however, due to funding, permissions and safety issues. Developing railway tourism requires physical infrastructure, large financial investments, market studies and environmental impact assessments, among other requirements. Careful consideration of these and additional factors discussed in the next section must be included in the planning and development stages. Next, we highlight some of these issues and success factors in developing railway tourist products drawn from the literature and case examples in Mexico and elsewhere.

Developing Heritage Railway Tourism: Key Issues

A review of the scarce literature on tourist routes and case examples of iconic heritage railway journeys provides insights into the factors that should be considered when developing railway tourism. The following were identified as key characteristics of successful tourist rail ventures around the world, including those that have been developed in Mexico:

Theme

Tourist train routes and products should be developed around a central heritage theme that links on- and off-board experiences, location, attractions and services (Carson & Cartan, 2011; Hardy, 2003). The heritage theme should also be extended to the design and look of the train and the appearance of train staff (IBIS Group, 2010). The Tequila Express and the Jose Cuervo Express, for example, developed their journeys around the theme of tequila; travelers are taken to the agave plantations, traditional haciendas where they can see tequila distilleries and the tequila museum and sample tequila. At one of the stops, riders take part in a cultural experience involving traditional cuisine, mariachi music, rodeo and folk dances.

Onboard experience

A positive traveler experience is important, particularly for long-distance journeys. As previous studies have found (e.g. Dallen, 2007), segments of the train traveler market see the activity as more than the need to travel between two destinations. Riders are motivated by enjoying the train ride, sightseeing and opportunities to socialize with fellow passengers. Services and amenities that provide added value to the trip are thus desirable. Some tourist trains provide onboard services ranging from basic dining facilities to sumptuous restaurants, personalized service, sleeping accommodation and even souvenir stores. Other trains, such as the Jose Cuervo Express and the Transcantabrico train in Spain, offer live entertainment. Luxury train services are not uncommon. The Orient Express offers luxury tourist train services across several countries; among the most popular are the Palace on Wheels in India, the Venice-Simplon Express in Europe, the Eastern and Oriental Express in Asia and the Rocky Mountaineer in Canada. The last train features carriages that offer 180-degree views of the Canadian landscape. As Hardy (2003) pointed out, however, care must be taken to include services and attractions that meet travelers' expectations rather than focusing exclusively on supply-driven products.

Link to heritage attractions and sites

In addition to unique scenery and landscapes and onboard experiences, tourist trains can link two or more sites that have cultural or natural significance and thus become a main draw for tourists. Popular tourist trains depart from and arrive at key tourist destinations or, as in the case of the 'trail and rail' routes, connect travelers to a region's natural and cultural heritage sites. For example, the Texas Eagle route, which connects San Antonio to Fort Worth (Texas), provides guided services to San Antonio missions. Likewise, the Lincoln Service, which connects St Louis (Missouri) with Springfield (Illinois), has links to the Jefferson National Memorial and Lincoln Home National Historical Site. In Mexico, El Chepe makes short stops at selected natural and cultural sites along the route, such as the Copper Canyon and indigenous site of the Tarahumara group. In addition to key destinations, several tourist trains offer all-inclusive excursion packages that provide access to secondary destinations and attractions within a region.

Interpretation

Because many tourist trains draw on natural and cultural resources to attract passengers, interpretation is of particular importance for travelers' enjoyment and understanding of local heritage and destinations and for promoting attitude change (Hardy, 2003). Interpretation can be provided before departure or during the journey using brochures, videos or talks by trained staff. For its 'train and rail' program, the National Park Service developed audio podcasts that provide information on the travel experience, points of interest and other information related to the sites and destinations experienced on the route.

Stakeholder support and cooperation

Another key factor in developing railway tourism is stakeholder participation and collaborative planning (Hardy, 2003). Train tourism development requires participation and coordination among multiple stakeholders on different scales including local government, private operators, tourism marketers, non-governmental organizations, trade associations and the local community. The involvement of all stakeholders should be encouraged from the inception to the management of the projects. National and local governments can play a key role in financing or subsidizing some of the initial infrastructure renovation, maintenance and operating costs, as well as costs associated with marketing and promotion. In some countries, the government runs and manages tourist trains. Private operators, such as the Orient Express, can provide the technical and management expertise to manage the day-to-day operations and to market the product to selected markets. Non-governmental organizations can assist with overseeing the environmental, social and cultural impacts of train operations and protecting heritage sites and railways. Trade associations, such as the Heritage Railway Association (HRA), which represents railway organizations in the UK, can provide members with advice and information about issues such as changing legislation, environmental regulation and safety issues, and can mediate in disputes between members, governments and the public (Morgan, 2002). Trade associations can also assist with traveler education, marketing and promotion, staff training, lobbying and fund-raising. Finally, local communities, which should benefit from the train business (e.g. through tourism income, jobs, community improvements and access to remote areas), should also be involved in developing, managing and interpreting their resources. Partnerships are important because, as Tillman (2002) pointed out, railways are joint public–private goods. An example of a public–private partnership initiative for railway tourism has been forged between the states of New Mexico and Colorado and Cumbres and Toltec Scenic Management Corp., to operate the Cumbres and Toltec Scenic Railroad in the United States.

At the same time, developing heritage railway tourism can be affected by several issues that must be considered in the early stages of planning and development. Among the most important are the initial financial investments, pricing structure, passenger safety and security, accessibility, and community support.

Financial investment

Converting old railways to functioning heritage tourism products requires significant financial investment to purchase, repair, renovate, and maintain train carriages for tourism; fix the rail beds; and build train stations and other tourism infrastructure, to name just a few. More often than not, a sole investor cannot cover these costs. Government investment and subsidies are often necessary to start the project and help sustain the business during its first years of operation. Many heritage railway projects in Mexico and around the world have not materialized or have stopped operating due to excessive costs, sometimes amounting to millions of dollars.

Pricing

The price for tourist rail journeys is normally high due to the capital and operating expenses associated with operating the train. To be economically sustainable, railway tourism must attract a market segment that can afford the price of the railway journey, which can range from a few dollars to thousands of dollars, depending on the season and the services sought. High pricing, however, discriminates against local people who cannot afford the tourist rates. Local people's access to tourism sites and resources is a matter of justice in tourism (see Camargo *et al.*, 2007) and developers must ensure that locals are not excluded, particularly via pricing, from enjoying railway or train tourism opportunities. Some companies offer different pricing schemes for local people, students, or senior citizens, although this is not the norm. Market studies are very important, because they can assess the market and revenue potential of heritage trains.

Accessibility

In addition to the price being affordable, railway companies must operate within national and international accessibility standards and there are often guidelines to provide access to people with disabilities, aging adults and families with children. Accessible railway transport fosters quality and dignified tourist and leisure experiences for everyone. It can also serve to attract the market segment of travelers with disabilities (see Buhalis *et al.*, 2012, regarding best practices in accessible tourism).

Passenger safety

Passenger safety and security are paramount to heritage railway tourism. Trains and railways, especially historic ones, must be very well maintained and monitored constantly to ensure safety. In addition, the route and destinations incorporated into railway tourism must be safe. In developing nations, particular Latin America, political instability, civil unrest and protests can jeopardize passenger safety. In Mexico, some railways are used by people seeking to migrate illegally to the United States; indeed, they use freight trains as a means of transportation to the Mexico–US border. Railway tourism developers should consider security indexes and indicators for the areas in which potential journeys are proposed.

Future developments

Despite the success of heritage railway tourism in some parts of the world, some stakeholders, particularly those from private industry, are skeptical, even pessimistic, about the real potential of this type of tourism, due to high costs and low ridership. Interviews with tour operators and cruise line officials on Vancouver Island (IBIS Group, 2010) revealed limited interest in the possibility of including train excursions in their offerings. Similarly, an interview with the director of one of the three operating tourist trains in Mexico (Morales *et al.*, 2011) revealed a pessimistic view of possibly expanding railway tourism in the country because of the costs associated with operating the train, the number of potential users and the lack of support from private train operators (which tend to focus on freight transport). Morales *et al.*'s study revealed, on the other hand, that local people and local business owners viewed railway tourism differently. In an exploratory study that sought to obtain the opinions and attitudes of community stakeholders to railway tourism in six communities identified as potential destinations for railways tourism in Mexico, Morales *et al.* found that the great majority of respondents favored tourism as an alternative economic activity in their communities. On average, more than 90% of respondents agreed with the idea of having a tourist train arrive in their community and expressed a willingness to support railway tourism.

Conclusion

In this chapter, we have argued for the development of railway tourism, in the form of rail journeys or rail itineraries, as a way to diversify tourist offerings in Mexico, a country visited primarily for its sun, sand and sea. The country has the rail infrastructure and immense cultural and natural resources to develop this type of tourism, which would attract different market segments. Although this effort may require heavy initial investments, heritage railway tourism can be economically sustainable in the medium and long term, as the Tequila Express and the Jose Cuervo Express have proven. Train journeys, however, must meet certain criteria to ensure their success. Such criteria include scenic views, links to primary and secondary tourist destinations and attractions, a heritage theme and interpretation, quality services and amenities onboard, and support from different stakeholders. We hope this chapter launches a research agenda that investigates key factors and issues in developing railway tourism, in particular for Latin American countries. Theoretical and methodological approaches to developing railway tourism and impact assessments are scarce.

As such, there is a pressing need to empirically investigate the factors that contribute to the success or failure of railway routes so that the potential of this type of tourism can be positioned and sold for success.

References

Bichis-Lupas, M. and Moisey, R.N. (2001) A benefit segmentation of rail-trail users: Implications for marketing by local communities. *Journal of Park and Recreation Administration* 19 (3), 78–92.

Buhalis, D., Darcy, S. and Ambrose, I. (eds) (2012) *Best Practice in Accessible Tourism: Inclusion, Disability, Aging Population and Tourism*. Bristol: Channel View Publications.

Camargo, B., Lane, K. and Jamal, T. (2007) Environmental justice and sustainable tourism: The missing cultural link. *George Wright Society Forum* 24 (3), 70–80.

Carson, D. and Cartan, G. (2011) Touring routes: Types, successes and failures. In B. Prideau and D. Carson (eds) *Drive Tourism: Trends and Emerging Markets* (pp. 296–307). New York: Routledge.

Charlton, C.A. (1998) Public transport and sustainable tourism: The case of the Devon and Cornwall Rail Partnership. In C.M. Hall and A. Lew (eds) *Sustainable Tourism: A Geographical Perspective* (pp. 132–145). Harlow: Addison Wesley Longman.

Dallen, J. (2007) Sustainable transport, market segmentation and tourism: The Looe Valley Branch Line Railway, Cornwall, UK. *Journal of Sustainable Tourism* 15 (2), 180–199.

Dickinson, J.E. and Lumsdon, L.M. (2010) *Slow Travel and Tourism*. London: Earthscan.

Dickinson, J.E., Lumsdon, L.M. and Robbins, D. (2011) Slow travel: Issues for tourism and climate change. *Journal of Sustainable Tourism* 19 (3), 281–300.

El Chepe (2012) Presentación. At http://www.chepe.com.mx/grales/prese.html (accessed 22 June 2012).

European Commission (2011) Passenger transport statistics. At http://epp.eurostat. ec.europa.eu/statistics_explained/index.php/Passenger_transport_statistics#Rail_passengers (accessed 13 June 2012).

Fu, S.T. (2009) A destination in transition: Lhasa after the Qinghai-Tibet railway. Unpublished masters thesis, Hong Kong Polytechnic University, School of Hotel and Tourism Management.

Grupo México (2009) *Desarrollo sustentable '09: Un reto continuo*. Mexico City: Grupo México. At http://www.gmexico.com.mx/pdf/InformeDS2009.pdf (accessed 13 June 2010).

Hardy, A. (2003) An investigation into the key factors necessary for the development of iconic touring routes. *Journal of Vacation Marketing* 9 (4), 314–330.

IBIS Group (2010) *E&N Railway Corridor Study: Analysis of Tourist Train Potential*. Victoria, BC: British Columbia Ministry of Transportation and Infrastructure.

Kosters, M. (1992) Tourism by train: Its role in alternative tourism. In V.L. Smith and W.R. Eadington (eds) *Tourism Alternatives: Potentials and Problems in the Development of Tourism* (pp. 180–193). Philadelphia, PA: University of Pennsylvania Press.

Lyons, G., Jain, J. and Holley, D. (2007) The use of travel time by rail passengers in Great Britain. *Transportation Research Part A Policy and Practice* 41 (1), 107–120.

Morales, M., Sens, G.M., Garza, C.G. and Gómez, K.G. (2011) Formulación de una propuestas de tren, como producto turístico, en territorio mexicano. Unpublished thesis, Universidad de Monterrey, San Pedro Garza Garcia, NL, Mexico.

Morgan, D. (2002) The role of umbrella organizations in the development of heritage railways. *Japan Railway and Transport Review* 32, 35–37.

National Park Service (NPS) (2012) Trails and rails. At http://www.nps.gov/findapark/trailsandrails/index.htm (accessed 10 June 2012).

Nichol, M. and Moore. T. (2010) *The Bellarine Railway: Economic Impact Analysis Report.* Report for the Bellarine Railway. Bendigo, Victoria: Compelling Economics Pty Ltd.

Page, S. and Ge, Y. (2010) Transportation and tourism: A symbiotic relationship? In T. Jamal and M. Robinson (eds) *The Sage Handbook of Tourism Studies* (pp. 371–395). London: Sage.

Pas, E.I. and Huber, J.C. (1992) Market segmentation analysis of potential inter-city rail travelers. *Transportation* 19, 177–196.

Pi-Sunyer, O., Thomas, R.B. and Databuit, M. (2001) Tourism on the Maya periphery. In V.L. Smith and M. Brent (eds) *Host and Guests Revisited: Tourism Issues of the 21st Century* (pp. 122–140). New York: Cognizant Communication Corporation.

Secretaria de Comunicaciones y Transporte (CST) (2010) *Anuario Estadistico 2009.* . At http://www.sct.gob.mx/informacion-general/planeacion/estadistica-del-sector/anuario-estadistico-sct (accessed 17 June 2012).

Secretariat of Tourism of Mexico (SECTUR) (2010) *Guias para el desarrollo de productos turisticos en las rutas conmemorativas.* At http://www.sectur.gob.mx/work/models/sectur/Resource/15601/IntroGuiaRutasTuristicas.pdf (accessed 10 June 2012).

Secretariat of Tourism of Mexico (SECTUR) (2011) *Bulletin 11: President Felipe Calderón Decrees 2011 as the Year of Tourism in Mexico.* At http://www.sectur.gob.mx/es/securing/Bulletin_11_President_Felipe_Calderon_decrees_2011_as_the_Year_of_Tourism_in_Mexico (accessed 10 June 2012).

Su, M.M. and Wall, G. (2009) Destination and en-route experiences among train travellers to Tibet. *Tourism Recreation Research* 34 (2), 181–190.

Tequila Express (2009) ¿Qué es 'Tequila Express'? At http://www.tequilaexpress.com.mx/que-es-tequila-express (accessed 22 June 2012).

Tillman, J.A. (2002) Sustainability of heritage railways: An economic approach. *Japan Railway and Transport Review* 32, 38–45.

Torres, R.M. (2002) Cancun's tourism development from a Fordist spectrum of analysis. *Tourist Studies* 1, 87–116.

Torres, R.M. and Momsen, J.D. (2005a) Gringolandia: The construction of a new tourist space in Mexico. *Annals of the Association of American geographers* 95, 314–335.

Torres, R.M. and Momsen, J.D. (2005b) Planned tourism development in Quintana Roo, Mexico: Engine for regional development or prescription for inequitable growth? *Current Issues in Tourism* 8, 259–285.

United Nations World Tourism Organization (UNWTO) (2011) UNWTO tourism highlights 2011. At http://mkt.unwto.org/en/content/tourism-highlights (accessed June 2012).

Velazco, J. (2011) Relanzan al Tequila Express. *El Informador*, 2 January 2011.

12 The Grand Canyon Railway

Fredrick Collison

Introduction

In the United States, where rail transportation was once predominant for the carriage of both freight (cargo) and passengers, market shares have declined for both sectors, especially the latter. Today, rail transportation of passengers is primarily found in urbanized areas, with a small amount in intercity (long-distance) service offered by the National Passenger Rail Corporation (Amtrak). About 280 tourist railroads exist in the US over short distances, devoted to carrying passengers primarily for sightseeing (Anonymous, 2011; Tourist Railroad Information Center, 2011); one such railroad is the Grand Canyon Railway (GCRy). Originally operated by the Atchison, Topeka and Santa Fe Railway (ATSF) as a spur line from Williams, Arizona, it was abandoned in 1968. Passenger service was revived in 1989 by Max and Thelma Biegert, private owners of the 'new' GCRy. The GCRy was subsequently purchased by Xanterra Parks and Resorts (Xanterra) in 2006, and Xanterra was then purchased by Philip Anschutz in 2008 (Grand Canyon Railway, 2012a, n.d.:a; Hotel Online, 2008)

History of US Transportation Systems

Although rail transportation was once dominant for the long-distance carriage of passengers in the US, this is no longer the case. Rail reached its peak in the mid-1890s, with about 95% of the intercity passenger transportation market in terms of passenger kilometers (km) or miles (mi) (National Association of Railroad Passengers, 2006). In the early 1900s the highway mode of transportation began to make inroads into the dominant market share of the railroads, with the introduction of the motor bus and the private automobile (including rental cars). Although the highway mode was complementary to the rail mode for passenger transportation initially, it quickly became a competitor. Air transportation began to provide competition after 1925, especially for long-distance travel (Bureau of the Census, 1975).

By the 1920s, the automobile form of travel overtook the rail mode of passenger transportation in passenger km/mi provided. By the 1950s, the private automobile became the dominant form of intercity passenger transportation, with market shares of over 90% of intercity passenger km/mi. The motor bus industry accounted for a very small portion of the highway mode of transportation's service and market share. Rail transportation of passengers is today a very small segment of the overall passenger transportation system in the US (Bureau of the Census, 1975; Youngs *et al.*, 2008).

Many reasons can be cited for these modal shifts. Perhaps foremost are the inherent advantages of the automobile (e.g. flexibility, privacy, availability). Road systems became much more widely developed by the 1950s, allowing automobiles to reach many more destinations than at the beginning of the 20th century. The disadvantages of intercity rail, such as lack of frequent service and limited points served, also led to the rapid modal shift from rail to highway for passenger transportation. In more recent years air transportation market shares grew, as this mode can provide rapid transportation speed over longer distances.

As a result of these modal shifts in passenger demand, many railroads saw once profitable passenger transportation become money-losing segments that they no longer wished to serve. In most cases, railroads provided poor passenger service, which decreased demand even further. The reason for this management behavior was the hope that a railroad could petition the Interstate Commerce Commission (ICC), which economically regulated railroads, to be allowed to cease a particular passenger service due to inadequate level of demand, which was regularly granted (Full Wiki, 2010; PBS, 2010; Slack, 2012).

The unprofitable operations of most scheduled passenger rail operations in the US led to the establishment in 1971 of the National Rail Passenger Corporation (Amtrak), via the Federal Rail Passenger Services Act of 1970 (National Association of Railroad Passengers, 2006; US Department of Transportation, 1978). Nearly all railroads with passenger operations opted to turn them over to the federal government, to be operated by Amtrak. Although Amtrak operates as a private sector corporation, it receives and has received significant subsidies from the federal government, especially for capital expenditures (US Department of Transportation, 1978).

One railroad that did not lower the level of service on its passenger segment, despite the profitability problems, was the ATSF. Level of service was maintained on a number of long-distance passenger trains that served the south-western US from the Midwest and southern California. The ATSF passenger trains continued to provide passenger transportation near a number of National Park Service (NPS) units in the area of the Colorado Plateau. The Super Chief service of the ATSF between Chicago and Los Angeles (with Williams, AZ, as an intermediate stop) was arguably one of the most famous and well regarded of all US passenger trains. This service had one train operating in each direction on a daily basis (American-Rails, n.d.; Pullano, n.d.). The ATSF did turn over its rail passenger services in 1971 to Amtrak (BNSF, n.d.; National Railroad Passenger Corporation, 2012), and although the Super Chief service did not survive, a somewhat equivalent service exists today in Amtrak's Southwest Chief service, following the same basic route as its predecessor (Amtrak, 2012).

The Grand Canyon Region

An interesting feature of the south-western US is the Colorado Plateau; within the 130,000 square miles of this region lie many wonders of nature. The plateau contains eight national parks (NPs), 20 national monuments (NMs) and numerous other nationally designated areas and huge tracts of national forests. Within the immediate vicinity of the Grand Canyon National Park (GCNP) (see Figure 12.1) are Zion and Bryce Canyon NPs to the north-west, Glen Canyon National Recreation Area (NRA) to the north-east and a number of NMs to the south (e.g. Wupatki NM, Sunset Crater NM, Walnut Canyon NM, as well as Lake Mead NRA). This wealth of natural features and the cultures of the various Native American tribes in the region have made the area an important destination for visitors, especially those interested in natural history and culture.

The 'crown jewel' for this region is generally considered to be the Grand Canyon, one of the seven natural wonders of the world. The Grand Canyon is 306 km/190 mi long, 1.6 km/1 mi deep, and between 6.5 km/4 mi and 29 km/18 mi wide. The Grand Canyon covers 4942 km²/1900 mi² of the Colorado Plateau and is home to over 1700 species of plants, 373 species of birds, 34 species of mammals and 17 species of fish (NPS, 2012a). A number of ancestral homelands of Native American tribes are found in the region of the Grand Canyon, including the Hopi, Navajo, Hualapai and Havasupai (NPS, 2012b). The latter two tribes live in parts of the canyon and its vicinity today and have done so for many years.

The principal attraction to visitors is the sheer size and beauty of the canyon itself. The walls of the Grand Canyon are made up of many layers of rock of varying ages, with widely varying textures and hues. This panorama

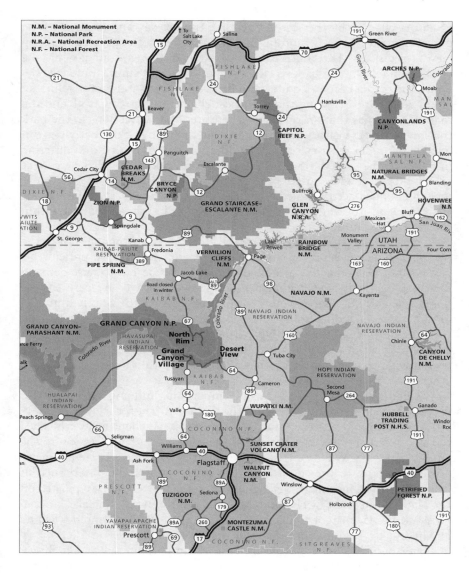

Figure 12.1 National Parks and Monuments in the Vicinity of Williams, Arizona
Source: Courtesy of the Williams (Arizona) Chamber of Commerce, at http://www.nps.gov/grca/planyourvisit/upload/GRCAmap2.pdf

of nature changes by the season, weather, time of day and location in the park. Generally, the early morning and late afternoon offer the most striking views for visitors. The South Rim in GCNP is open year-round, while the North Rim (also in the park) is closed in winter. In the summer months the South Rim often becomes quite crowded with visitors and motor vehicles.

In addition to viewing the geological characteristics of GCNP and the many panoramas that are available, there are other attractions in the park that may interest visitors, regardless of how they arrive. Such activities can include hiking excursions of varying duration and difficulty, and differing in what can be seen during the walk, and trail rides. The NPS rangers at GCNP present a wide variety of programs highlighting aspects of the park, including ranger-accompanied hikes. Many exhibits are located throughout the various visitor centers at the park as well as in other buildings within the park (NPS, 2012c).

Consideration has been given by the NPS to ban automobiles from the park and to move visitors around the park by shuttle buses. At present this ban has not been enacted, although it might be expected to raise demand for the GCRy if it is ever implemented. However, there are park shuttle buses available that serve a number of areas within the South Rim area of the park, including some areas where personal vehicles are banned throughout much of the year (NPS, 2012d, 2012e). Motor coach tours from a large number of locations throughout the US Southwest and elsewhere also provide transportation for their passengers within the areas of GCNP where they are permitted to operate.

Williams, Arizona, serves as one important 'jumping off' point for visitors traveling to GCNP, with the South Rim of the canyon only 101 km/63 mi north of the town. Williams is closely identified with travel to the canyon and has even registered the trademark 'The Gateway to the Grand Canyon'®. Williams is at an elevation of 6800 feet. There are many attractions both in the town itself and in the surrounding area, such as lakes for swimming and fishing, horseback riding and a downtown listed on the National Register of Historic Places. The surrounding Kaibab National Forest in the vicinity of Williams offers opportunities for camping, fishing and hiking, for both visitors and residents alike.

The town has for many years been an important rail and highway transportation hub. Williams is closely identified with Route 66, which connected Chicago, Illinois and Santa Monica, California, long before the interstate highway system was developed. Williams has the last stretch of the original Route 66 bypassed by the interstate system (in this case I-40). Even before highways became highly developed, Williams served as a railroad terminal (since 1882) for the forerunners of the ATSF; the railroad, now part of the Burlington Northern Santa Fe Railroad (BNSF), continues to serve the town today, though with a freight-only service (Richmond, 2005; Rothman, 1996; Runte, 1998).

National Park Development in the US West

The development of national park tourism to any significant degree in the western US was begun in the late 1800s, led by railroads: the Northern Pacific Railroad (Yellowstone NP and Glacier NP) being the first and the ATSF to the South Rim of Grand Canyon National Park (GCNP) in 1901 (Grand Canyon, AZ, n.d.; Kelly, 2001; Richmond, 2005; Rothman, 1996; Runte, 1998) This latter service by the ATSF was via a branch line of 110 km/63 mi that connected at Williams Junction via motorcoach service to the GCRy. The ATSF was not only involved in rail passenger and freight transportation between Williams and GCNP but also in the provision of lodging and dining services at the Grand Canyon and elsewhere along its tracks. These services for the ATSF were provided for many years by the Fred Harvey Company of Kansas City, in partnership with the railway company, replacing what was regarded as poor dining service by the ATSF itself. The original agreement began with the establishment of a Harvey House dining operation located in Topeka, Kansas, along the main line tracks of the ATSF. Fred Harvey dining and lodging operations were eventually established along the entire main line of the ATSF, from Kansas City to the US west coast (Weigle, 1989). These developments included the Fray Marcos Hotel in Williams, which was replaced by the Grand Canyon Railway Hotel in present times (Wheels Museum, Inc., 2007).

The Fred Harvey Company had a significant influence at GCNP and not just in the provision of dining services within the park and on the long-distance trains that brought visitors to the vicinity of the park where they connected to the GCRy for final travel to the park. Many of the lodgings and other buildings at the park were designed by an architect in the employ of Fred Harvey. Mary Jane Colter was well known for her distinctive 'pueblo' style of architecture, which incorporated her interests in 'Native American history, architecture, and landscape of the American Southwest' (Perry, 2012; see also Shaffer, 2004; Weigle, 1989).

Following later was the Union Pacific Railroad (UPRR), in the early 1920s, with what it called the 'Grand Tour', which included Bryce Canyon NP, Zion NP, the North Rim of GCNP, Cedar Breaks NM and Kaibab National Forest, with connecting highway travel based out of the railroad's newly developed rail depot in Cedar City, Utah. Unlike the ATSF, the UPRR did not provide rail transportation directly to the rim, as did the former railroad

(Kelly, 2001; Scrattish, 1985; Strong, n.d.). The Utah Parks Company, a subsidiary of the UPRR, handled not only the connecting highway travel, but also the lodging and dining segments of the 'Grand Tour' (Runte, 1998; Scrattish, 1985; Strong, n.d.). In a sense, the Utah Parks Company played a role equivalent to what the Fred Harvey Company did for the ATSF and the GCRy. The UPRR's 'Grand Tour' lasted only until 1958, after which it was abandoned due to increasing use of the automobile for national park visitations (Kelly, 2001).

The Grand Canyon Railway

Railroad history

Historically, rail freight service on the GCRy line began in the late 1800s, transporting ore from the Anita mines 72 km/45 mi north of Williams, south to the ATSF main line. Passenger service was initiated in 1897, with the ATSF taking over this service and completing the track in 1901 to GCNP. The ATSF built a number of the now historic structures on the Grand Canyon's South Rim, including the passenger terminal and the iconic El Tovar Hotel, which were managed via contract with the Fred Harvey Company, which provided a similar service among railroads throughout the south-western United States (Xanterra Parks and Resorts, n.d.-a; Weigle, 1989).

Passenger service on the GCRy was abandoned in the 1960s due to economic pressures from the automobile form of travel. Freight service by the ATSF on the Grand Canyon branch was abandoned in 1974, with no maintenance work performed on the track between Williams and the Grand Canyon from then until 1989, when the GCRy was re-established. Rail service between Williams and GCNP was not only abandoned by the ATSF but the track was very nearly torn up in 1983 (Runte, 1998), which would have undoubtedly prevented the restart of rail passenger service to the national park.

After several proposals to restart this passenger service were un-successful, one was accepted by the ATSF (which owned the rail track and infrastructure) that resulted in approximately $20 million being invested to re-initiate service. The new owners were Max and Thelma Biegert, retired entrepreneurs who came out of retirement and invested their own financial resources to restart GCRy (Arizona State University, W.P. Casey School of Business, 2012; Grand Canyon Railway, 2012a).

This project included rehabilitating the railroad tracks, refurbishment of the Williams terminal, construction/refurbishment of a hotel complex in Williams adjacent to the Williams terminal and old Fray Marcos hotel, and the purchase and reconstruction of railway equipment (locomotives and passenger cars) (Grand Canyon Railway, n.d.-a). The NPS restored the Grand Canyon terminal in Grand Canyon Village near the South Rim in 1987. This terminal is one of only three remaining wooden log terminal buildings in the national parks and the only one currently in operation (Grand Canyon Railway – historic depots, n.d.-b; Harrison, 2001; Youngs, n.d.). The work to get the GCRy running was monumental, since all engines and passenger cars had to be acquired and completely rebuilt. All of this equipment was obtained from various sources and were in varying conditions of repair. In addition, the depot at Williams and the adjoining hotel (now known as the Grand Canyon Railway Hotel) were in need of substantial refurbishing. In the depot, operating offices, ticket offices, a waiting room and souvenir shop had to be built and furnished. All of this work was accomplished in a span of seven months, to be ready for the September 1989 opening.

There have been a number of ownership changes for both the GCRy and the concession operations at GCNP since re-establishment of the rail service in 1989 (and before this date). Amfac Corporation, then based in Hawai'i, bought the Fred Harvey Company in 1968, with the organization subsequently being purchased in 1988 by JMB Realty of Denver. The organization was renamed Xanterra Parks and Resorts in 2002, which continues to the current day (Fred Harvey Company, n.d.). The subsequent takeover of the railroad by Xanterra occurred in 2007 (Grand Canyon Railway, n.d.-a, 2012)

The most popular way for visitors to get from either Williams or Flagstaff (51 km/32 mi to the east of Williams) to GCNP is by motor vehicle, although contemplated restrictions by the NPS on vehicles within the park might be expected to change this somewhat. The distances by road to GCNP are 130 km/80 mi from Flagstaff and 101 km/63 mi from Williams. The highway and rail lines within the vicinity of Williams and between Williams and GCNP are shown in Figure 12.2. An attractive alternative for some visitors is to travel between Williams and the Grand Canyon by rail. The GCRy offers this option with one round trip per day. This rail service, which operates purely as a tourist railroad, began operations in September 1989 and has provided a daily service since that day (except for Thanksgiving and 24 and 25 December).

Railroad operations

Today, the GCRy provides an interesting and nostalgic way for visitors to travel to the canyon. In the earliest years of operation, a daily round-trip rail service was provided by steam locomotive during the summer season, while in the winter diesel locomotives were used due to the severity of weather

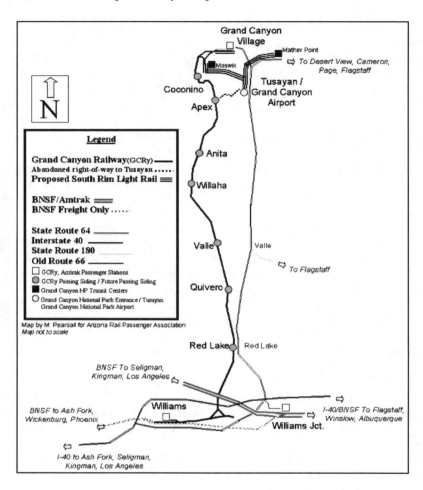

Figure 12.2 Transportation corridor: Williams, Arizona, to the Grand Canyon National Park (as of 2002)
Source: Pearsall, M. (2002) Arizona Passenger Rail Association; and Pearsall, M. (2002) Transportation corridor: Williams, Arizona, to the Grand Canyon National Park (as of 2002). Arizona Passenger Rail Association

conditions on the plateau. More recently the operation has been converted to an all-diesel service due to its lesser environmental impact. Additionally, the cost of operation of diesel engines is lower, due to the improved efficiency of diesel engines and cheaper maintenance and repairs (Krug, 2012; Locomotives-and-Trains.com, 2011). The roster of GCRy's diesel and steam locomotives is presented in Tables 12.1 and 12.2 (Grand Canyon Railway, 2007, 2009, n.d.-c).

Occasionally, due to continuing requests for the former type of service, a steam engine is used in regular service to GCNP. For 2012, these dates were 22 April (Earth Day), 2 June (Kick-Off to Summer), 4 July (Independence Day) and 15 September (GCRy Anniversary Day; actually 17 September for both the initial service and the renewed service) (Arizona Rail Passenger Association, 2009; Naylor, 2012; Your West Valley, 2012). At the time of writing these were the only full services to GCNP on the railroad operated by steam. In order to further accommodate the demand for steam service, however, on 12 and 13 May and 9 June, shorter (8-mile) runs on the hour between 10 am and 4 pm were operated on what is known as the 'Cataract Creek Rambler'. The price for the latter service was $15 for adults and $10 for children, while for the former there was no additional charge beyond the price charged for the normal diesel service (Grand Canyon Railway, 2012b).

For all service, passengers travel in railcars that date from 1923 onwards and which are reconditioned to approximate the time period of initial service. A list of the passenger cars owned by the GCRy is given in Table 12.2, including their dates of initial construction and their entry into service on the GCRy (Grand Canyon Railway, 2009). The types of passenger equipment vary from standard rail coaches of the first half of the 20th century to a luxury parlor car with an open observation platform. Some of the passenger cars are dedicated to a particular class of service (a dome car, for example) on the normal run to/from GCNP, while others may be used for services such as the Polar Express or the Cataract Creek Rambler, which are shorter runs that do not access the park.

Departure from Williams is currently at 9.30 am and arrival at Grand Canyon NP is at 11.45 am, in the center of the park's historic district at the 1910 Grand Canyon Depot. There have been periods in the past when two trains per day were operated, due to high levels of demand. The train currently departs from the Grand Canyon at 3.30 pm and arrives back in Williams at 5.45 pm. No smoking is allowed on the train in any of the passenger railcars. One of the difficulties faced by the passengers on the GCRy is that their time to explore the Grand Canyon and its environs is extremely limited. Motor coach service in the park provided by Xanterra and GCRy do provide a limited, narrated tour of portions of the South Rim,

Table 12.1 Grand Canyon Railway locomotive equipment

Equipment designation	Equipment type	Date built	Date entered service
Diesel Engine No. 2134	GP-7[a]	1953	
Diesel Engine No. 6773	FPA4-A unit[b]	1959	1991
Diesel Engine No. 6793	FPA4-A unit[b]	1959	1996
Diesel Engine No. 6776	FPA4-A unit[b]	1959	1998
Diesel Engine No. 6871	FPA4-B unit[b]	1959	1998
Diesel Engine No. 6860	FPA4-B unit[b]	1959	2001
Diesel Engine No. 237	F-40PH[a]	1979	
Diesel Engine No. 239	F-40PH[a]	1979	2004
Diesel Engine No. 295	F-40PH[a]	1979	2009
Steam Engine No. 29	Consolidation 2-8-0		1996
Steam Engine No. 539	Mikado 2-8-2	1917	
Steam Engine No. 4960	Mikado 2-8-2	1923	1989

[a]Built by Electro-Motive Division of General Motors Corporation.
[b]Built by American Locomotive Company (ALCO).

Sources: Grand Canyon Railway (2009, n.d.-c).

Table 12.2 Grand Canyon Railway passenger equipment

Equipment type	Date originally built	Date entered service
Budd Coach cars		2006
Pullman Harriman-style Coach cars[a]	1923	2006
Bright Angel Class cars		2004
Buckley O'Neil Class cars[b]		
The Colorado River car	1948	2000
The Yavapai car	1950	1998
The Coconino car[c]	1954	1997
The Grand View coach[d]		2004
Kokopelli coach[c]		2000
The Santa Fe car	1948	2004
The Chief car		2002
The Max Biegert car[e]	1954	2006

[a]Used exclusively for Polar Express service.
[b]Cars named for original owner of Grand Canyon Railway.
[c]Dome coach.
[d]Vista Dome coach.
[e]Luxury parlor car; named after individual responsible for restoration of rail service to GCNP.

Sources: Grand Canyon Railway (2009, n.d.-c).

covering a much bigger area than would be possible for the passengers by other means. Visitors can purchase packages that include an overnight stay in GCNP, thus allowing considerably more time to enjoy the park than if they take the train back to Williams on the same day. At the present time, overnight lodging at GCNP is provided for GCRy passengers at Maswik Lodge, which is close to the center of Grand Canyon Village and the South Rim of the park.

Railway product and pricing

Reservations can be made by calling a toll-free number, 1–800-THE TRAIN. Information about the train ride, as well as reservations, are also available on the railroad's website, www.thetrain.com. Different classes of service are offered to travelers, depending upon the fare paid and the car in which a passenger rides, with the following prices in effect as of 1 June 2012 (children's fares for ages 2–15). Coach-class service is priced at $75.00 per adult and $45.00 per child. Snacks and beverages are available for purchase in the 1950s era railcar café car. First class provides recliner chairs, a full continental breakfast (including fresh fruit, pastries, coffee and juice) with snacks and soft drinks in the afternoon, and the availability of alcoholic beverages for purchase. In 2012 fares for first class were $140 per adult and $110 per child (Grand Canyon Railway, 2012c).

'Observation dome' class represents a further upgrade. The service level is nearly the same as first class, but with a champagne toast on the return trip to Williams. Passengers ride in an upper-level enclosed dome, which provides excellent views of the surrounding landscape. The price for this service was $170 for adults (with children under 16 not permitted). The highest class of service, luxury parlor class, is provided in a railcar with an open-air rear platform; complimentary continental breakfast, coffee, tea and juice are provided in the morning and champagne and snacks in the afternoon. This class of service was priced at $190 per person (again, children under 16 not permitted). For both observation dome class and luxury parlor class, alcoholic beverages are available for purchase (Grand Canyon Railway, 2012c).

For all classes, the individual entrance fee to GCNP ($12 for 2012) is an additional charge, along with taxes. For those passengers with a National Park Pass, there is no additional entrance fee for the park. Other services are also available from the GCRy for additional charges. Continental breakfast is served in the terminal's Grand Depot Café until the train departs (Grand Canyon Railway, n.d.-d). A narrated motor coach tour of the South Rim of the Grand Canyon is available from Xanterra Resorts (the concessionaire for

GCNP as well as owner of the railroad) for $33.50 per adult and $23.50 per child, which can include lunch at the Maswik Cafeteria for $12 extra (Grand Canyon Railway – Grand Canyon tours, n.d.-e). Packages are available which may include one or two nights at the Grand Canyon Railway Hotel in Williams and one night at the Maswik Lodge in GCNP (Grand Canyon Railway, n.d.-f)

For example, travel packages (including prices) available for summer 2012 included the following, all of which were for coach-class service:

- the 'Railway Express Plus' – round-trip train travel to GCNP, and two nights at the GCRy Hotel (in Williams), for $225 per adult and an extra $32 per child;
- the 'Railway Getaway Plus' – same as the previous but two breakfasts and two dinners per person, for $283 per adult and $66 per child;
- the 'Canyon Limited' – one night at the GCRy Hotel, one night at the Maswik Lodge in GCNP, motor coach rim tour, and one breakfast and one dinner per person, for $308 per couple and $69 per child;
- the 'Canyon Limited Plus' – same as the 'Canyon Limited' but with an extra night at the GCRy Hotel and two breakfasts and two dinners per person, for $421.50 per adult and $86 per child.

All of the meals included in any of the above packages are for buffet dining at the GCRy's Grand Depot Café at the Williams terminal (Grand Canyon Railway, n.d.-f).

During the ride between Williams and GCNP many natural venues can be seen, including ponderosa forests, high desert plains and small arroyos, along with wildlife such as pronghorn, mule deer, prairie dogs and elk (Naylor, 2012; Newberg, 2004). There is formal narration for some of these venues that provides background information to the passengers; a printed guide is available for purchase, which describes these sights and provides a history of the GCRy. Interestingly, only a very limited and brief view of the Grand Canyon is available from the train, just as it arrives at and departs from the park.

Each railcar has an attendant who serves beverages, goes around with snacks for sale and engages in conversations with the passengers, including about the railroad and scenery. During the summer, many of these attendants are college students on break from their studies. The Grand Canyon Railway uses costumed performers in a number of different ways to simulate an earlier time period, and thus includes cultural aspects as well as physical aspects of the rail service (Youngs et al., 2008). Before the train departs from Williams, performers stage an 'old West' gunfight, just as might have been seen some 100 years ago in this area. Performers also move among the railcars, often singing songs of the 'old West', during the trip to the Grand Canyon. Passengers are encouraged to sing along with the performers. All of the performers are costumed in the type of dress found at the turn of the century.

On the return trip, the activities are slightly different. A group of performers stage a train robbery, as was sometimes found during earlier times in the south-western US. Passengers are included in portions of the action, but none are actually robbed. Eventually, the sheriff captures the train robbers and takes them away to be put in jail. Passengers, especially younger children, enjoy this, which makes the trip back to Williams seem much shorter than it actually is. The other activity that some engage in is to take a nap, since many are tired due to their activities at the high altitude and low humidity of the Colorado Plateau.

A number of seasonal products have been introduced by the GCRy over the last few years. Beginning in 2001 the GCRy began operating a Polar Express in the Christmas season, based on the book and more recently the movie of the same name. GCRy is not alone in doing this, as a number of other heritage railroads are also offering a similar type of seasonal service. This service was offered on select days in the latter half of November, nearly all days in December (not on Christmas Eve or Christmas Day, however) for 2012, and a couple of days in January 2013 that follow. The departures for this service were at both 5.30 pm and 7.30 pm on most days and 3.30 pm on occasional weekend days. Current prices for the Polar Express were typically $32 for adults and $ 20 for children in 2012 and a package could be purchased that also included an overnight stay at the Grand Canyon Railway Hotel in Williams, along with breakfast and dinner buffet meals at the railroad's Grand Depot Café (Grand Canyon Railway, 2012d).

On 24 December a special 'Christmas Eve Limited' is offered, also based on the *Polar Express* story. In this case, however, this product is offered on only one night, Christmas Eve, and has enhanced elements not found in the Polar Express product, such as special gifts from Santa. Both the Christmas Eve Limited and the Polar Express products include a visit to the 'North Pole', a brief visit to Santa and his reindeer, and hot chocolate and cookies. For the Christmas Eve Limited the 2012/13 prices were $62 for adults and $40 for children, with all prices exclusive of taxes (Grand Canyon Railway, 2012d).

A 'Pumpkin Patch Train' service to celebrate Halloween was inaugurated in 2011 with three trains daily for selected weekends in October. In addition to a round-trip ride on a train, every child in a family gets to pick a pumpkin to take home and gets to participate in activities at the depot in Williams, including a free hay maze, decorating their pumpkin, and face painting. Refreshments such as apple cider can be purchased as well. Tickets for this service were $20 for adults and $15 for children in both 2011 and 2012, with refreshments costing extra (Arizona Republic, 2011; Grand Canyon Railway, 2012e).

Demand for GCRy

The actual demand in terms of annual passenger numbers that visit GNCP on the GCRy is shown in Figure 12.3 for the years 1991 through 2011. It should be noted that these passenger numbers do not include passengers on the Cataract Creek Rambler, Christmas Eve Limited, Polar Express and Pumpkin Patch Train. In terms of annual passengers (which are shown by a solid line), relatively consistent growth was experienced, particularly after 1997, until 2006, when demand peaked at just over 238,000 passengers. This was followed by two consecutive years of passenger declines, with only 200,000 passengers in 2008, although annual demand increased to nearly 218,000 passengers in 2009. The last two years for which data were available saw precipitous declines to just over 132,000 passengers in 2011, while the number of visitors to the South Rim declined only 160,000 from a peak of about 4,150,000 in 2010 (NPS, 2012f).

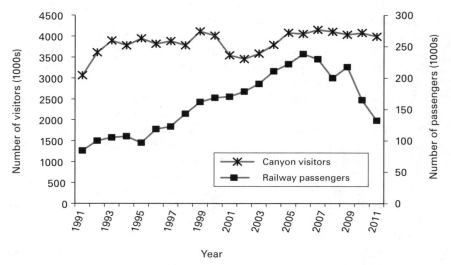

Figure 12.3 Grand Canyon National Park: Annual numbers of recreational visitors to the South Rim and by Grand Canyon Railway, 1991–2011

Figure 12.3 also includes the annual number of recreational visitors to GCNP's South Rim (dashed line) (NPS, 2012f). Generally, the plot for the South Rim's annual visitors is similar to that found for GCRy's passengers (solid line). The period 1991 through 2006 comparatively saw train visitors growing faster than South Rim park visitors as the two scales in Figure 12.4 are similar in lowest and highest values. The actual average annual increases were 6.9% for GCRy and 1.5% for GCNP. After 2006 these two demand measures (GCRy passengers, South Rim park visitors) diverged dramatically, with the train passengers declining much more rapidly than GCNP South Rim visitors. The demand for GCRy declined 11.1% (compounded) from the 2006 peak, while the demand for GCNP declined only 2.2% from its 2010 peak.

The number of passengers by month on GCRy's service to the park is shown in Figure 12.4 for 2005 through 2011. The months generally with the smallest number of passengers are November through February for essentially all years shown. These periods correspond for the most part to the winter season, with lower temperatures and potentially periods with snow. The peak months for rail service demand to GCNP tends to be somewhat more variable, with June and/or July typically having the largest number of passengers. A secondary peak is also found during the months of March and/or April (NPS, 2012f). In the first case, the peak months correspond to

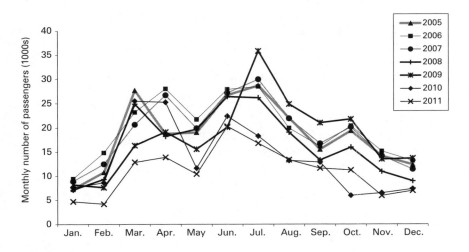

Figure 12.4 Grand Canyon Railway passenger numbers, by month, 2005–11

the summer tourist season, while the latter correspond to the time period when spring break occurs for schools at all levels of education in the US.

Another measure of how the GCRy's service rates can be found at the website 'America's Best and Top 10', which contains ratings of train trips that are arguably considered the best in the US. The top four in 2012 relied heavily on the scenery encountered en route:

(1) White Pass and Yukon Route, Alaska;
(2) Alaska Railroad;
(3) Durango and Silverton Narrow Gauge Railroad in Colorado;
(4) Great Smoky Mountain Railroad.

GCRy (ranked number 7) relies less on the en-route scenery than it does on what lies at the outbound destination, GCNP. The trains ranked 5 and 6 were both dinner trains and thus represented a very different experience from the trains listed above, although scenery is part of the experience for these two trains as well (America's Best and Top 10, 2012). GCRy's service was also rated in the top 10 of the best North American train trips, where the top 10 also included Amtrak services, unlike other ratings shown above and below (Duckett, 2010).

At the website Tourist Trains Worldwide (n.d.), the quick-search function can be used to produce a list of trains of different kinds by geographic location, and the listing includes brief details of each train service. The US is one such geographic area, and the list can be broken down by type of train, type of propulsion and track style, specific themes of at least some services, and operational periods. Each individual entry for a train service includes the number of 'hits' on this website for that service. In evaluating the number of hits, the following tourist trains (not including Amtrak) in the US south-west had the highest number of 'hits' (list ranked by number of hits for all hits >10; seasonality and state shown in parentheses):

- Cumbres and Toltec Scenic Railroad (seasonal; Colorado and New Mexico), 32;
- Durango and Silverton Narrow Gauge Railroad (all year; Colorado), 30;
- Grand Canyon Railway (all year; Arizona), 29;
- Georgetown Loop Railroad (seasonal; Colorado), 20;
- Pueblo Railway Museum (seasonal; Colorado), 20;
- Rio Grande Scenic Railway (seasonal; Colorado), 20;
- Verde Canyon Railway (all year; Arizona), 19;
- Virginia & Truckee Railroad (seasonal; Colorado), 18;
- Nevada Southern Railway at Nevada State Railroad Museum (seasonal; Nevada), 17;

- Heber Valley Railroad (all year; Nevada), 15;
- Nevada Northern Railway Museum (all year; Nevada), 15;
- Santa Fe Southern Railway (all year; New Mexico), 13.

GCRy ranks quite high on the number of 'hits', with only the Cumbres and Toltec, and Durango and Silverton receiving more, albeit only by a small amount. These 'hits' serve only as a proxy for demand for any tourist railroads since they indicate only that potential passengers accessed the information for individual railroads on the website. The above indicates that, in a comparative sense, the GCRy ranks quite high compared with other tourist railroads in the south-west.

The website TripAdvisor permits travelers to provide evaluations of travel attractions and this includes visitor attractions in Williams, Arizona. In terms of Williams, Grand Canyon Railway is rated by travelers as the third most recommended attraction, with the Williams Depot as the fifth most recommended (out of a total of 22 attractions) (TripAdvisor, 2012b). Grand Canyon Railway had 466 reviews posted with TripAdvisor. The breakdown of their ratings was as follows (TripAdvisor, 2012a):

- excellent, 263;
- very good, 105;
- average, 53;
- poor, 30;
- terrible, 15.

Thus, although there were a few reviews that considered the Grand Canyon Railway a 'poor' or 'terrible' attraction, the vast majority considered it 'very good' or 'excellent' (nearly 79% of all reviewers).

The above ratings for the GCRy indicate that the railroad's service is generally perceived as above satisfactory. In many cases the degree to which the railroad's service is perceived as satisfactory or not relates to what the passenger's expectations were prior to riding on the railroad. Passenger satisfaction also derives from the varied experiences during the round-trip ride and from the Grand Canyon itself, with the latter experience under control of the NPS and nature itself rather than the GCRy and Xantera (except for bus tours and meals, which are controlled by the latter).

Management challenges

The GCRy faces a number of managerial challenges in terms of the current and future environment experienced by the railroad and what management might do to respond to those challenges. Perhaps first and foremost among these challenges is the significant decline in demand that has occurred since 2006, representing a decrease of over 55% in total (Figure 12.4a). With the exception of 2009, all years after 2006 had an annual passenger decline from the previous year. Although the implementation of other revenue generators such as the Polar Express, Christmas Eve Limited, Pumpkin Patch Express and Cataract Creek Rambler services can help to mitigate the passenger declines on the GCNP main service, they probably do not overcome that large decline in passengers and revenue for the service to/from GCNP.

A significant component to the recent declines in demand may well be the US economic environment from the late 2000s, with years of low or negative economic growth, higher than normal levels of unemployment and reduced levels of consumer discretionary spending (Strassner & Wasshausen, 2012; US Department of Commerce, Bureau of Economic Analysis, 2012b; US Travel Association, 2012). Although some recovery in leisure travel demand occurred in 2010/11, current economic trends may be negative for further recovery (Cook, 2012; US Department of Commerce, Bureau of Economic Analysis, 2012a). GCRy services, which are particularly attractive to families with children, can be expensive. For a family with two adults and two children, the cost for the GCRy service to visit the park for a few hours one day is $240, not including taxes, GCNP admission and other incidental costs. Over the last 10 years or so of operation, the prices for the various classes of service have increased, especially for children in coach and first class, on the order of 130% and 220%, respectively. Most adult fares in all classes have increased only on the order of 50–70%, other than adult first class (120%) (Collison, 2003).

Another component to the GCRy demand decline could be the near elimination of summer steam engine services that Xantera implemented starting in 2008 (Arizona Rail Passenger Association, 2009). After the takeover of the GCRy by Xanterra, the environmental impact of the railroad became a more important element of decision-making due to the environmental sustainability initiatives undertaken by the parent organization (Xanterra Parks and Resorts, n.d.-a, n.d.-b). Xanterra's environmental sustainability effort carried over to the railroad as well and led to numerous awards for its efforts in this area (Grand Canyon Railway, n.d.-g). Regular steam locomotive service was eliminated, although very limited service has since been restored using recycled vegetable oil as fuel. This may not be sufficient to recover from the potential loss in demand from steam train enthusiasts as they may decide to drive to GCNP and/or ride other tourist trains that offer a steam service.

In the current economic environment, costs of operation can be a major concern for GCRy. One difficulty facing the railroad is that many of the individual cost elements are either fixed or semi-fixed. It may be difficult to reduce to any significant degree these types of costs, which result from providing a scheduled service. For example, in providing scheduled train service to/from the Grand Canyon, once the train is actually operating, certain costs are incurred, such as fuel and the engineer's compensation, even if only the engine(s) is(are) operating. As a result, operating (and some other) costs are not directly proportional to the number of passengers carried, but must still be covered by operating revenue, which is composed of not only the transportation price paid, but also the purchase of food and beverages, incidentals and souvenirs.

Marketing represents a particular challenge for GCRy in the economic environment noted above, as the demand for the railroad's service to/from GCNP has declined considerably over the last few years. In order to be more successful in this situation, it may require a better understanding of current markets and the identification of new, untapped markets, especially for service to/from GCNP. Concurrent with this, GCRy management might consider ways to improve the customer reach of some of its marketing components, such as advertising, public relations, website and use of intermediaries. An element of GCRy's service that may need increased marketing exposure is that of environmental sustainability. With more marketing efforts devoted to presenting to actual and potential passengers the improvements in sustainability with the use of diesel locomotives and the advantages compared with the automobile, demand for the rail service to/from GCNP may be increased.

Despite the challenges facing the GCRy and Xanterra, the railroad has a role to play at GCNP. Although some might question the need for GCRy (Repanshek, 2009), it is definitely part of the historical record of the park and provides an alternative for visitors to access the park. Time will tell whether GCRy will be more successful than in the present period.

References

American-Rails (n.d.) The legendary Super Chief, flagship of the Santa Fe. At http://www.american-rails.com/super-chief.html (accessed 12 June 2012).

America's Best and Top 10 (2012) Best train trips in the USA. At http://www.americasbestonline.net/train.htm (accessed 12 June 2012).

Amtrak (2012) Southwest Chief. At http://www.amtrak.com/servlet/ContentServer?c=AM_Route_C&pagename=am%2FLayout&cid=1241245650447 (accessed 12 June 2012).

Anonymous (2011) *Tourist Trains Guidebook* (3rd edition). Waukesha, WI: Kalmbach Books.

Arizona Rail Passenger Association (2009) Steam is back at the Grand Canyon. At http://www.azrail.org/tag/grand-canyon (accessed 14 June 2012).

Arizona Republic (2012) Pumpkin Patch Train ready to roll in Williams. At http://www.azcentral.com/arizonarepublic/arizonaliving/articles/2011/09/17/20110917willi ams0917.html (accessed 19 June 2012).

Arizona State University, W.P. Casey School of Business (2012) Edward Jones Spirit of Enterprise Award – Grand Canyon Railway. At http://wpcarey.asu.edu/Spirit/ grand_canyon.cfm (accessed 25 June 2012).

BNSF Railway (n.d.) The history of the BNSF – a legacy for the 21st century. At http:// www.bnsf.com/about-bnsf/our-railroad/company-history/pdf/hist_overview.pdf (accessed 2 May 2012).

Bureau of the Census (1975) *Historical Statistics of the United States: Colonial Times to 1970 Part 2.* Washington, DC: US Department of Commerce. At http://www2.census. gov/prod2/statcomp/documents/CT1970p2-04.pdf (accessed 14 May 2012).

Collison, F.M. (2003) Case 17: The Grand Canyon Railway. In P. Kotler, J. Bowen and J. Makens (eds) Marketing for Hospitality and Tourism (pp. ¿¿¿–¿¿¿). Upper Saddle River, NJ: Pearson Education, Inc.

Cook, S. (2012) US Travel Association's US travel outlook – Research and trends. At http://www.ustravel.org/sites/default/files/page/2009/09/Outlook-expanded1_0. html (accessed 25 July 2012).

Duckett, R.H. (2010) Top ten North American train trips – travel – National Geographic Traveler. At http://travel.nationalgeographic.com/travel/top-10/north-american-train-trips (accessed 23 June 2012).

Fred Harvey Company (n.d.) Harvey Houses – Civilizing the old west. At http://www. harveyhouses.net/fredco.html (accessed 17 May 2012).

Full Wiki (2010) Rail transport in the United States: Wikis. At http://www.thefullwiki. org/Rail_transport_in_the_United_States (accessed 28 May 2012).

Grand Canyon, AZ (n.d.) At http://archive.azrail.org/station/az/grandcanyon/index. htm (accessed 3 May 2011).

Grand Canyon Railway (2007) Grand Canyon Railway acquires a new steam locomotive, No. 539. At https://www.thetrain.com/No.-539-1274966091-7111.html (accessed 25 June 2012).

Grand Canyon Railway (2009) Rail equipment. At http://www.thetrain.com/Locomo-tives-&-Passenger-Cars-5685.html (accessed 25 June 2012).

Grand Canyon Railway (2012a) The only way to experience the Grand Canyon! At http://www.american-rails.com/grand-canyon-railway.html (accessed 3 July 2012).

Grand Canyon Railway (2012b) Cataract Creek Rambler – National Train Day – May 12 & 13, 2012. At http://www.thetrain.com/national-train-day-8037.html (accessed 25 June 2012).

Grand Canyon Railway (2012c) Grand Canyon Train – rates. At https://www.thetrain. com/grand-canyon-train-5677.html (accessed 5 June 2012).

Grand Canyon Railway (2012d) The Polar Express. At http://www.thetrain.com/polar-express-5679.html (accessed 29 June 2012).

Grand Canyon Railway (2012e) Pumpkin Patch Train. At http://www.thetrain.com/ pumpkin-train-8498.html (accessed 25 June 2012).

Grand Canyon Railway (n.d.-a) Railway history. At http://www.thetrain.com/Railway-History-5683.html (accessed 12 April 2012).

Grand Canyon Railway (n.d.-b) Historic depots. At http://www.thetrain.com/Historic-Train-Depots-5684.html (accessed 17 June 2012).

Grand Canyon Railway (n.d.-c) Steam in the 21st century. At http://www.thetrain.com/ grand-canyon-railway-steam-7275.html (accessed 25 June 2012).

Grand Canyon Railway (n.d.-d) Grand Depot Café. At https://www.thetrain.com/
Grand-Depot-CafÃ©-5688.html (accessed 17 June 2012).

Grand Canyon Railway (n.d.-e) Grand Canyon tours. At https://www.thetrain.com/
Grand-Canyon-Tours-5701.html (accessed 5 July 2012).

Grand Canyon Railway (n.d.-f) Search for your vacation package. At https://secure.
thetrain.com/reserve/packages (accessed 17 June 2012).

Grand Canyon Railway (n.d.-g) Environmental initiatives. At http://www.thetrain.com/
Environmental-Initiatives-5712.html (accessed 1 July 2012).

Harrison, L.S. (2001) National Park Service: Architecture in the parks (Grand Canyon
Depot). At http://www.nps.gov/history/history/online_books/harrison/harrison7.
htm (accessed 7 July 2012).

Hotel Online (2008) Philip Anschutz, the Denver, Colorado billionaire, acquires Xanterra
Parks and Resorts – News for the hospitality executive. At http://hotel-online.com/
News/PR2008_4th/Oct08_Xanterra.html (accessed 3 July 2012).

Kelly, J. (2001) Summer tours and western travel. *Classic Trains Magazine*. At http://ctr.
trains.com/en/Railroad%20Reference/Operations/2001/07/Summer%20tours%20
and%20western%20travel.aspx (accessed 15 March 2011).

Krug, A. (2012) Steam vs. diesel. Railway technical web pages. At http://www.railway-
technical.com/st-vs-de.shtml (accessed 12 June 2012).

Locomotives-and-Trains.com (2011) – Diesel locomotive advantages over steam
locomotives. At http://www.locomotives-and-trains.com/diesel-locomotive-vs-
steam-locomotive.html (accessed 12 June).

National Association of Railroad Passengers (2006) Brief chronology of railroad history,
with passenger emphasis. At http://www.narprail.org/cms/index.php/resources/
more/railroad_history (accessed 15 May 2011).

National Railroad Passenger Corporation (Amtrak) (2012) Company history. At http://
www.referenceforbusiness.com/history2/64/National-Railroad-Passenger-Corpora-
tion.html (accessed 6 May 2012).

Naylor, R. (2012) Grand Canyon Railway rolls out steam train for Earth Day. At http://
www.azcentral.com/arizonarepublic/arizonaliving/articles/2012/04/20/20120420gr
and-canyon-railway-steam-train.html (accessed 16 June 2012).

Newberg, J. (2004) Arizona excursion trains. The Arizona Republic. At http://www.
azcentral.com/travel/arizona/features/articles/archive/0702trains.html?&wired
(accessed 16 June 2012).

NPS (2012a) Grand Canyon National Park, Arizona – Animals. At http://www.nps.gov/
grca/naturescience/index.htm (accessed 29 June 2012).

NPS (2012b) Grand Canyon National Park, Arizona – Archeological resources. At http://
www.nps.gov/grca/historyculture/arch.htm (accessed 12 May 2012).

NPS (2012c) The guide – Grand Canyon National Park – The official newspaper. At
http://www.nps.gov/grca/parknews/upload/2012SRsummer_letter.pdf (accessed 20
May 2012).

NPS (2012d) Grand Canyon National Park, Arizona – Public transportation. At http://
www.nps.gov/grca/planyourvisit/publictransportation.htm (accessed 17 June 2012).

NPS (2012e) Grand Canyon National Park – Getting around Grand Canyon. At http://
www.nps.gov/grca/parknews/upload/2012SRsummer-guidemap_letter.pdf
(accessed 20 June 2012).

NPS (2012f) Public Use Statistics Office. At http://www.nature.nps.gov/stats/park.cfm
(accessed 27 February 2012).

PBS (2010) General article: Interstate Commerce Act. At http://www.pbs.org/wgbh/

americanexperience/features/general-article/streamliners-commerce (accessed 27 June 2012).

Perry, R.M. (2012) All hikers – historical figures – Mary Jane Colter. At http://www. allhikers.com/Allhikers/History/Historical-Figures/Mary-Jane-Colter.htm (accessed 17 May 2012).

Pullano, J. (n.d.). The Santa Fe Railroad and its famous passenger trains. At http://ezinearticles.com/?The-Santa-Fe-Railroad-And-Its-Famous-Passenger-Trains&id=1105355 (accessed 2 June 2012).

Repanshek, K. (2009) Should the trains keep rolling into Grand Canyon National Park? National Parks Traveler (Blog). At http://www.nationalparktraveler.com/2009/06/ should-trains-keep-rolling-grand-canyon-national-park (accessed 14 July 2012).

Richmond, A. (2005). Rails at both rims. In M.F. Anderson (ed.) *A Gathering of Grand Canyon Historians: Ideas, Arguments, and First-Person Accounts* (Proceedings of the inaugural Grand Canyon History Symposium, January 2002). Grand Canyon, AZ: Grand Canyon Association. At http://www.grandcanyon.org/booksmore/epubs/ historians/pdfs/chapter_02.pdf (accessed 28 January 2011).

Rothman, H. (1996) Selling the meaning of place: Entrepreneurship, tourism, and community transformation in the twentieth century American west. *Pacific Historical Review* 65 (4), 525–557.

Runte, A. (1998) *Trains of Discovery: Western Railroads and the National Parks* (4th edition, revised). Boulder, CO: Roberts Rinehart Publishers.

Scrattish, N. (1985) Historic resource study – Bryce Canyon National Park. Denver: United States Department of the Interior, National Park Service, Rocky Mountain Regional Office, Branch of Historic Preservation. At http://www.nps.gov/history/ history/online_books/brca/hrs.htm (accessed 16 August 2010).

Shaffer, M.S. (2004) 'The west plays west': Western tourism and the landscape of leisure. In W. Deverell (ed.) *A Companion to the American West* (pp. 375–389). Malden, MA: Blackwell.

Slack, B. (2012) Rail deregulation in the United States. At http://people.hofstra.edu/ geotrans/eng/ch9en/appl9en/ch9a1en.html (accessed 25 June 2012).

Strassner, E.H. and Wasshausen, D.B. (2012) BEA briefing – Prototype quarterly statistics on U.S. gross domestic product by industry, 2007–2011. At http://www.bea.gov/scb/ pdf/2012/06%20June/0612_industryaccounts.pdf (accessed 12 July 2012).

Strong, S. (n.d.) The Grand Tour: Explore the red-rock country of southern Utah and northern Arizona, areas that were first championed by an unlikely advocate. An article from *Camping Life* digitally published at http://www.amazon.com/The-Grand-Tour-championed-advocate/dp/B000972WSM (accessed 11 January 2011).

Tourist Railroad Information Center (2011) North America. At http://www.touristrailways.com/namerica/index.html (accessed 02 June 2012).

Tourist Trains Worldwide (n.d.) At http://www.touristtrains.net/cgi-bin/index.pl (accessed 15 June 2012).

TripAdvisor (2012a) Grand Canyon Railway – 466 reviews of Grand Canyon Railway. At http://www.tripadvisor.co.uk/Attraction_Review-g31407-d126897-Reviews-Grand_Canyon_Railway-Williams_Arizona.html (accessed 12 July 2012).

TripAdvisor (2012b) Things to do in Williams – 29 Williams attractions. At http://www. tripadvisor.co.uk/Attractions-g31407-Activities-Williams_Arizona.html (accessed 12 July 2012).

US Department of Commerce, Bureau of Economic Analysis (2012a) National income and accounts tables – table 1.5.1. Percent change from preceding period in gross domestic product, expanded detail. At http://bea.gov/iTable/iTable.cfm?ReqID=9&step=1 (accessed 17 July 2012).

US Department of Commerce, Bureau of Economic Analysis (2012b) U.S. economy at a glance: Perspective from the BEA accounts. At http://www.bea.gov/newsreleases/glance.htm (accessed 28 June 2012).

US Department of Transportation (1978) *Preliminary Report to Congress and the Public: A Reexamination of the Amtrak Route Structure*. At http://www.fra.dot.gov/downloads/rrdev/reex-may78.pdf (accessed 16 May 2011).

US Travel Association (2012) U.S. travel forecasts. At http://www.ustravel.org/sites/default/files/Forecast_Summary.pdf (accessed 14 July 2012).

Weigle, M. (1989) From desert to Disney World: The Santa Fe Railway and the Fred Harvey Company display the southwest. *Journal of Anthropological Research* 45 (1), 115–137.

Wheels Museum, Inc. (2007) The story of the Fred Harvey Company. At http://www.wheelsmuseum.org/harveyhouse.html (accessed 17 May 2012).

Xanterra Parks and Resorts (n.d.-a) About us – the Fred Harvey legacy. (2012). At http://www.xanterra.com/our-fred-harvey-legacy-326.html (accessed 5 June 2012).

Xanterra Parks and Resorts (n.d.-b) Environment – introduction. At http://www.xanterra.com/Environmental-Action-364.html (accessed 28 June 2012).

Xanterra Parks and Resorts (n.d.-c) Environment – Xanterra's environmental policies and management. At http://www.xanterra.com/environment-374.html (accessed 28 June 2012).

Youngs, Y. (n.d.). NCHGC. Sites and sounds: South Rim: Grand Canyon Railway Depot. At http://grandcanyonhistory.clas.asu.edu/sites_southrim_railwaydepot.html (accessed 5 June 2012).

Youngs, Y.L., White, D.D. and Wodrich, J.A. (2008) Transportation systems as cultural landscapes in national parks: The case of Yosemite. *Society and Natural Resources* 21, 797–811.

Your West Valley (2012) Grand Canyon Railway schedules runs. At http://www.your-westvalley.com/valleyandstate/article_753826f8-6879-11e1-b3ee-001871e3ce6c.html (accessed 5 July 2012).

13 Railways as Heritage Attractions: The Malaysia–Singapore Line

Joan Henderson

Introduction

This chapter examines aspects of railway heritage with specific reference to Singapore and the line which once crossed the island, connecting it via a causeway with Malaysia, and the former main station of Tanjong Pagar and the smaller suburban Bukit Timah Station. The case is interesting because the railway has colonial origins and historical circumstances resulted in it belonging to and being run by a state-owned Malaysian company. The latter situation was a source of tension between the neighbouring countries, but an agreement was reached in 2010 whereby the railway was closed and the terminus moved to the causeway. The stations are to be conserved, but the purpose of the buildings has yet to be decided and there is uncertainty about the future of the track, which forms a corridor of greenery. The meaning and significance of the heritage of Singapore's railway and the merits of alternative new uses are discussed in the chapter, which begins with an account of the broader framework, followed by a summary of the history of the railway. Attention is then given to matters of conservation and popular and official positions on the subject, before a final conclusion.

Setting the Scene

The Malay peninsula traditionally was divided into individual states, each with its own ruler or sultan. The British sought to extend their influence in the region in the 19th century, leading to the formation of the Federated Malay States (FMS) in 1896, which became part of the British Empire, although not all sultanates chose to join. Singapore, at the southern tip of the peninsula, was governed as a British crown colony, known as the Straits Settlements, in which it was combined with Malacca and

Penang for administrative purposes. Imperial rule continued in Malaya and Singapore until the World War II, when both were occupied by the Japanese, after which there was fairly rapid movement towards independence. The Malayan Union was formed in 1946 as an alliance of the states on the Malay peninsula, but collapsed in 1948 due to anxieties among rulers about loss of sovereignty and the granting of citizenship to non-Malays. It was replaced by the Federation of Malaya, later called the Federation of Malaysia, and independence was attained in 1957 (Turnbull, 1989).

Singapore had acquired internal self-rule in 1959, when the People's Action Party (PAP), led by Lee Kwan Yew, won the election, and joined the federation in 1963. The union failed and Singapore was expelled in 1965, leaving a legacy of bitterness and mutual recrimination. Despite questions about its viability as an independent entity, the republic flourished there-after and PAP policies delivered one of the highest standards of living in Asia. The PAP has remained in office and Prime Minister Lee appointed Goh Chok Tong as his successor in 1990. Lee's son assumed the job in 2004 and the two former Prime Ministers stayed in the Cabinet as Minister Mentor and Senior Minister respectively until after the 2011 election.

The administration is characterised by its pursuit of order and control (Economist Intelligence Unit, 2008) and it governs a society of almost 4 million citizens of mixed ethnic origin. Immigration after Singapore became an East Indian Company trading post in the 19th century meant that the original Malay inhabitants were eventually outnumbered. Malays now comprise around 14% of the population, while ethnic Chinese account for 75% and Indians 9% (Singapore Statistics, 2009). Race is a sensitive matter due to the pre-eminence of the Chinese, fears of the marginalisation of the other ethnic groups (Lai, 1995; Rahim, 1998) and official apprehension about a repeat of the 1964 race riots. Averting strife and the cultivation of a sense of national identity and nationhood, founded on multiracialism and notions of a shared history, have been major objectives of the government.

Despite divergences in economic and political systems and philoso-phies and in approaches to managing ethnicity and religion, Malaysia and Singapore are united by historical experiences and both have seen political continuity in terms of firmly entrenched ruling parties which engage in long-term planning. There are socio-cultural affinities and economic inter-linkages (Chang, 2003) and both belong to the Association of South East Asian Nations (ASEAN), which aims to foster unity among the 10 partici-pating states. Nevertheless, these bonds have not mitigated the mistrust and occasional hostility which has existed since separation in 1965 (Shiraishi, 2009). Antagonism is of necessity accompanied by pragmatism (Nathan, 2002) and images of a family are often invoked, members inescapably bound together yet prone to rivalry and bickering. The complexities, dynamics and outcomes of bilateral relations are illustrated and illuminated by the story of the railway, which is one example in a series of long-standing disputes of varying severity and raises issues observed in other contexts of 'contested trans-national heritage' (Beaumont, 2009: 298).

The History of the Railway

The history of Singapore's railway is not very well documented and certain details cannot be confirmed, but the imperative of having a railway system appears to have been recognised in the second half of the 19th century. Production of Peninsular Malayan rubber, tin, palm oil and copra was growing and the produce needed to be transported. Singapore was a major international trading port and an obvious outlet. The line traversing the island of Singapore was not, however, built until the early years of the 20th century, under the supervision of the general manager of the Federated Malay States Railway (FMSR). The FMSR had been founded in 1901 in an initiative to integrate the separate railways installed by members of the Federated Malay States (Stanistreet, 1974). It had been encouraged by the colonial Governor, who was keen on the idea of uniting Singapore with India by rail (Vernon, 1997). The original Singapore line opened in 1903 and ran from Tank Road through the town to Bukit Timah Station and then to Kranji. The northern terminus was adjacent to the jetty from which ferries crossed the Straits of Johor to the mainland, where rail passengers could continue their journeys on FMSR services to the Malayan capital of Kuala Lumpur and elsewhere (Singapore Railways, 2010; Tyers, 1976).

The track was extended southwards in 1906–07, connecting it to the wharves and docks, and covered almost 32 km in total. Six locomotives with 26 passenger coaches and 46 goods wagons were deployed by what was, until the end of 1912, called the Singapore Government Railway. Operations were transferred to the FMSR in 1913 but then in 1918 the railway was sold, including station and track land, for S$4,136,000 (US$3,199,258) on a 999-year lease. It seems that the heaviest passenger traffic was on Sundays, when Singaporeans visited 'gambling farms' run by Johor businessmen, who paid their return fares (*Straits Times*, 2011a).

Shortly after, a Singapore Railway Transfer Ordinance authorised the building of a causeway across the Straits of Johor. Work on the 1056 m causeway began in 1919 and the two-track railway opened to passenger and goods trains in 1924, after a ceremony which was attended by the Governor and the Sultan of Johor. The result was possibilities for uninterrupted rail travel and transportation of goods between Singapore and Malaya, as well as Siam (Thailand), to the north. There were ambitions of eventually being able to reach Europe and China through an expanded rail network (PMB & URA, 2011).

Activity on the railway increased, but the Tank Road–Bukit Timah line came to be seen as something of an inconvenience, as the town became busier and there was competition for space. It was decided to construct a larger station on reclaimed swampland on Keppel Road, served by a separate line from Bukit Timah. The Tank Road stretch became obsolete and was removed, together with the overhead bridge (Tyers, 1976). The new station was named Tanjong Pagar and was opened by the Governor in the presence of the Sultan of Perak in 1932, the former speaking of Singapore developing into a 'great industrial centre' from where 'Malayan goods may be conveyed by land and sea to all parts of the world' (*Straits Times*, 2011a). The location was near the harbour, facilitating freight distribution, and the railway line and station were to play an essential part in the region's international trade. Tanjong Pagar was one of the busiest stations on the FMSR West Coast Line and it was the only one with buffer stops. The method of signalling was inherited from the British and the 24-lever box was mechanically operated. The station, like those in Ipoh and Kuala Lumpur, incorporated a hotel managed by Chinese contractors, which in its heyday was acclaimed as being on a par with the more famous Raffles Hotel (Tan, 2000). Bukit Timah Station was much less grand; there were also several smaller stations along the line as it passed through suburban areas.

The railway and its stations thrived in subsequent decades, with some minor modifications to the track and trackside buildings. However, World War II saw the invasion of Singapore by the Japanese in 1942 and disruption to everyday life and business. Prior to the occupation, Tanjong Pagar Station was crowded with Malayan rolling stock, which had been moved south in a bid to prevent it falling into enemy hands. The Japanese forces unexpectedly struck from Malaya, after landing on its north-east coast, and the causeway was bombed by the retreating British in an effort to thwart the onslaught of General Yamashita's troops. The ensuing breach was quickly repaired, enabling its use by the Japanese (Vernon, 1997), and the causeway acquired a strategic and historic importance. After the war and the restoration of British colonial administration, FMSR was renamed the Malayan Railway Administration in 1948 and then Keretapi Tanah Melayu (KTM) on Malaysia's independence. The Singapore line and Tanjong Pagar Station continued to be vital to the entrepôt trade on which Singapore's economy depended, although changes were underway by the early 1970s. Traditional exports started to decline and emphasis shifted in Singapore to promoting the services sector and the port container reshipment business.

The departure of Singapore from the Federation of Malaysia in 1965 was another turning point in the history of the railway. There was an agreement that KTM would retain ownership and control of the stations, track and railway land in accordance with the original lease (NHB, 2010). As suggested in the previous section, however, these circumstances were a cause of contention between Malaysian and Singapore authorities and the railway became a symbol of their difficult relationship. Holding of land by a foreign power was irksome for the city state's government and had potentially undesirable consequences for national security (Nathan, 2002). The Malaysian administration was loath to cede ownership, appreciative of its monetary worth as well as more intangible value at the negotiating table. The problem was raised often at talks held in the aftermath of separation, but there was little sign of resolution until the Points of Agreement (POA) were brokered in 1990. Under the accord, Tanjong Pagar Station would be moved to Woodlands, near the causeway, and Malaysia would be given plots of land in recompense; these would be managed by a development company in which Malaysia would have a 60% share and Singapore 40% (Lee, 2003). There was wrangling about implementation of the POA in the years that followed and Singapore went ahead with the building of a new customs and immigration complex at Woodlands for travellers using the causeway. Rail arrivals were processed there after the completion of facilities in 1998, but Malaysia refused to move its officers. Malaysian procedures were carried out as usual at the end of the journey, in Tanjong Pagar, so that, officially, travellers reached Singapore before leaving Malaysia. By this date, railway traffic was dwindling, being superseded by alternative modes of transport, and KTM was running only three trains a day in 2010.

It seemed that these arrangements would persist indefinitely, but a breakthrough occurred in 2009, when a new Prime Minister was elected in Malaysia. After joint ministerial committee meetings, he met his Singapore counterpart at a leaders' retreat. They later agreed that Tanjong Pagar Station, together with the Malaysian customs and immigration services, would move to Woodlands by July 2011 and land would be allocated and developed as planned in the POA. The deal was finalised in late 2010 and lauded as a landmark achievement by the second generation of political leaders looking to the future and less shackled by the past than their predecessors. The Singapore Prime Minister commented that the POA was 'not something which should drag on, because we do not want outstanding legacy issues to affect our core relationship'. His Malaysian counterpart concurred by saying that 'we cannot allow it to fester because it will always be seen as an impediment preventing us from progressing and moving forward in terms of our bilateral ties' (Prime Minister's Office, 2010). A commitment to save Tanjong Pagar Station was made and there was also a promise that due regard would be given to preserving Bukit Timah Station (SGPress Centre, 2010). Doubts were expressed, however, about how the sites would be developed and the uses to which the reincarnated stations might be put, as well as the fate of the land occupied by the track.

Singapore's Railways Heritage and Its Conservation

At the time of its closure in 2011, Tanjong Pagar Station was shabby and neglected, in striking contrast to the ultra-modern structures of the nearby Central Business District (Henderson, 2011). Nevertheless, it was agreed that it still had aesthetic appeal and was of historic interest (*Sunday Times*, 2010). The station was reputed to be the work of a renowned Singapore firm of architects, Swan and MacLaren, and was hailed by planners as an 'exemplary piece of Modern Architecture with Neo-Classical and Art-Deco influences and an integration of public art and local design motifs' (PMB & URA, 2011). The building was dominated by a vaulted space over 21 m high above the main waiting hall and palatial facades on three sides. Four figurative sculptures representing agriculture, commerce, transport and industry adorned the building and signified the sources of Malaya's wealth in the 1930s. A set of murals on rubber tile panels inside depicted traditional scenes of rice planting, rubber tapping, tin mining and seafaring. The entrance porch roof was covered with green glazed Chinese-style tiles, while Moorish-style plaster moulding decorated the porch. Cast iron canopies were embellished with classical Greek motifs and the window parapets had moulded lion heads. Again, according to officials, the building 'successfully showcases the harmonious blending of Eastern and Western aesthetics in a Modern way', which makes it a 'local, national and international landmark' (PMB & URA, 2011). Bukit Timah Station, too, was an 'endearing local landmark' with its 'cosy cottage appearance' (PMB & URA, 2011). As a simple brick building with an open-sided waiting hall, it was reminiscent of traditional small-town stations common in the UK and Malaya in the pre-war years and the only extant Singapore suburban station.

Awareness of the importance of the stations is revealed in decisions made in early 2011 about their status by the Preservation of Monuments Board (PMB) and Urban Redevelopment Authority (URA). The PMB is part of the National Heritage Board, which oversees heritage and aims to make it an 'enriching part of everyone's life and enable a better appreciation of our cultures, heritage and national history and to give us a sense of purpose and belonging' (MICA, 2011). The URA deals with national planning directed towards sustaining economic growth and maximising the revenue-earning potential of scarce land, but it has acquired conservation duties. These include selecting buildings and areas to be conserved and devising regulations and guidelines about good practice (URA, 2011a). It was announced that Tanjong Pagar Station was to be preserved as a national monument by the PMB, while the station at Bukit Timah would be listed as a conserved building by the URA. Designation as a national monument requires that a building's form be unaltered, although changes are permitted to interiors if they are in compliance with official guidelines. The front of a conserved building must be retained, but the sides and back can be altered subject to approval.

The PMB and URA said in a joint statement that the awards were inspired by the 'deep historical significance' of the stations and the need to 'protect physical reminders of our rich heritage'. The railway had once been a critical mode of transport for passengers and goods, thereby playing a part in Singapore's economic development that should be remembered and celebrated. A representative argued that the railway buildings were 'part of the collective social memory of Singaporeans' and that the URA's Conservation Programme was 'set up to keep these physical reminders of our built heritage'. Tanjong Pagar Station was especially notable because of its unique structure, key operational role and ability to communicate the 'sense of elegance and grandeur' of rail travel in the past. The hope was expressed that it would remain a 'landmark even in its adaptive re-use to reflect the nature and strength of ties between both countries as well as amongst its people' (PMB & URA, 2011). The lines and other equipment were the property of the operator and to be removed, but the URA stated that it would 'study the possibility of marrying development and greenery' regarding the land (*Straits Times*, 2011b). The option of amalgamating the track into the existing network of park connectors (pathways linking parks and other green spaces) and planned 150 km round-island route were raised by officers, who engaged in talks with the National Parks Board and Singapore Nature Society, forming a consultation group which was to meet every two months. Public feedback about the rail corridor was invited on a dedicated website, which contained a forum where ideas, memories and photographs could be exchanged. The website promised that the corridor would be accessible to the public once clearance work was finished (URA, 2011b).

The news that the station buildings would have a degree of protection met with a generally favourable reaction and prompted public discussion about possible uses and the overall development of railway land. Concerns were voiced about the stations being overwhelmed by construction at the sites and losing their dignity and sense of history. There were fears of absorption and transformation into amenities such as shopping malls, entertainment nightspots and expensive hotels, which are already ubiquitous in Singapore (*Straits Times*, 2011c). A Facebook group was set up and advocated a museum as the most desirable option (*Straits Times*, 2010a; *Sunday Times*, 2010). Thoughts were also put forward about what to do with the track and included green pathways for cyclists and walkers. Such a recreational purpose would be in keeping with its countryside feel created by the plant and animal life, which includes rare birds and butterflies, inhabiting the narrow strips of land beside the rails. The stance was backed by nature and cultural heritage groups, which argued that protection was merited because the line linked a range of natural habitats and historic sites associated with World War II.

Its imminent demise as a working station drew many residents to Tanjong Pagar Station. Sales of miscellaneous souvenirs were high and events were organised to mark the occasion, such as a film screening. Those interviewed by the press spoke about reliving happy memories of train rides to Malaysia and wanting to share these experiences with their children (*Straits Times*, 2011d; *Sunday Times*, 2010). The final school holiday before the closure saw a number of student parties making a trip to Malaysia and KTM reported a dramatic increase in ticket sales, with almost all long-distance services fully booked (Channel News Asia, 2011). In addition, the PMB organised a series of walking tours of the station designed to give participants a greater 'understanding of Singapore's cultural heritage' and an 'appreciation of our newest national monument' (*Straits Times*, 2011e). These pre-booked tours were quickly sold out, leaving many disappointed. Crowds gathered on the evening of 30 June to see the last scheduled service depart, followed by a special train carrying 600 invited guests and the Sultan of Johor, who was at the controls. Entry to the station was denied from July 2011, when the lifting of the rails commenced. However, in response to popular demand, the line was open to the public for a two-week period, and a 3 km stretch was open for a month. Bukit Timah Railway Station and 1.5 km of track were also made accessible after removal works had been completed. The outing proved popular with walkers and especially family parties.

Public interest in the future of the stations and rail corridor and official actions are indicative of heightened engagement in conservation matters among Singaporeans (MICA, 2009; NHB, 2011; URA, 2010). Nevertheless, there are obviously tensions between the demands of conservation and urban development; much built heritage and open space has already been sacrificed and that which survives is at risk. The instance of the railway stations and land is indicative of the current approach, in which a greater willingness to conserve is tempered by economic pragmatism, requiring that heritage and land should make money whenever possible. To this end, the URA allows 'flexible negotiations for adaptive reuse of old buildings as driven by the market', with a view to enabling 'modern redevelopment' while 'keeping the past for people' (Teh, 2007: 26). Adaptive reuse (Langston *et al.*, 2008) can, however, pose practical problems and be very costly if major structural alterations are necessary (Bullen & Love, 2010; Feilden, 2003; Kincaid, 2002). Adaptations and new tenants may be deemed inappropriate by some stakeholders and exclude locals, thereby denying them their heritage. The damaging effects of fundamental change in usage on a transport building's historic meaning are evidenced by Clifford Pier, dating from 1933 and of an art deco design (National Library Singapore, 2010). The destiny of the pier was subject to deliberations similar to those about Tanjong Pagar Station, with which it has attributes in common. The President of the Singapore Heritage Society urged that the site be devoted to a maritime museum, but URA officials said that the reinvention of the waterfront as a 'lifestyle and retail hub' had given Clifford Pier a 'new lease of life' (Fu, 2006; *Straits Times*, 2010b). It is now occupied by an expensive Chinese restaurant, where, 'amid all the marble and fancy furniture', there is no sign that this 'landmark was once an important destination for generations of migrants arriving at, or departing from the colony' (Wu, 2009), apart from two small plaques on external walls.

Conclusion

Whether the difficulties inherent in adaptive reuse and securing a satisfactory accommodation between conservation and development can be resolved with regard to Singapore's railway heritage is at present unknown, as final decisions had not been made at the time of writing. Potent arguments can, however, be made for turning Singapore's main station into a state-run museum and the track into a recreational green corridor based on the socio-cultural benefits accruing. Such moves would give due regard to the station's former standing and its function as a repository of individual and collective memory. Singaporeans would also be provided with a novel natural environment for outdoor pursuits, enhancing both physical and psychological well-being. The case for a museum is strengthened by the distinctive political context, whereby the history of the railway mirrors that of the two countries, divided yet inextricably linked by assorted ties. Narratives of the railway thus afford insights into wider changes and there is scope for a museum devoted to Malaysia–Singapore relations which extends beyond questions of transport to those of economics, politics and international affairs. Addressing and exploring a relationship of complexity and sensitivity through railway heritage poses formidable challenges, but meeting these would mark a step forwards on the journey to nationhood and promote understanding of the past and its repercussions among the citizenry of both Singapore and Malaysia. Such a museum would also create an interesting and informative visitor attraction rooted in the local and a welcome contrast to certain recent projects which have favoured the emergence of a somewhat bland and homogenised international tourism landscape.

References

Beaumont, J. (2009) Contested trans-national heritage: The demolition of Changi Prison, Singapore. *International Journal of Heritage Studies* 15 (4), 298–316.

Bullen, P. and Love, P. (2010) The rhetoric of adaptive reuse or reality of demolition: Views from the field. *Cities* 27, 215–224.

Chang, L.L. (2003) Singapore's troubled relations with Malaysia: A Singapore perspective. In D.J. Singh and K.W. Chin (eds) *Southeast Asian Affairs* (pp. 259–274). Singapore: Institute of South East Asian Studies.

Channel News Asia (2011) Tanjong Pagar Station sees surge in passenger load. At http://www.channelnewsasia.com/stories/singaporelocalnes (accessed 29 May 2011).

Economist Intelligence Unit (2008) *Country Profile 2008 Singapore*. London: EIU.

Feilden, B.M. (2003) *Conservation of Historic Buildings*. Oxford: Elsevier.

Fu, G. (2006) Building an endearing home through conservation. Speech by Minister of State for National Development at the 2006 URA architectural heritage awards, 25 September. At http://www.mnd.gov.sg/newsroom (accessed 28 May 2011).

Henderson, J.C. (2011) Railways as heritage attractions: Singapore's Tanjong Pagar Station. *Journal of Heritage Tourism* 6 (1), 73–80.

Kincaid, D. (2002) *Adapting Buildings for Changing Uses: Guidelines for Change of Use Refurbishment*. London: Spon.

Lai, A.E. (1995) *Meanings of Multiethnicity: A Case Study of Ethnicity and Ethnic Relations in Singapore*. Oxford: Oxford University Press.

Langston, C., Wong, F., Hui, E. and Shen, L.Y. (2008) Strategic assessment of building adaptive reuse opportunities in Hong Kong. *Building and Environment* 43, 1709–1718.

Lee, P.O. (2003) The water issue between Singapore and Malaysia: No solution in sight? Economics and Finance No. 1. Paper. Singapore: Institute of Southeast Asian Studies.

MICA (2011) Heritage. At http://app.mica.gov.sg/Default.aspx?tabid=69 (accessed 26 May 2011).

MICA (2009) Speech by Mr Sam Tan Chin Siong at the launch of 'Colours of Heritage'. Ministry of Information, Communications and the Arts Press Releases and Speeches, 28 September.

Nathan, K.S. (2002) Malaysia–Singapore relations: Retrospect and prospect. *Contemporary Southeast Asia* 24 (2), 385–410.

National Library Singapore (2010) Singapore pages. At http://infopedia.nl.sg (accessed 23 March 2010).

NHB (2010) Heritage trails. Bukit Timah trail: Bukit Timah Railway Station. At http://heritagetrails.sg/content/199/Bukit_Timah_Railway_Station.html (accessed 7 June 2010).

NHB(2011) Our brand: Living heritage, dynamic cultures. At http://www.nhb.gov.sg/www/brand.html (accessed 24 May 2011).

PMB and URA (2011) Historic railway stations to be kept for future generations. Preservation of Monuments Board and Urban Redevelopment Authority. Media release, 8 April.

Prime Minister's Office (2010) News: The *Straits Times*, 25 May. At http://www.pmo.gov.sg/News/Transcripts/Prime+Minister/Points+of+Agreement++A+20+year+saga.htm (accessed 6 June 2010).

Rahim, L.Z. (1998) *The Singapore Dilemma: The Political and Educational Marginality of the Malay Community*. Kuala Lumpur: Oxford University Press.

SGPress Centre (2010) Joint statement by Prime Minister Lee Hsien Loong and Prime Minister Dato' Sri Mohd Najiob Tun Abdul Razak at the Singapore–Malaysia Leaders' retreat on 24 May. Press release.

Shiraishi, T. (ed.) (2009) *Across the Causeway: A Multi-Dimensional Study of Malaysia–Singapore Relations*. Singapore: Institute of South East Asian Studies.

Singapore Railways (2010) Overview. At http://members.multimania.co.uk/railsing/Singapore/SRhistory.htm (accessed 7 June 2010).

Singapore Statistics (2009) *Yearbook of Statistics Singapore 2009*. Singapore: Singapore Statistics.

Stanistreet, J.A. (1974) *Keretapi Tanah Melayu: The Malayan Railway*. Lingfield: Oakwood Press.

Straits Times (2010a) Old station, new platforms, 5 June.

Straits Times (2010b) Why Clifford Pier had to be adapted, 30 March.

Straits Times (2011a) All aboard, last trains chug across Singapore, 1 July.

Straits Times (2011b) Unbroken green stretch along railway land? 2 July.

Straits Times (2011c) Tanjong Pagar Station a national monument, 8 April.

Straits Times (2011d) All aboard for that last ride from Tg Pagar train station, 23 May.

Straits Times (2011e) Take heritage walk at Tanjong Pagar rail station, 7 May.

Sunday Times (2010) Inside Tanjong Pagar Station, 30 May.

Tan, B. (2000) Tanjong Pagar Railway Station. At http://infopedia.nl.sg/articles/SIP_954_2005-01-10.html (accessed 2 June 2010).

Teh, L.Y. (2007) Built heritage conservation in Singapore: A public–private partnership. In UNESCO *The Preservation of Urban Heritage in Cambodia* (pp. 25–26). Phnom Penh: UNESCO.

Turnbull, C.M. (1989) *A History of Malaysia, Singapore and Brunei*. Sydney: Allen and Unwin.

Tyers, R. (1976) *Singapore: Then and Now*. Singapore: University Education Press.

URA (2010) *URA Lifestyle Survey 2009*. Singapore: Urban Redevelopment Authority.

URA (2011a) Information guide. At http://www.ura.gov.sg/conservation/mod2.htm (accessed 27 May 2011).

URA (2011b) Rail corridor. At http://www.ura.gov.sg/railcorridor (accessed 12 September 2011).

Vernon, C.T. (1997) Singapore–Johor causeway. At http://infopedia.nl.sg/articles/SIP_992004-12-30.html (accessed 6 June 2010).

Wu, D. (2009) Restaurants: One on the Bund. *Time Out Singapore*. At http://wwwtimeoutsingapore.com (accessed 22 March 2010).

14 The Rhaetian Railway in the Albula/Bernina Landscapes: A Masterpiece of Railway Engineering

Philipp Boksberger and
Martin Sturzenegger

Introduction

Doubtless the development of the Rhaetian Railway was one of the pioneering efforts in railway engineering in Switzerland in the late 19th century. Recently listed as a UNESCO World Heritage site, the Rhaetian Railway is not only a heritage tourism attraction but it also plays an important role in the public transport system of Switzerland. This case study highlights the dilemmas of commercial transport tourism in the past, present and future.

The Rhaetian Railway and Graubünden

General Alpine tourism dates back to the first half of the 19th century, driven by artists, poets, sportsmen as well as scientists and their common desire for adventure, romance and an experience of nature (Luger & Rest, 2002). Later on, the positive health effects of the climate increased the flow of guests and tourists towards the Alps (Kaspar, 1995). From the middle of the 19th century, the development of railway systems, highways and bypasses to and within the Alps accelerated travel and made it safer. Gradually, peripheral and remote regions of the Alps were opened up by railways and roads. This expansion and development of traffic infrastructure facilitated the rapid expansion of mass tourism, because tourists from all over Europe were able to access almost every Alpine holiday destination rapidly and comfortably. The increasing development of transportation infrastructure led to a continuously rising number of regions, valleys and villages taking part in a booming tourism business (Keller, 2001; Pechlaner & Tschurtschenthaler, 2003). Over time, Alpine tourism evolved slowly but steadily from a niche market to mass tourism, that saw a significant and lasting change of seasonality and shifts in demand (Schuckert *et al.*, 2007).

Switzerland was one of the first countries in the world to have become a tourist destination, exemplified by the early 19th-century British mountaineers climbing the main peaks of the Bernese Alps or Britain's Thomas Cook Company first sending tour groups to Switzerland about 150 years ago. The world has changed a lot since tourism started to discover Switzerland but the mountains of the Swiss Alps have lost nothing of their magnificence, splendour and fascination (SCCIJ, 2011). Today, with revenues of US$34 billion and 5% of gross domestic product (GDP), tourism is Switzerland's biggest export industry (BfS, 2011). In 2010, the country received 17 million overnight guests with 36 million commercial overnight stays (STV, 2011). Switzerland offers a wide diversity of experiences and attractions for all – providing a paradise for winter sports, hiking, biking and wellness and spas, art and culture. But Switzerland offers not only splendid mountains, tranquil meadows and a wonderful landscape to marvel at: the country is internationally known for its spectacular railway journeys. Within Switzerland, Graubünden is the undisputed main destination for railway enthusiasts (Harris & Clarke, 2005).

Graubünden, the largest canton in Switzerland, is a typical mountain region, with its 150 valleys, 615 lakes and 937 peaks (its highest peak, Bernina, rising to 4049 m above sea level) and a settlement history of over 11,000 years. Graubünden is not only the most important visitor destination in Switzerland, with 5.8 million commercial overnight stays (STV, 2011) in 2010 and with its world-famous holiday destinations such as Engadin, St Moritz, Davos, Klosters, Arosa and Flims Laax, but is also the home of the ibex, a species of mountain goat, the fictitious children's book character Heidi and the source of the Rhine River (Boksberger *et al.*, 2011). The Rhaetian Railway (RhB; see Figure 14.1) is Graubünden's very own narrow-gauge railway system, providing access to this part of the Alps and giving visitors from all over the world an unrivalled panorama of Graubünden.

From very early times the Alpine passes played a vital role in people's life in 'Rhaetia' – the Latin name for the area. Cart tracks from the Roman era were found on Julierpass and Septimerpass. However, for long stretches, cliff paths were necessary, and gorges such as the Viamala presented construction problems for any kind of transport. The first real roads were built across the Alps from around 1816: the historical one crossing Splügenpass is still in very good condition. The idea of building a mountain railway in Graubünden first arose in 1888. Thanks to the initiative of a Dutchman named Willem-Jan Holsboer, the narrow-gauge railway company Schmalspurbahn Landquart–Davos AG (now the Rhaetian Railway) was

Rhätische Bahn

RhB UNESCO Welterbe

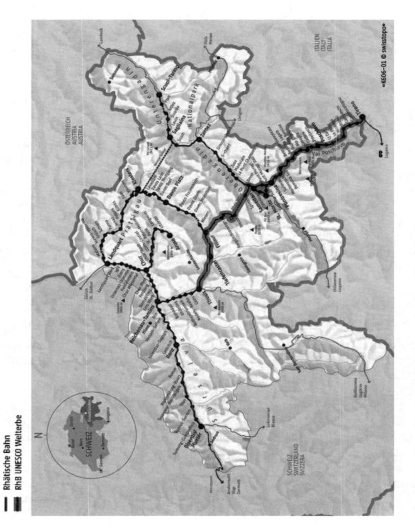

Figure 14.1 Rhaetian Railway (RhB), running from Thusis to Tirano

founded (RhB, 2012a). The ceremonial first sod of turf was cut in that same year, and steam trains began to ply the route from Landquart up to Davos in 1890 (Schönborn, 2009). Thomas Mann described his train journey up to Davos in his 1924 novel *The Magic Mountain*:

> The train was winding through a narrow pass; you could see the forward cars and the laboring engine emitting great straggling of brown, green, and black smoke. Water roared in the deep ravine on his right; dark pines on his left struggled up between boulders toward a stony gray sky. There were pitch-black tunnels, and when daylight returned, vast chasms were revealed, with a few villages far below.… Magnificent vistas opened onto regions toward which they slowly climbing, a world of ineffable, phantasmagoric Alpine peaks, soon lost again to awestruck eyes as the tracks took another curve. (Mann, 1996: 5)

The network was expanded slowly but steadily to 384 km of rail line, 114 tunnels as well as 592 bridges, not only for commuters but also for tourists (Schönborn, 2009). RhB employs some 1400 people, transports 11 million passengers and around 800,000 tons of freight every year over its high-altitude Alpine rail network (RhB, 2012b).

The Rhaetian Railway and UNESCO World Heritage

The line across Albula and Bernina, now more than a century old, was rendered possible by an exceptionally creative exploitation of technical, economic and socio-cultural forces. An important goal which was promoted by the construction of the railway was to preserve the diverse cultural and linguistic areas within the canton of Graubünden.

In view of the topography, the Albula line was laid out as a narrow-gauge railway, but its design and operation followed the pattern of a mainline (standard-gauge) railway. The aim was to facilitate access to the Engadin, in both summer and winter. Thus the railway contributed to the development of a new branch of the economy, namely winter (sports) tourism. Indeed, tourism was to become the main industry in the region. The railway line was integrated subtly into the diversified cultural landscape and continues to enrich it today.

The Bernina line was a product of the hydroelectric projects built on Italian initiative, to generate power for the Lombard metropolis of Milan, and exploited the capital released by these projects (UNESCO, 2008). Moreover, the concerns of tourism were taken into account by aligning the track to ensure an exceptional 'mountain experience' from the comfort of the train. To satisfy these special conditions, the latest technology was used to construct the high alpine railway as an electrical surface operation. As a UNESCO World Heritage site, the Rhaetian Railway in the Albula/Bernina Landscapes is a masterpiece, created by a unique and diversified interplay between economics, politics, engineering, culture and nature (RhB, 2006).

The Rhaetian Railway in the Albula/Bernina Landscapes is a mountain railway integrated into an alpine landscape. The Albula line, with its spectacular alignment and original engineering structures that represent a most impressive technical achievement, is an outstanding 'product' of the golden age of high-altitude railways. From the outset, it was recognised as a passenger transport route most harmoniously embedded in the unique landscape. 'What is more, the development of its alignment was planned with a view to the best possible integration into the surrounding landscape' (RhB, 2006: 364). The Albula/Bernina line, as a railway that traverses an entire mountain range, links three distinct linguistic and cultural regions. To this day, it remains in full service, transporting both passengers and goods. Since July 2008, the Albula and Bernina lines of the RhB have been on the UNESCO list of World Heritage sites (UNESCO, 2008).

Albula/Bernina Railway Engineering

The Albula/Bernina lines of RhB constitute the central element of the UNSECO World Heritage site. The Albula railway was completed in 1903; the Bernina railway in 1910. The combination of two different kinds of mountain railway – the one with crest tunnels (and the equally technically demanding spiral tunnels) and the other a surface electric railway crossing a high-altitude mountain pass in the open – make the Albula/Bernina line simultaneously unique and typical, an outstanding example of a railway in the mountains. Its major role in the history of railway construction and the quality of the achievement established the basis for the worldwide recognition it has enjoyed ever since it was first brought into service. It is essentially different from the mountain railways already on the World Heritage list: the Albula line, as a masterpiece, constructed with lavish planning and excellent craftsmanship, represents the archetype of the mountain railway from the golden age of rail. With its many stone viaducts of varying heights and lengths, the complex, sometimes overlaid structures of the helical tunnels and the long crest tunnel, the meticulous and architecturally valuable design of the elevated structures, and finally the actual operation itself, it displays all the characteristics of a mainline railway, even though it was constructed with a narrow gauge. The Bernina line, on the other hand, an electric surface railway at a high altitude and with the extreme gradient of 70‰, opened up new technical territory and introduced a new type of railway, which would soon become widespread (RhB, 2006).

The Albula/Bernina section represents a special type of high-altitude mountain railway: over a distance of some 130 km and with a maximum altitude of 1700 m it crosses a mountain range from one side to the other. While the Semmeringbahn UNESCO World Heritage site marks the beginning of accessing mountainous areas by rail, the Albula/Bernina line represents the golden age of mountain railway construction (Figure 14.2): it was only with the development of mechanical tunnelling machines in the second half of the 19th century that long tunnel constructions and special types of tunnel (such as spiral tunnels) could be erected within acceptable time and cost constraints (RhB, 2006).

Various specialists were engaged to construct the Albula railway (Thusis–St Moritz – see Figure 14.1). The layout of the route and all engineering structures were designed in compliance with the most advanced mountain railway construction standards of the day. The Albula railway was constructed as a classic mountain railway for operation with steam

Figure 14.2 Construction of parts of the Rhaetian Railway in the second half of the 19th century

engines. The layout of the line and the engineering structures built of locally quarried stone mark the zenith of the classic era of railway building. The Bernina railway (St Moritz–Tirano) is an innovative adaptation of an electric overland railway, with an exceptionally skilful layout in a high Alpine landscape. It immediately became the model for many projects throughout the Alps and the recognised standard for several railways that were built later. Today the Bernina railway is quite unique: it is the highest-altitude trans-Alpine railway, and one of the steepest adhesion railways in the world (RhB, 2006).

The engineering structures of the Albula and Bernina lines (bridges, station buildings, signal complexes, tunnels and their portals) are in harmony with the striking topography. The layout, in particular of the Bernina line, was largely designed to highlight the attractions of the spectacular mountain landscape for tourism. Both railways were designed, in terms of both the route layout and accompanying structures (buildings), to blend into the landscape (UNSCO, 2008).

Albula/Bernina Landscapes

Even when the railway was being built, the outstanding quality of the landscape to be traversed was recognised and deemed worthy of preservation. Emphasis was put on harmonious integration of the railway infrastructure, while at the same time the alignment – particularly in the case of the Bernina line – was planned, as far as possible, to present the landscape to the traveller in all its magnificence. The structurally created measures to enhance perception of the landscape during the rail journey, together with the railway landscaping realised during construction, are unique in the early 20th century. The experience of the exceptional views is an inherent element of the quality of the property. The Rhaetian Railway in the Albula/Bernina Landscapes displays emblematically this synthesis of nature, culture and technology, which has exerted a powerful influence on how the Alps have been perceived over the years: a vignette of cultural history (RhB, 2006).

The Albula/Bernina line is a unique example of a railway that has managed to integrate harmoniously into a high mountain region. This happy symbiosis between landscape and railway did not come about by chance; it was the result of careful forward planning, the fortuitous availability of certain technical innovations and careful consideration of the terrain. This is why the UNESCO World Heritage site covers both the railway itself and the countryside around it. Along the winding route through abruptly sloping Alpine valleys the line includes monumental landmarks such as the

Figure 14.3 The Landwasser Viaduct

Landwasser Viaduct (Figure 14.3), the series of winding tunnels between Bergün and Preda, and the Circular Viaduct at Brusio (UNESCO, 2008).

Three buffer zones are defined, in addition to the core zone comprising the line itself. The qualified buffer zone, which is adjacent to the core zone, contains significant and valuable cultural sites that are classed as being of national importance. The immediate buffer zone includes all those areas that are adjacent to the core zone, but which are not classed as part of the qualified buffer zone. This zone includes residential properties of more recent construction and small commercial and industrial areas. The distant buffer zone covers all the remaining landscape that can be seen from the railway (RhB, 2006).

The Rhaetian Railway and Tourism

The RhB runs through the cultural landscapes of the Albula/Bernina area, a popular destination for tourism. It forms part of the tourism-related infrastructure of Graubünden, which includes over 668 hotels with 39,081 beds, plus a further 125,000 beds are available in the self-catering sector (BfS, 2011). The region offers a whole range of tourist attractions, including the spectacular Viamala Gorge, the wooded Alpine slopes of the Albula Valley, the splendid isolation of Val Bever, bustling St Moritz, the mountain splendour of the Bernina Pass, and the southern, almost Mediterranean, ambience of Puschlav. The one element that links all these fantastic locations is the RhB. Its UNESCO World Heritage status is in recognition of the unique combination of technical wizardry, cultural diversity and harmony.

More Than Railway Heritage

While the RhB earns around 20% of its revenue from its two premium train operations, the Glacier Express and the Bernina Express, railway tourism remains a niche market for the region (RhB, 2012a). Even though these heritage railway products are both tourist attractions in their own right and iconic representations of Graubünden, the RhB provides canton-wide transport for thousands of commuters and leisure travellers in general, and skiers, hikers, mountain-bikers and day-trippers in particular. Targeted development of the tourist sector is now taking place along the UNESCO World Heritage route, including a new system of signage (Figure 14.4), as well as information given in the trains.

Figure 14.4 The new system of signage for the World Heritage Rhaetian Railway

Figure 14.5 The promotion of family hiking by the Rhaetian Railway as part of the World of Leisure initiative

New attractions are constantly being added under the brand of UNESCO World Heritage 'World of Leisure'. The World of Leisure initiative provides 'bridging products' between the premium train operations and other leisure travellers, as well as between the destinations along the entire World Heritage line. Therefore, the RhB is seen as the mean of transport in a series of integrated tourism-related products; for example, a hiking track was opened in 2010 that is divided into 10 stages and follows the route of the Abula/Bernia line (Figure 14.5). Tourists are able to book packages that include hotel accommodation and luggage transport in a single step. Since families are a key target group for the RhB, a large railway museum in Bergün, which opened in 2012, combines entertainment with learning as part of an overall tourism experience in Graubünden.

A Great Tagline in Marketing

The marketing of UNESCO World Heritage status naturally supposes important challenges when it comes to providing the right mix of cultural duty and commercial necessity. In order to go beyond the niche of railway

Figure 14.6 Online marketing of the Rhaetian Railway

heritage or cultural tourism, it is vital to establish communications with a wider community. Many visitors may not even be immediately aware of what the status actually refers to, but still they will be exposed to certain elements during their stay. Thus, the UNESCO World Heritage status is used as a tagline in the marketing of the Bernina Express, in order to make the route stand out in the highly competitive railway tourism sector and to provide tour operators with a good sales pitch. Moreover the tagline is used for a series of up-to-date communications tools to support the World of Leisure initiative (Figure 14.6). The 'Switzerland's Rich Heritage' campaign is being disseminated directly via various social media, including a Facebook page that allows people with an interest to post material. The online community can then vote on the most original contributions. The activities centred on social media are designed to provoke an exchange of information and discussions about the UNESCO World Heritage status – while using the latest in social media to give the common cultural traditions a contemporary spin.

Culture and Commerce – A Sensible Combination?

The RhB was originally built to serve the tourism sector. Around 100 years ago, steel bridges and tunnel engineering were the high-tech achievements of their day, while the backbreaking construction of stone viaducts and difficult sections of track also helped ensure the best possible view from the line. The intention was to provide visitors with a unique experience based on the high-altitude landscapes of the Alps. The current heritage thus originally stemmed from commercial considerations, which provide a link with the present-day approach to tourism products and tourism marketing. The RhB is not only a heritage railway but a key part of a fiercely contested tourism industry that seeks, just as it did 100 years ago, to attract tourists from all over the world.

References

BfS (2011) *Schweizer Tourismusstatistik 2010*. Neuchâtel: Bundesamt für Statistik der Schweiz.

Boksberger, Ph.E., Anderegg, R. and Schuckert, M. (2011) Structural change and reengineering in tourism – A chance for destination governance in Grisons, Switzerland? In E. Laws, H. Richins, J. Agrusa and N. Scott (eds) *Tourist Destination Governance: Practice, Theory and Issues* (pp. 145–158). Wallingford: CABI.

Harris, K. and Clarke, J. (eds) (2005) *Jane's World Railways 2005–06*. Surrey: Janes Information Group.

Kaspar, C. (1995) *Tourismuslehre im Grundriss*. Bern: Haupt.

Keller, P. (2001) Tourism growth and global competition. In P. Keller and T. Bieger (eds) *Tourism Growth and Global Competition* (pp. 11–25). St Gallen: AIEST.

Luger, K. and Rest, F. (2002) Der Alpentourismus: Konturen einer kulturell konstruierten Sehnsuchtslandschaft. In K. Luger and F. Rest (eds) *Der Alpentourismus: Entwicklungspotentiale im Spannungsfeld von Kultur, Ökonomie und Ökologie* (pp. 11–29). Innsbruck: StudienVerlag.

Mann, T. (1996) *The Magic Mountain* (trans. J.E. Woods). New York: First Vintage International Edition.

Pechlaner, H. and Tschurtschenthaler, P. (2003) Tourism policy, tourism organisations and change management in Alpine regions and destinations: A European perspective. *Current Issues in Tourism* 6 (6), 508–539.

RhB (2006) *Candidature UNESCO World Heritage – Rhaetian Railway in the Albula/Bernina Cultural Landscape*. No. 1/14. Switzerland: RhB.

RhB (2012a) Past and present. At http://www.rhb.ch/Past-and-present.86.0.html?&L=4 (accessed March 2012).

RhB (2012b) About us. At http://www.rhb.ch/About-us.20.0.html?&L=4 (accessed March 2012).

SCCIJ (2011) *Swiss Tourism Goes 'Natural and Authentic'*. Tokyo: Swiss Chamber of Commerce and Industry in Japan.

Schönborn, H.B. (2009) *Die Rhätische Bahn: Geschichte und Gegenwart*. München: Geramond.

Schuckert, M., Möller, C. and Weiermair, K. (2007) Alpine destination life cycles: Challenges and implications. In R. Conrady and M. Buck (eds) *Trends and Issues in Global Tourism 2007* (pp. 121–136). Berlin: Springer.

STV (2011) *Schweizer Tourismus in Zahlen 2010 – Struktur- und Branchendaten.* Bern: Schweizer Tourismus-Verband.

UNESCO (2008) *Decision – 32COM 8B.38 – Examination of Nomination of Natural, Mixed and Cultural Properties to the World Heritage List – Rhaetian Railway in the Albula/Bernina Landscapes.* Quebec City: UNESCO.

15 Regional Railway Revival: Connecting Heritage and Tourism in the Spa Centre of Australia

Leanne White

Introduction

This chapter examines links between railway heritage and tourism in Australia's leading spa tourism area – the Daylesford/Hepburn Springs region of Victoria. The chapter explores the railway-related heritage of the region, examines the current state of play in the heritage rail volunteer industry and highlights its links to tourism in the area. The chapter explores the fascinating case study of the Central Highlands Tourist Railway (CHTR), which operates under the name of Daylesford Spa Country Railway (DSCR), from a range of perspectives. The collection of heritage trains ranging from the 1920s to the 1970s is the largest of its kind in Victoria. A 2007 study undertaken by Heritage Victoria assessed the collection to be of major significance.

The chapter ties in with a number of the overarching themes of this book, including: railway attractions and destination development; conservation and preservation issues in rail heritage; visitors and markets for railway attractions; interpretation, authenticity and the tourist experience; and nostalgia, cultural memory and identity as they relate to railway tourism. The essentially qualitative analysis is undertaken by addressing the above themes while also examining this railway attraction through the theoretical lens of destination marketing. While the railway systems of Australia were once a dominant part of the economic and social landscape, they have evolved to become an integral part of the cultural fabric of the nation.

When exploring our past, we are delving deeper into our own heritage and also that of the nation. Underlying this suggestion is the proposition that heritage is a 'cultural and social process' that is 'ultimately intangible' (Smith, 2006: 307). With this in mind, this chapter aims to demystify the ways in which the often intangible concept of heritage is imagined, and examines the decisions made by those associated with the rail heritage of Daylesford. In particular, the meanings conveyed in the presentation of the region's rail heritage are highlighted. By focusing on railway heritage and the historic town of Daylesford, we can rethink our understanding and 'awareness of the role' that heritage plays 'in our everyday lives' (Waterton, 2010: 206). Others have argued that heritage has the ability to 'guide and cement national identities' (Gammon, 2007: 1).

For the tourist visiting the rail museum or taking a trip on the DSCR, heritage becomes somehow embodied and personified by the rail volunteers involved with the experience and images of past railway workers and enthusiasts on display at the museum. If we understand heritage as a process that constructs meaning about the past, then the construction of rail heritage in Daylesford is illustrative of this process. It is, essentially, a construction of heritage based upon restored trains, museum pieces and stories passed down (in written and oral form) by committed volunteers. Contrary to popular notions of heritage that situate it as 'object based', this example offers a new interpretation of heritage that builds on the work of Smith, Waterton, Gammon and others.

Spearritt and Walker recognised that popular culture in Australia had been largely ignored as a subject worthy of academic analysis. They argued, 'The battle for Australia's symbols was really won or lost in tourist pamphlets and encyclopaedias' (Spearritt & Walker, 1979: 58). Many studies in tourism have considered the role of heritage attractions in helping create a national identity. Pretes (2003) notes that tourists receive messages sent to them by the creators of the places they visit, and these sites of significance, presented as aspects of national heritage, help to shape a common national identity, or imagined community among a diverse population. Rojek (1997: 58) argues that 'most tourists feel they have not fully absorbed a sight until they stand before it, see it, and take a photograph to record the moment'. If tourism sites can help create a common identity or imagined community, can photographs taken at these destinations help to develop a better understanding of the place visited? Morgan et al. (2004: 4) argue that travel for the purpose of leisure is 'a highly involving experience, extensively planned, excitedly anticipated and fondly remembered'. The photographs that capture the highlights of the travel occasion constitute a vital element of both remembering the event and sharing the experience with others.

The Popular Tourist Town of Daylesford

Daylesford in regional Victoria was founded in 1852 and currently boasts a population of just over 3000. The town is located approximately

120 km north-west of Melbourne, at an altitude of 650 m. The town is named after Daylesford in England. The population grew rapidly with an influx of thousands of miners following the discovery of gold in the 1850s. Gold was discovered in 1851 at the Jim Crow goldfield (the area now known as Daylesford and Hepburn Springs) and by 1855 a substantial number of people had settled in the area (Gervasoni, 2005: 28). Many thousands of European settlers (including about 2000 from the border regions of Italy and Switzerland) were attracted to Daylesford's cool climate, ample mineral water and the prospect of finding gold.

Prior to the discovery of gold in the region, the Dja Dja Wurrung indigenous population lived in the area. The Daylesford and Macedon Ranges Regional Tourism Board's *Official Visitor Guide* acknowledges the original inhabitants of the land: 'The region that centres around Daylesford and the Macedon Ranges has been a gathering place for thousands of years. A sacred place for aboriginal nations since time began' (Daylesford and Macedon Ranges Tourism, 2011: 3).

After the Daylesford railway station opened in March 1880, timber and agricultural products were sent to Melbourne and other parts of Victoria by train. The railway also played an important role in the development of tourism in the area. The town and rail authorities promoted the region with the slogan 'Delightful Daylesford' (Davidson & Spearritt, 2000: 76). Before the railway came to Daylesford the town generally relied on horse-drawn carriages for transport – one example being the famous Cobb and Co. service. The appeal of the region increased during the early 20th century as affluent Melburnians were attracted by the supposed healing powers of the mineral springs. As a tourist destination, Daylesford went through a period of stagnation in the 1960s and 1970s. A resurgence of the area occurred slowly from the late 1980s.

With its emphasis on day spas and good food, the historic gold-mining town is considered a perfect weekend destination for many Melburnians. Daylesford and the neighbouring town of Hepburn Springs (featuring an impressive bath house built in 1895) boast 72 mineral springs. This represents 80% of Australia's mineral springs and the highest concentration in the Southern Hemisphere. As a result, Daylesford authorities promote the town as the 'Spa Centre of Australia' (Figure 15.1). The pursuit of indulgent weekends away has led to a rise in 'wellness tourism' for the town. Over the past couple of decades, the destination has recaptured the popularity that it enjoyed as a spa destination during the Victorian era, when tourists flocked to the town to 'take the waters' (bathe in the warm mineral springs). More than 100 day spa and health/wellness businesses in the area actively embrace the concept, offering services such as spa treatments, relaxation,

Figure 15.1 Daylesford is branded the 'Spa Centre of Australia'

massage and various holistic therapies. The offerings in the region are exceptionally varied. For instance, the boutique hotel Lake House offers yoga, tai chi, forest walks, spa treatments, gourmet cuisine, seminars and cooking demonstrations. These sorts of activities are designed to provide participants with a balance for mind, body and spirit.

Unlike many destinations, the region can boast substantial visitation during the cooler months of the year. The winter weather is actually featured as part of the charm of the destination, with much of the promotional imagery focusing on food and wine and the cozy warmth of an open fire – even a 'Words in Winter' writers' festival.

In 2005, Daylesford received international coverage by topping a worldwide list of 'funky towns'. The British Airways *High Life* in-flight magazine awarded Daylesford the coveted prize, explaining that the town has a reputation for diversity and tolerance. The town holds a number of popular festivals and events, including (since 1997) the annual 'Chillout' Festival for gay couples and lesbians. The Lonely Planet guide to Australia claims that

Daylesford attracts 'hedonists, spirituality seekers and escapees from the city rat race' (Smitz *et al.*, 2004: 535). Offering more than 200 accommodation options, the region is deliberately marketed as satisfying a wide range of interests and target audiences including gays, straight couples, families and retirees, those in search of pampering, gourmands, alternative lifestyle seekers and artists. The area's success as a tourist destination owes much to its social diversity. The Daylesford area has also been the beneficiary of the phenomenon known as a 'tree change', where city dwellers move to the country to enjoy a less hectic lifestyle (Burnley & Murphy, 2004).

The Conservation and Preservation of Daylesford's Rail Heritage

After much lobbying by residents, a railway line was established which linked Daylesford to Melbourne and other destinations in Victoria. When the line was opened on 17 March 1880, a temporary terminus was set up in East Street Daylesford. In 1881, a permanent brick station, featuring a verandah with ornate wrought iron columns and delicate lacework, was built near the present-day site at Raglan Street (Figure 15.2). Passengers who travelled from Melbourne had to change trains at Woodend to make the trip to Daylesford. Activity at the Daylesford railway station steadily increased, and at the height of its operation, in 1891, 22 trains either passed through or stopped at Daylesford on a daily basis (Osborne, 1978: 17). Indeed, the economically prosperous periods of the 1890s represented the boom period for the rail line. In 1890, 34,479 passenger journeys through the Daylesford station were undertaken. By 1930, the figure had dropped to 11,913 journeys, and just 5403 by 1975 (Osborne, 1978: 75).

The rail line served as a popular means of commuting between Melbourne and Daylesford. As commuter numbers dwindled over the years, the decision was made to close the service, almost 100 years after it had opened. Locals fought almost as fiercely as their ancestors had done a century earlier for their beloved train line. In 1977 a committee with the exceedingly long name of Keep the Daylesford–Trentham–Carlsruhe Branch Railway Line Open Upgraded and Maintained met regularly in a desperate bid to save the local train service. It was estimated that around A$4 million would be needed to keep it running. Unfortunately for the town, decades of neglect had resulted in a service that was slow and unreliable for the very few who chose to take the journey.

On 24 June 1978 local train enthusiasts organised for a special final train journey out of the station before the line was officially closed on 3 July (Osborne, 1978: 22). If Daylesford locals wanted to commute to Melbourne

Figure 15.2 One of two remaining Leyland Railmotors at Daylesford station

by train, they would first have to make their way by car or bus to larger towns such as Woodend. Ironically, by the time the track closed in the late 1970s, the journey took longer than it had in the 1880s, due to the poor condition of the track. In its final years the train line was described as a 'goat track' by Melbourne's newspaper *The Age* (Osborne, 1978: 38).

It did not take long, however, for the Daylesford community to rally behind their beloved train. While they could not restore the service as a commuter train to Melbourne, they understood the potential of the historic station and train as a tourist attraction in the area. At a meeting in 1980 it was agreed that the CHTR be established. A Tourist Railway Bill was passed in the Victorian Parliament the following year, and the Daylesford Railway Station was listed on the Historic Buildings Register in 1982 and formally recognised by the Australian Heritage Commission a decade later.

In September 1990, the CHTR (which has operated under the trading name of DSCR since 2002) officially opened its first tourist service between Daylesford and the nearby town of Musk. The platform at Musk is earth with timber surrounds and a ramp at each end. It has remained essentially the same since 1882. Despite the fact that hundreds of similar platforms were constructed by Victorian Railways, it is the only one of its type still in use today. By 1997, a group of committed volunteers who had invested much time and money restored the service to Bullarto – 9 km down the track and the highest railway station in Victoria (747 m above sea level). Unfortunately, track damage caused by the devastating 2009 bushfires in Victoria resulted in a return to the shorter journey – less than 2 km from Daylesford station. Bushfires in the nearby Wombat State Forest caused around $250,000 worth of damage to the line, as 2000 sleepers were destroyed and many rails buckled in the extreme heat.

The railway operates every Sunday and raises revenue by coordinating the adjacent Sunday market (Figure 15.3). The Daylesford Sunday market operates all year round, and the $25 fee paid by each market stall holder is a significant revenue raiser for the DSCR. The market provides a mix of trash and treasure for the tourists to pass by and fossick through. Antiques, tools, spare car parts, plants, second-hand books, clothes, hot food and fresh produce are just a few of the types of items that can be found at the eclectic market next to the railway station. The DSCR greatly benefits by being in this location, as the Sunday market is frequented by many of the town's tourists and a regular supply of locals.

As outlined above, visitors seeking tangible heritage can often find this through images of past railway workers and enthusiasts that are on display at the free museum (Figure 15.4). In 2006, the DSCR became the

Figure 15.3 The DSCR benefits from the passing trade of the Sunday market

Figure 15.4 Visitors can experience Daylesford's rail heritage at the free museum

first railway to become accredited in the Australian Museum Accreditation Program (MAP). The accreditation effectively means that the DSCR has been assessed as achieving industry standards in the managing, conserving and interpreting of heritage assets. The mission statement of the DSCR is proudly displayed at the museum located in the heritage-listed station. The mission emphasises the argument made by Waterton and others about the role heritage plays in our everyday lives. The organisation's mission statement manages to capture the passion and excitement that many associate with heritage train journeys by using alliteration, with words like 'sights, sounds and sensations':

> To develop a living-history railway museum of State significance between Daylesford and Trentham, based on the philosophy that the most effective way of encouraging an interest in the historical importance of railmotors and railways to the development of Victoria, is for visitors to experience as passengers the sights, sounds and sensations of a real railmotor journey as it was in the days of the Victoria Railways.

As outlined, the ultimate goal of the DSCR is to run the heritage train from Daylesford to Musk, Bullarto, Lyonville and, eventually, Trentham. Passengers waiting for their train ride often wander around the displays and may come across this mission statement while waiting for their train journey.

The DSCR normally runs six trains each Sunday with regular departure times between 10.00 am and 2.30 pm. The trip from Daylesford to Musk and return takes 35 minutes and costs $10 for adults and $8 for children, or a family ticket can be purchased for $25. To entice passengers to board the heritage train, the DSCR brochure includes phrases such as 'Take a trip through the forest', 'step back in time' and 'a true heritage experience'. Also promoted in the brochure is the monthly Saturday night 'Silver Streak Champagne Service', where would-be riders are encouraged to 'experience the red carpet treatment onboard the premium food and wine train', where a 'regionally inspired seasonal grazing menu' can be enjoyed. The experience is promoted as 'the perfect way to wrap up your day in the Spa Country'. A separate brochure promotes 'The Silver Streak Champagne Train' as 'a top of the range experience', while the DSCR website encourages prospective diners to 'indulge in a pre-dinner warm fuzzy glow' while being entertained by a local music band, The Travelling Concessions.

The organisation's brochure cleverly promotes the regular Sunday train service, the monthly Saturday evening food-and-wine service, the opportunity to charter the train for special events and the Sunday Market; importantly, it also takes the opportunity to recruit new volunteers. The reader of the brochure is told that 'Volunteers are the lifeblood of the railway; without them it wouldn't exist'. All are made to think that their potential volunteer services would be welcome, with words such as 'Whether you'd like to get your hands dirty with the track gang, join the crew running the trains, or assist in the administrative side of the railway, there is a role for you, no matter what your interest' (DSCR, 2011).

The DSCR conducts at least two 'Working Bees' every month, with track maintenance a regular focus. Volunteers are enthusiastic and dedicated to their hobby (although the devotion can easily turn into an expensive and time-consuming sideline for some). DSCR director Barry Fell explained that the voluntary organisation applied for grant money 19 times over a period of 27 years before it was successful in obtaining $80,000 from the Victorian government to build a storage facility to keep their carefully restored trains out of the weather and free from attacks by vandals (DSCR, 2010). The activity became fondly known as the Shed Project and was completed in 2010. The shed houses the majority of the DSCR's railmotor fleet.

The group's magazine for members is *The Turntable* – named after the 70-foot turntable at Daylesford station. Although the glossy colour magazine is meant to be published on a quarterly basis, in recent times it has not proved possible to do four editions in the year. This can be a relatively common situation for volunteer organisations. Nonetheless, since *The Turntable* was first published, more than 100 editions have been distributed. The format of the magazine has remained much the same for many years, with some of the standard features being: Editorial, Board of Directors, President's Report, Out on the Track, Rolling Stock Report, Volunteers, Safety Page, Grants, Trolley Branch Report, Origin of Station Names and often a final section simply headed 'Other News'.

Like any well planned tourist attraction, the DSCR features a souvenir shop; it is positioned next to the ticket booth and at the entrance of the station. The shop sells postcards, books, glasses, mugs, coasters, stubby holders, magnets, pens and other souvenirs of the heritage train experience (Figure 15.5). The purchasing of souvenirs enables the visitor to remember the service experience after it has been consumed. As discussed above, photographs taken by tourists at the site serve to capture the highlights of the occasion and constitute another way of remembering the event and sharing the experience (often via social media) with others.

Figure 15.5 Souvenirs at the Daylesford Spa Country Railway shop, reminders of the heritage experience

Rail Heritage and Tourism in Daylesford and Beyond

The heritage rail sector contributes to the Australian economy through employment, tourism expenditure and the intangible benefits of volunteering (Breydon & Doubleday, 2008: 2). In Australia this sector consists of more than 75 operators – with most being non-profit organisations that operate on weekends and public holidays. In 1901, when Australia became a federated nation rather than group of colonies, a significant legacy was that the states operated with different rail gauges. While broad (5 ft 3 in), standard (4 ft 8.5 in) and narrow (3 ft 6 in) gauge lines were in existence, standard gauge was agreed to be the uniform width to connect the large continent (Testro, 1972: 38).

The rail heritage phenomenon seen in Daylesford is one that is replicated across Australia and the rest of the world. The Australian Railway Historical Society (ARHS) was founded in 1933 and was originally known as the Australasian Railway and Locomotive Historical Society. The main aim of the ARHS is to 'record and preserve history, past and present, of Australian Railways' (Osborne, 1978: 82). Its logo features a train wheel on a track displaying the Latin motto 'Historia nostra via peregrinari ferrea', with the English translation 'For all who are interested in railways'. The ARHS has more than 2500 members and has branches in each state of Australia and the Australian Capital Territory; it operates a railway museum in Williamstown, Victoria. The star attraction of the museum is 'Heavy Harry' – the largest and heaviest steam locomotive in Australia (Carroll, 1976: 94).

The DSCR is a member of the Association of Tourist and Heritage Railways of Australia (ATHRA). Formed in 2004, the ATHRA is the national body which aims to represent the interests of the country's numerous tourist and heritage rail organisations. The Association maintains a common safety manual and examination system for members, develops codes of practice and tries to ensure that members have access to affordable public liability insurance. The group also promotes Australia's heritage train and tram journeys through its website, which has links to the various rail heritage experiences around the country. A survey in 2006 revealed that the ATHRA has 1894 volunteers and an annual turnover of $9.9 million (Breydon & Doubleday, 2008: 9). It also indicated that rail heritage volunteers are generally male and are often retired, and were likely to be former or current transport workers, or individuals with trade skills. Many of the prospective passengers who are likely to take a journey on a heritage train also fall into these categories.

Some of the many tourist railway experiences in Australia coordinated by the ATHRA include: Puffing Billy Railway (a daily service promoted as

'Australia's favourite steam train' – featured in Chapter 6 of the present volume), Victorian Goldfields Railway, Zig Zag Railway (in the Blue Mountains, west of Sydney), Bally Hooley Steam Train, Pichi Richi Railway (a significant tourist attraction in the Flinders Ranges of South Australia) and the West Coast Wilderness Railway. Great trains with commanding names such as the Indian-Pacific, the Spirit of Progress, the Southern Aurora and the Ghan have also played a key role in shaping the nation and its people. However, the real strength of the train in Australia has been in 'moving the nation's produce rather than its people' (Carroll, 1976: 7).

Conclusion

As reviewed in this chapter, the railway holds an important place in the heritage, popular culture and identity of Australia. This is reflected in the 'Spa Centre of Australia', where visitors can learn about the rail heritage by visiting the rail museum and heritage train. This chapter has revealed how Australia's intangible and tangible rail heritage is experienced and has been imagined by visitors. There are also signs that the country's rail heritage has become part of the national identity. In an age where car is king, rail heritage as experienced by the tourist has become synonymous with Australia's present-day rail industry. Heritage rail helps put a human face on the sector. The heritage train journey can bring an enormous amount of nostalgia for adults and represents a novel experience for children. The moment is often savoured by purchasing a souvenir or taking photographs.

Despite numerous management and operational challenges, the fact that the DSCR is still operating – with the support of occasional hard-won government grants, some local shire support, business donations, member subscriptions and the tireless work of dedicated volunteers – is evidence that a core group of people value the rail heritage of Daylesford. Rail heritage, although recognised as part of national identity in Australia, is thus both historic and contemporary, integrated into the tourism gaze not only through heritage-related tourism but also through the visitors' overall experience of the region.

References

Breydon, G. and Doubleday, W. (2008) *Profile of the Tourist and Heritage Railway and Tramway Sector in Australia*. Background briefing paper for Australian and state government originations' staff and consultants. Port Adelaide: Association of Tourist and Heritage Rail Australia.

Burnley, I. and Murphy, P. (2004) *Sea Change: Movement from Metropolitan to Arcadian Australia*. Sydney: University of New South Wales Press.

Carroll, B. (1976) *Australia's Railway Days: Milestones in Railway History*. South Melbourne: Macmillan.

Davidson, J. and Spearritt, P. (2000) *Holiday Business: Tourism in Australia since 1870*. Melbourne: Miegunyah Press.

Daylesford and Macedon Ranges Tourism (2011) *Daylesford and the Macedon Ranges Official Visitor Guide*. Daylesford: Designscope.

DSCR (2010) Trains to get a new home at Daylesford. At http://www.dscr.com.au/newsDetail.php?id=2&year=2010 (accessed January 2014).

DSCR (2011) *Daylesford Spa Country Railway: Heritage Train Rides*. Brochure. Dayleford: DSCR Marketing.

Gammon, S. (2007) Introduction: Sport, heritage and the English. An opportunity missed? In S. Gammon and G. Ramshaw (eds) *Heritage, Sport and Tourism: Sporting Pasts – Tourist Futures* (pp. 1–8). London: Routledge.

Gervasoni, C. (2005) *Bullboar, Macaroni and Mineral Water: Spa Country's Swiss Italian History*. Hepburn Springs: Hepburn Springs Swiss Italian Festa Inc.

Morgan, N., Pritchard, A. and Pride, R. (2004) *Destination Branding: Creating the Unique Destination Proposition*. Oxford: Elsevier.

Osborne, M. (1978) *Timber, Spuds and Spa: A Descriptive History and Lineside Guide of the Railways in the Daylesford District, 1880–1993*. Melbourne: Australian Railway Historical Society (Victorian Division).

Pretes, M. (2003) Tourism and nationalism. *Annals of Tourism Research* 30 (1), 125–142.

Rojek, C. (1997) Indexing, dragging, and social construction. In C. Rojek and J. Urry (eds) *Touring Cultures: Transformations of Travel and Theory* (pp. 52–74). London: Routledge.

Smith, L. (2006) *The Uses of Heritage*. London: Routlege.

Smitz, P., Ashworth, S., and Bain, C. (2004) *Australia* (12th edition). Footscray: Lonely Planet Publications.

Spearritt, P. and Walker, D. (eds) (1979) *Australian Popular Culture*. Sydney: George Allen and Unwin.

Testro, R. (1972) *Australian Trains and Railways*. Melbourne: Lansdowne Press.

Waterton, E. (2010) *Politics, Policy and the Discourses of Heritage in Britain*. Basingstoke: Palgrave Macmillan.

16 The Future of the Yunnan–Vietnam Railway: A Political Economic Perspective

Libo Yan and Xingcheng Zhuang

Introduction

The Yunnan–Vietnam Railway (YVR) celebrated its 100th birthday in 2010, but the French-built railroad is now facing uncertain future. In mass media and scholarly articles have discussed controversies about its future. Some would say the railway has come to the end of its life due to its low freight efficiency relative to that of its highway counterpart. In addition, the Trans-Asian Railway's Yunnan section is under construction, and its east line was due to be completed in 2014. In south-east Yunnan the newly built railway is undoubtedly an efficient substitute for the old one. Despite the negative opinions about the future of the YVR, others would suggest that it has significant value in understanding the history of Yunnan: its early life related to the French exploitation together with its socio-cultural influence on the area, its subsequent contribution to Yunnan's economic development, its significance to the victory of the war against the Anti-Japanese War (1937–45), as well as its role in economic interactions between China and Vietnam. It also had important meanings to the ethnic communities along the line. Accordingly, it should be preserved and developed as a cultural tourism resource. And given that the YVR is at a critical point in its history, it should seek to become a Word Heritage site.

Despite the enthusiasm of scholars, experts, fans and locals, the railway, like its heritage, has been quietly left to itself to decay, except for several major sites on the list of national and provincial heritage lists. To a large extent, there is still no official policy regarding a heritage railway: its conservation and preservation, its governance and sustainable management, not to mention its potential in terms of tourist use. This case study aims to examine the cause of the situation in which the YVR now finds itself, through an exploration of the conflicting ideologies, the application for

World Heritage status, different understandings of its value and potential, as well as development strategies.

Past and Present

The railway is 854 km long, built on Yunnan and Vietnam's formidable terrain. Its Yunnan section is 465 km and the Vietnam section 389 km. The former winds its way from Kunming, the provincial seat of Yunnan, to Hekou, the border city adjacent to Vietnam (see Figure 16.1). The

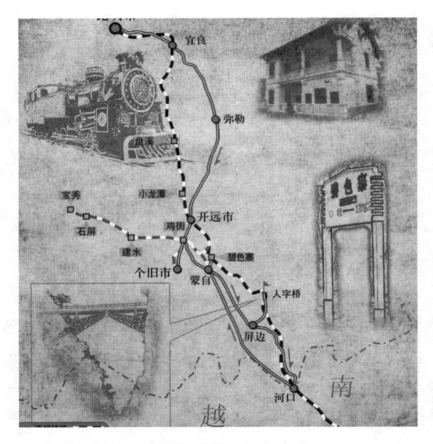

Figure 16.1 Map of the Yunnan–Vietnam Railway
Source: Gao (2011)

construction of the Vietnam section was begun in 1901 and completed in 1903, while the Yunnan section was built from 1903 to 1910 (Zhuang, 1992). Construction of the Yunnan section employed over 60,000 laborers in extreme conditions, who managed to build 425 bridges crossing deep valleys and 155 tunnels (these account for 36% of the total length of this section). Apart from Chinese laborers, more than 3000 foreign engineers, technicians and contractors were involved in the construction. They were French, American, British, Italian and Canadian. It was one of the most magnificent projects in the history of railroad construction. The railway represents the highest level of engineering technology in the early 20th century, with 80% of its length traversing precipitous mountains.

Apart from its technological significance, the railroad had a deep influence on the socio-economic development of Yunnan, both the cities and the rural communities along the line. The following quotation describes the economic and cultural impacts of the railroad, offering a glimpse into the old Kunming and its changes, beginning with the operation of the railroad:

> It was an epoch-making revolution for ancient, mysterious Yunnan to accept this European culture and new technology that was so completely different from Chinese tradition ... the steam engine drew remote Yunnan closer to the world at one fell swoop. And from this point on, tranquil Kunming became a city on the international traffic arteries; advanced French steam trains would shuttle day and night between Hekou and Kunming, carrying Michelin rubber tires and passenger carriages. The trains brought various Western goods to the people of southern Yunnan, and filled the commodity markets of Kunming. Well-off families adopted pocket watches and irons; women took to wearing nylon stockings and French bread appeared on the dinner tables; later, in towns along the railroad, black, bitter-tasting coffee became the drink of choice for the elderly when they were chatting....In 1918, Kunming introduced technology and equipment from France to build waterworks, making it the first city in China to have tap water. In 1923, telegraph and telephone networks were established in Kunming.... At the same time, the Yunnan–Vietnam Railroad also brought French-style architecture, culture, religion and arts to cities along its route. (InKunming, 2011)

According to Zhuang (1996), after the outbreak of the war against the Japanese, the railway was predominantly used to transport military supplies and played a significant role in the war. In 1940, to prevent a Japanese invasion from Vietnam, the Hekou Bridge connecting Hekou and Vietnam was destroyed, and some parts of the railway's Yunnan section were dismantled. In 1946, China regained the sovereignty and management of the section after negotiations with France. In 1957, eight years after the foundation of the People's Republic of China, the railway's Yunnan section was renamed the Kunhe Railway and operated again. In 1965, commercial communication between China and Vietnam was interrupted as northern Vietnam was frequently bombed by US warplanes. The railway played its part in transporting various goods to support Vietnam in its war against America. In the late 1970s, with the deterioration of the relationship between Vietnam and China, the line again stopped working. The Vietnamese section was in part destroyed while the Yunnan section kept running except for the part from Hekou to Mengzi. In the late 1980s, with the relationship between the two countries improving, the railway operated again, and played a significant part in Yunnan's international trade.

Despite the grandeur in its past, the aging railway is now facing an awkward reality:

> Passenger operations ended in 2003, and freight operations will be phased out over the next few years. Old, French-style stations have been converted into houses by rural residents, and villages that used to be connected via a short train ride are now veiled in isolation. Merchants, who once used the train to sell their wares in different villages, now trudge alongside the old train tracks, bringing along their merchandise. (China Radio International's English Service, 2011)

The above is quoted from a post reporting a French photographer's fieldwork along the old railway. The post further explains the photographer's visual presentation of the railway and its relationship to the life of people living along the line:

> Her photos show the aging railroad against Yunnan's breathtaking countryside and the old, abandoned stations constructed in French style of architecture, but she also captures life around the railroad. Two of her most interesting photos show the modern role of an old station as a villager's house. Laundry now hangs outside the yellow-painted station, and ticket windows inside the building help to serve as shelves. Other photos capture villagers trekking alongside the railroad, lacking any alternative transportation, and children playing in surrounding towns. Her collection succeeds in capturing a segment of Yunnan's civilization that developed and flourished around the railroad, but is now all but forgotten as their lifeline nears its end. (China Radio International's English Service, 2011)

In short, the railway is of historical significance in three important respects (Lee, 2003): its contribution to the victory in the war against Japanese in the 1940s; the death toll of Chinese workers during the process of construction; and the engineering achievements which the line represents. In addition, its heritage value relates to the part it played in the cultural relationship between Yunnan and France, and its impact on the communities along the line.

Conservation and Preservation

Since the late 20th century the rapid development of transportation has left many of the railways constructed over 100 years ago largely redundant as transport lines. Some of them are abandoned, while some others have become a form of transport heritage (Halsall, 2001). The legacy left by generations before us is now understood as railway heritage:

> the rich treasuries of railway archives, buildings such as railway stations and engine sheds and railway works, lesser structures such as signal boxes, technical equipment of many kinds … major structures in the landscape such as bridges and viaducts, and minor artifacts that nevertheless convey the local distinctiveness of the various companies, such as clocks, benches and other furniture. (Burman, 1997: 19)

This quotation indicates that railway heritage refers to a series of interrelated items, not limited to locomotives and tracks. And the mention of 'railway archives' suggests that besides the material elements, the railway heritage includes cultural elements. The concept of railway heritage embraces both tangible and intangible aspects. Accordingly, while most scholars focus on the tangible assets of the YVR's heritage, others stress the importance of the intangible assets, such as oral histories, including various stories, anecdotes, folk tales and articles (Hu, 2010).

'Cultural routes' as a concept emerged in the mid-1990s, reflecting an expanded interest in heritage conservation 'from a concern with individual monuments to broad landscapes' (He, 2008: i). As defined by the International Committee on Cultural Routes (CIIC) of the International Council on Monuments and Sites (ICOMOS), the concept refers to:

> a land, water, mixed or other type of route, which is physically determined and characterized by having its own specific and historic dynamics and functionality; showing interactive movements of people as well as multi-dimensional, continuous and reciprocal exchanges of goods, ideas, knowledge and values within or between countries and

regions over significant periods of time; and thereby generating a cross-fertilization of the cultures in space and time, which is reflected both in its tangible and intangible heritage. (CIIC of ICOMOS, 2003, cited in He, 2008: 2)

As suggested by this definition, there are various forms of transport heritage, such as canals, roads and railways (Wang & Zhao, n.d.). The YVR falls into the category of cultural route, which is in part similar to the situation of two railways already inscribed on the World Heritage list, namely the Semmering Railway in Austria and the Darjeeling Himalayan Railway in India. There are many types of cultural routes (Chairatudomkul, 2008: 17–18). The route in question is related to aggression and imperialism, exchange between different peoples, trade activities and special moments in history. It is also a route associated with historically important people.

Among the major reasons for heritage conservation and preservation in Western societies are national pride and nostalgia, economics, aesthetic and artistic value, and the fear of rapid modernization (Timothy & Boyd, 2006). To a large extent, they also apply to the situation of the YVR.

First, it has many characteristics that distinguish it from other railways in China. It was a railway connecting Yunnan to a foreign country rather than to a neighboring province. In addition, the symbol of the railway, the Inverted 'V' Bridge, became a legend for its engineering design and endurance. France built the railway to bring Yunnan under control and to obtain economic benefit mainly through opening mines in the region. Trading ports were opened up in Mengzi, Hekou and Kunming after the Opium War. Mengzi possessed the first customhouse in Yunnan, and located 10 km from Mengzi, Bisezhai, the former top-grade station on the YVR, became a prosperous town that saw the convergence of businessmen from different countries.

Second, the YVR was related to many historical events, such as the 1908 Hekou uprising indirectly led by Sun Yatsen, and the basis for the insurgence was the presence of the large number of laborers constructing the railway (Zhao, 2009). Since the YVR began operation in 1910, the railway has been closely related to historic events. Its role during the war against the Japanese is a good example, through its transfer of university students and professors, as well as its transportation of goods and supplies supporting the Chinese army:

During the Anti-Japanese War, Yunnan acted as the rear area, and many factories, schools and universities from both inland and coastland were moved to Yunnan....

Kunming became an important industrial area and the center of education in China during the Anti-Japanese War.... The Kunming Vietnam Railway, the Kunming Burma Road, China India Road and the Tuofeng Airline were the only ways to the outside world. Yunnan therefore was called the Lifeline of the Anti-Japanese War. (China Discover, n.d.)

Among the professors and students moved to Yunnan were those of the Southwest Union Universities, who sojourned in Mengzi for one year and then moved to Kunming. Their stay in Yunnan left many relics. The historic events associated with the railway become a collective memory of the Yunnanese, especially those living in Kunming City and Honghe Prefecture. These collective memories stimulate the sense of place identity, pride of place, as well as the concerns with preservation and conservation (see Yu, 1992).

Third, economic considerations are also an important reason for the conservation and preservation of the YVR. The railway played a significant role in the social and economic development of the communities along the route (Wang & Wang, 2007). The route connected numerous villages, towns and cities. During its operation, many ethnic communities had convenient access to the traffic. People sold fruits and produce at the railway stations, whether to businessmen or to passengers. Each time the train came, the stations became a living market. However, when the trains stopped running, residents in these communities, without alternative transportation, had to walk several miles to the highway and they lost their customers, the train passengers. Under this circumstance, the economy and mobility of ethnic communities along the route become a concern in considering the conservation and preservation of the railway.

Fourth, the aesthetic value of the railway's heritage has been recognized in recent years. Fan (2008) conducted a masters study on the landscape of the railway and produced an overall evaluation of the railway as a tourism resources. The study points out there are four types of resources with tourism potential: stations, engineering accomplishments, nature tourism resources and historical or 'red' tourism resources. There are 34 stations on the Yunnan section and an additional 20 stations on its branch line, the Gebishi line. Stations along the route present the French culture and can thus be regarded as an important resource. Typical stations such as Yiliang, Bisezhai and Jijie are well preserved today and available for touristic use. Engineering achievements are always regarded as an important aspect of heritage value. In certain regards, this can be related to the aesthetic value of the railway, especially the Inverted 'V' Bridge. The construction of the railway was an excellent example of problem-solving: how can a railway climb mountains? The route was chosen to follow the valleys, and the line is parallel to three water courses: Nanpang, Nanxi and Honghe Rivers. For this reason, the railroad traverses gorgeous, diverse landscapes. The 'red' tourism resources refer to the fact that many historic events as well as figures were closely related to the YVR, as discussed above, and this association might also have tourism potential.

Fifth, while the Vietnam section is still in use, its Chinese counterpart has stopped operation. The difference lies in the different stages of moderniz-ation of the two countries. There is a fear that rapid modernization will lead to the neglect of the heritage value of the YVR, especially in light of the operation of the Yunnan section of Trans-Asian railway scheduled for 2014.

Having considered the conceptual issues and the justification for the conservation and preservation of YVR, the author would like to turn to the protection of the heritage route under discussion. As mentioned above, there are more than 50 stations scattered along the route and its branch line, but only a few of these are protected. However, as a heritage route, the value of the historic railway cannot be represented by merely a small part of it. As pointed out by Conti, 'The concept of cultural route implies a value as a whole which is greater than the sum of its parts and gives the route its meaning' (cited in Orbaşli & Woodward, 2008: 166–167). That is, only as an integrated entity can the heritage route make sense. This leads to the conclusion that it is unreasonable for parts of the railway to be selectively conserved. To protect the railway heritage as a whole, two issues should be addressed: first, resolution of the ideological conflicts; and second, the establishment of related laws, regulations and policies.

The railway was a product of colonialism. Its early history was closely related to France's control and exploitation of Yunnan. The past con-nection with colonialism continuously stirs up a mix of patriotism and anti-imperialism in the minds of some Chinese people. According to the stereotype, the historic railway was an everlasting symbol of shame for being invaded, oppressed and exploited; and more than 10,000 lives were lost in its construction (see Ding, 1982; Long & Long, 1990; Luo, 2010; Miao, 1986; Zhao, 2011). While that sort of thinking still has a certain purchase, there is an increasing voice for an objective understanding or evaluation of the historical sense of the railway. Some scholars note that the railway's sover-eignty and management were retrieved three years before the foundation of the Peoples' Republic of China, and thereafter the railway largely served the economic development of Yunnan province until the turn of the 21st century. Realizing this, scholars of the second category would like to rectify the overemphasis of the early part of the railway's history, and advocate a balance in understanding the railway's dual meanings to the Chinese, and the Yunnanese in particular (e.g. Peng, 2008; Wang & Wang, 2010). They would like to explore the other side of the railway's meanings to Yunnan, such as its influence on:

- the cultural relationship between France and China (Zhang, 2003);
- social values (Che, 2007);
- cultural assets and heritage (Liu, 2006);
- ethnic communities (Wang & Wang, 2007; Yang & Li, 2011);
- socio-economic development (Zhuang, 1992, 1996);
- industrial development (Che, 2010; Wang & Fan, 2010).

Now it is necessary for an objective, not emotional, understanding of the colony culture brought by the French-built railway; it is time to offer the railway a fair evaluation (Peng, 2008; Wang & Zhao, n.d.). To enhance the awareness of the cultural asset as well as its conservation, it has been suggested that schools and institutions of tertiary education be asked to include the YVR in their syllabuses, or even required to do so, through official regulation. Indeed, while considerable analysis of the value of the railway provides an intellectual basis for its protection, in reality it is likely to be necessary to enact and implement laws, policies and regulations for its conservation. The reasons for calling for legislative intervention fall into two categories: first, heritage management could otherwise encounter the problem of lacking coordinated policies to protect the cultural asset as a whole; second, heritage usually resides in diverse settings, and different locations could have different priorities and management practices (Orbaşli & Woodward, 2008). The latter even troubles the water. Extending in the mountains for several hundred kilometers, segments of the old railway is vulnerable to destruction by villagers, conscious or unconscious. Facing these complexities, the protection work needs to be facilitated by a law specially made for railway heritage. An integrated law will contribute to effective protection of the cultural asset (Wang & Zhao, n.d.). Besides its coordinating role, a law would also keep the asset from inappropriate uses that would have a destructive effect on the historical landscape. It is also anticipated that a law would protect each part of the heritage line: with a designated institution or organization; with a protection area, and a buffer area where construction can be under strict control; with on-site signs; and with archives. The law would also help solve the problem of unclear ownership and responsibility at certain points where the line between adjacent administrative areas is unclear.

Comprehensive conservation should consider the development of rural communities along the route. In other words, communities within the buffer zone should be integrated into the conservation framework, as emphasized in a project focusing on the sustainable development of Darjeeling Himalayan Railway in India (Galla, 2005). Community participation is an important factor in the conservation of railway heritage. In his blog where many opinions reported in the mass media are aggregated, the social scientist Yang Fuquan points out that the conservation of the railway should be combined with the preservation of the associated folklore, as well as the cultural and natural landscapes, of communities which had been connected by the railway (Yang, 2010). Echoing Yang, a French diplomat notes that the heritage railway can be used to facilitate the development of an 'en route' community. Community-based tourism can increase the income of locals, thus keeping younger residents in the villages. It will be helpful for female employment and promote traditional handicrafts. Based on the heritage railway, rural tourism development can help to protect that heritage. Yang believes that the increased income from the heritage would give the locals a sense of dependence and help them to appreciate their heritage. Accordingly, they will protect the heritage, if only to maintain their livelihoods. There is still another reason for integrating community development into the conservation of heritage: the history and culture of the YVR was formed in the interaction between the railway and residents along the route.

The current focus is on just a few notable parts of the railway, such as the Inverted 'V' Bridge, Bisezhai station, Jijie station and Yiliang station, which are relatively well protected. But good conservation demands an impartial understanding of the railway's past and value, a holistic picture of the line's heritage, and the enacting and implementing of laws and regulations. While these considerations focus on on-site protection, some off-site work has been conducted. The latter type of conservation work refers to the development of a museum. At present, the Yunnan Railway Museum, located at the starting point of the railway's Yunnan section, Kunming North Railway Station, is devoted to the conservation of diverse articles and objects related to the YVR. It is one of the four earliest railway museums in China, which were all built in the first decade of the 21st century. With a floor area of 3176 m², the museum has a collection of approximately 10,000 pieces, from pictorial and written materials, such as historic pictures, relics, documents and archives, to objects such as locomotives and carriages. As the major location of the railway, Honghe Prefecture also contributes to conservation through a museum. A hall exhibiting collections related to the YVR can be found in the Museum of Honghe. Apart from governmental efforts, there are also some private initiatives in terms of collecting various objects related to the railway's heritage. Typical among them is the collection of a railway policeman, Huang Qing, whose interest in conserving articles relating to the railway started at the mid-1980s. In his collection are various old telephones that had been used on the railway route, tickets from 90 years ago, hurricane lamps, railway sleepers and deserted gauges.

Different from the situation in Western countries, where heritage railway conservation associations have been established, China still lacks such institutions. Certain associations, such as the Yunnan Dian–Vietnam Railroad Research Institute, located at Mengzi, and a similar one associated with Kunming Railway Bureau, have been founded but their major concern is not conservation and preservation. The former appear to be a government consultancy for the cultural and economic exploitation of the heritage railway; its mission does not highlight conservation.

Application for World Heritage Status

While on-site and off-site conservation and preservation as well as related laws and regulations significantly contribute to heritage protection, some scholars note that the best protection method is to have the site attain UNESCO World Heritage status. As stated above, the YVR is usually compared with two heritage railways that already have attained the designation, namely the Darjeeling Himalayan and the Semmering Railways. China has other railways which can be regarded as heritage sites, such as the Beijing–Kalgan Railway, built by Chinese engineers in 1909, and the Chongqing–Kunming line, built in the 1960s, during the Cultural Revolution. But the first was rebuilt and the second built to advance the revolution; accordingly, they are secondary to the YVR in terms of their prospects of achieving World Heritage status (Lee, 2003).

Twenty years ago, applying for UNESCO World Heritage designation was aimed mainly at the preservation and protection of heritage sites. More recently, socio-economic considerations have entered into play (VanBlarcom & Kayahan, 2011). Some potential sites would like to use World Heritage status as a marketing tool to boost tourism development. This applies to of the YVR. As the major location of the railway, the Honghe Prefecture government is the major power supporting the application. The provincial government had already successfully achieved World Heritage status for several sites and developed the surrounding area: in the south-west is Xishuangbanna, a destination popular with tourists for its rainforest and the ethnic culture of the Dai people; in the north-west is Dali, with the Bai ethnic culture and the ancient town of Lijiang (of Naxi ethnic culture); and Shangri-La, with its Tibetan ethnic culture. Furthermore, between the provincial capital, Kunming, and Honghe Prefecture is Shilin, popular for its Geopark and its Yi ethnic culture.

The situation in Honghe is quite different. Its eagerness to achieve World Heritage status for the YVR can be understood from two perspectives: in comparison with other destinations in Yunnan, and its own ethnic makeup. As described above, it is adjacent to many well known destinations in the territory. In addition, Honghe has a well preserved majority ethnic Han culture and, as a result, is perceived to be at less risk from a cultural perspective. In contrast to the popular destinations mentioned above, Honghe has received far fewer tourists, both international and domestic. Facing the situation that the Han culture (in the ancient town of Jianshui and elsewhere) cannot win a desirable marketshare, the local government began to adopt alternative strategies for tourism development. This can be seen in its early efforts to promote the Hani ethnic culture (the Honghe Hani Rice Terraces were inscribed on the World Heritage List in 2013) and recently in the pursuit of World Heritage status for the YVR. Provided the latter effort is successful, the designation would be a catalyst for local economic development.

However, it is possible to overestimate the economic benefits that might be brought about by World Heritage status. As noted by VanBlarcom and Kayahan (2011), there is a myth that that status necessarily means more tourist arrivals. Furthermore, in a sense, merely regarding the railway as a tourism resource would ultimately spoil it (Dilemma, 2010). The intangible elements of the heritage route deserve serious attention. The railway means a lot to the communities along the route. What the railway brought were not only goods and commodities, but their livelihoods as well as a culture that had a significant effect on them.

Ironically, while high expectation of economic benefit has been expressed through the mass media, the cost of obtaining World Heritage status is seldom carefully examined. As observed by VanBlarcom and Kayahan (2011), with the increasing level of competition, the bidding costs tend to soar. They offer a case from China where a county spent more than ¥1 billion (approximately US$170 million) to have its site inscribed on the World Heritage list. Besides expenditure in the bidding process, the costs also cover the investment for meeting the 'UNESCO requirements such as monitoring, periodic reporting and maintenance of the sites' (VanBlarcom & Kayahan, 2011: 147). Furthermore, the costs before and after obtaining designation are difficult to estimate, since they are site specific. Nevertheless, the components of costs should be carefully considered before making the decision to apply.

The application itself can be time-consuming, but the conservation work cannot wait. Accordingly, some experts and scholars would like to suggest that protecting the railway from natural and human destruction should be the prime concern. Furthermore, a successful application may further conservation of the YVR, but alternative arrangements should also be considered in the event that an application is not successful.

The mainstream, represented by most of the Chinese governmental officials and scholars, tends to be enthusiastic in terms of World Heritage application. Indeed, it is difficult to find different opinions expressed in academic journals. Nonetheless, there are different viewpoints. An interesting discussion has taken place on the website of the social scientist Yang Fuquan. In response to the host's emphatic point that, in the Chinese context, World Heritage application is a justification of heritage conservation, a visitor warns that it should never be forgotten that the railway was initially accompanied by exploitation and oppression (referring to the semi-colonial past), as well as death (referring to thousands of lives sacrificed during the seven-year-long construction). While admitting the railway had much history and should be protected, the visitor argues that the attempt to designate it a World Heritage site is inappropriate, since such a label means forgetting elements of the past. And he/she worries about that while, theoretically, becoming a World Heritage site can facilitate protection, in reality such sites might see no essential action in conservation, as illustrated by the World Heritage Commission's warning to the ancient town of Lijiang. Echoing these ideas, a post on the website states that it is unbelievable to say World Heritage application will facilitate conservation (Label of the YVR, 2011). While supporting the application, the post points out that it is important to seriously consider what label should be chosen for the heritage site. Considering the colonial past and the nightmare of construction, he/she thinks that it is a railway of blood, rather than a railway of culture. Accordingly, it is inappropriate to name it as a cultural route; instead, it should apply in the name of suffering culture.

Today, the YVR is in the process of being labeled as a heritage site (Li & Peng, 2009), which is affected by different powers and stakeholders, including governments, investors and scholars. Under this circumstance, the provincial government's overall development planning of the cultural asset turns out to be a negotiation or comprise among these powers. Accordingly, the future of the railway is still uncertain, and its heritage is facing different possibilities in terms of its future use.

Tourism Development

While sites of heritage value should be conserved for the benefit of future generations, their contemporary use should not be neglected or rejected. According to a study by Garrod and Fyall (2000), the mission of heritage protection covers dimensions such as conservation, accessibility, education, relevance and recreation. In a sense, while the first dimension is more concerned with the benefit of future generations, the latter four are related to contemporary use of heritage sites. People should have access to the heritage area, and have some individual, recreational experiences there. Further, the heritage asset should be well interpreted to enhance tourists' understanding of its significance, or its cultural value to the present and future societies. And the presentation and interpretation of the site should help the visitors understand the linkage between the heritage and themselves, the locals and the nation, as well as the linkage between the heritage and the place. All of these aspects contribute to making a public site accessible for the majority rather than a minority. And more importantly, efforts in these directions, as Garrod and Fyall point out, help in the sustainable development of a site.

To varying degrees, historic railways have been developed as tourist attractions around the world. Leading this tide is the UK, followed by India. And 'a growth in reviving steam and historic railways and museums can also be seen in the United States, China, Japan, the Middle East, and in a number of African countries' (Orbaşli & Woodward, 2008: 168). If used as tourism assets, historic railways can offer experiences such as rides on an old train or a journey on a heritage route, appreciation of stations, which are interpreted to facilitate tourists' understanding, as well as railway museum visitation (Orbaşli & Woodward, 2008). Further, the cultural and natural landscapes along the route can enrich tourists' experiences.

The YVR faces a specific problem, namely the competing ideas and proposals from different sectors and places along the line for the use of the asset. Different powers are involved in considering the conservation and development of the heritage asset, and different sectors and different places produce different proposals (Keeping Operation, n.d.). The situation can be glimpsed in the case of the small part of the railway traversing the urban area of Kunming. For a long time there had been disputes about its development. While the railway bureau insisted on its operation, the municipal government emphasized its conservation. Recently, an agreement has been reached, and both sides have agreed to its protective development, that is, its transformation into a sightseeing route.

The local government is not waiting for World Heritage status before developing the railway. With the major part of the railway in its territory, the Honghe Prefecture has already begun to develop some heritage sites related to the railway for tourism purposes. Currently, there are two major ongoing projects in three counties of the prefecture. The first is the development of Bisezhai (see Figure 16.2) into an exotic French town (Bisezhai

Figure 16.2 Bisezhai Station
Source: Honghe website at http://www.hh.cn

Project, 2010). The construction area is 1362 hectares; the estimated investment is ¥300 million, approximately US$46 million. At present the 10 km
road connecting the railway station at Bisezhai and the current prefecture
seat, Mengzi, has been paved. It is noted that the construction is based on
the development plan, but the project's objectives need to be re-examined.
As the project signpost says, the economic potential of the project arises
because the local area, a city group consisting of Gejiu, Kaiyuan and Mengzi,
has a relatively well developed economy and thus the city residents have a
certain capacity for the consumption of tourist experiences. In other words,
the target market is locals rather than visitors. It is a somewhat doubtful
market positioning. As an important part of the YVR heritage, the relic
of the old station has a certain degree of potential in both domestic and
overseas markets. With such a potential, it appears unreasonable to develop
the site for merely local recreation.

    The second project refers to the building of a resort at the Inverted 'V'
Bridge (see Figure 16.3) (Inverted 'V' Bridge, 2010). As one of the miracles
of railway bridge construction in the 20th century, the bridge is the symbol
of the YVR. Since 2006 it has been included in the national heritage list.
The bridge, 100 m above the valley, together with the mountain setting,
has a sense of the sublime. Many people would like to visit the bridge but
cannot due to the poor condition of the road. Under this circumstance and
in the context of the booming economy of Yunnan, the Pingbian County
government is attempting to develop the historic site into a high-level
scenic area. Apart from the rail infrastructure, the project involves in a

Figure 16.3 The Inverted 'V' Bridge
Source: Honghe website at http://www.hh.cn

series of construction projects: a French-style church; a French-style hostel; wall displays on the history of the railway bridge; a statue of the designer of the Inverted 'V' Bridge; a rebuilt a Miao ethnic village; an area for performance and exhibition; the governance of the river below the bridge; a history museum on the YVR (with a floor space of 1400 m²); a toy train for tourist use; re-creation of a 27 km meter-gauge railway; rolling stock; the reconstruction of four French-style stations; and a shopping street with exhibitions on the cultures of China, France and Vietnam. Unlike the first project, which focuses on the infrastructure and heritage conservation, the second project will invest more on construction, to solve the problems of accessibility, to diversify the attractions and to enrich the tourist experience.

Furthermore, the Kaiyuan (another county of Honghe) government is also taking advantage of the historic railway to develop rural tourism along the route. In the territory are several relics of the YVR: the abandoned Yulinshan Station, the Seven-Hole Bridge and the Dahua Steel Bridge. Near the Seven-Hole Bridge is Faxing village, which is one of the rural tourism sites promoted by the Kaiyuan city government. The theme of community tourism is the YVR. A folk railway museum has been founded, several French-style houses have been built and a French-style bar is operating.

Conclusion

There are different interpretations of the YVR (referring to the Yunnan section): as a scar on the land for its colonial past, as a lifeline during the war against Japanese invasion; as a stimulator and facilitator of the social culture and regional economy; and recently as a heritage site. Accordingly, the significance of the railway is interpreted either negatively or positively. The diverse interpretations play different parts in the conservation and development of the heritage.

The railway's future is still up to the negotiations between stake-holders and the application for World Heritage status. Its conservation and development still face considerable problems. Notably, although Vietnam and China will jointly apply for its World Heritage status, the railway's connection with Vietnam is seldom studied. Despite the eagerness of the World Heritage application, the economic and temporal costs are seldom carefully estimated or examined. This applies to the criteria of the World Heritage Committee. Further, while the railway has always been compared with the two-meter gauge railways inscribed on the World Heritage list, the foreign experience in terms of conservation is seldom borrowed. At the theoretical level, all agree with the conservation of the historic railway; however, there are controversies in terms of how to conduct the protection work. Some insist on a holistic approach, while others propose selective conservation. And it appears that much of the conservation work will depend on the result of applying for World Heritage status – although in fact the conservation work cannot afford further delay.

In addition, the foundation for conservation appears to depend on the genuine understanding of the significance of the railway or the ideologies of the governmental officials, as suggested by a railway enthusiast's travelogue reporting a visit to the 100-year-old Bisezhai station:

> There was no suspense in our mind when we were approaching Bisezhai. We regarded it as an old friend. We had already been very familiar with it before visiting, since the old station had been shot by considerable photographers, reported by considerable newsmen, and identified as cultural assets under government protection. However, at the entrance we sadly found that the track-switching equipment and a part of the

rails had been dismantled; the characters of the station's name were faded to a blur... All of these mean that it had already stepped down the historic stage as a station. We still could not believe the fact before our eyes: the well known, historic railway station was not treated as it deserved to be. Despite a signpost stating that a major cultural asset stood there, the old station received no repair and maintenance. Without an interpretation system, nor guardians, it looked like a deserted child, exposed to the rain and wind.... Ironically enough, the 'major cultural asset' signpost itself had become a relic, with its Chinese characters now difficult to read.... We were leaving for Mengzi [the seat of Honghe Hani and Yi Autonomous Prefecture], and then could visit the large modern building complex [the prefecture government office building] which has a nickname, 'The Palace of Hani' [Hani, one of the major ethnic groups in the territory, as the full name of the prefecture suggests]. I could not help thinking: maybe the cost of one of the lawns encompassing the building complex is enough for the conservation of the provincial-level cultural asset. (Bisezhai, 2011; author's translation)

References

Bisezhai (2011) Bisezhai: Along the 100-year-old railway. At http://qcyn.sina.com.cn/travel/sdy/2011/0617/10032840906_4.html (accessed 2 November 2011).

Bisezhai Project (2010) The Bisezhai Project. At http://www.hhzly.cn/P1013/ShowArticle.asp?ArticleID=1603 (accessed 17 July 2011).

Burman, P. (1997) Philosophies for conserving the railway heritage. In P. Burman and M. Stratton (eds) *Conserving the Railway Heritage* (pp. 18–33). London: E. & F.N. Spon.

Chairatudomkul, S. (2008) *Cultural Routes as Heritage in Thailand: Case Studies of King Narai's Royal Procession Route and Buddha's Footprint Pilgrimage Route.* Bangkok: Silpakorn University.

Che, L. (2007) Yunnan–Vietnam Railway and the changes of social ideas in Yunnan from 1910 to 1949. *Journal of Yunnan Normal University (Humanities and Social Sciences)* 3, 40–44.

Che, L. (2010) The function of Yunnan–Vietnam Railway on the industrial transformations of the cities along the railway in 1910–1949. *Journal of Yunnan Agricultural University (Social Sciences)* 4 (6), 103–108.

China Discover (n.d.) Yunnan history. At http://www.chinadiscover.net/china-tour/yunnanguide/yunnan-history.htm (accessed 31 July 2011).

China Radio International's English Service (2011) Death of a railroad: Adeline Cassier documents the Yunnan-Vietnam Railroad at the end of its life. At http://english.cri.cn/6566/2011/03/10/1881s625291.htm (accessed January 2014).

Dilemma (2010) To be or not to be: The dilemma of a 100-year-old railway. At http://www.chinanews.com/cul/news/2010/04-26/2247168.shtml (accessed 18 July 2011).

Ding, S. (1982) The construction of the Yunnan–Vietnam Railway and its impact. *Yunnan Social Sciences* 3, 69–76.

Fan, Y. (2008) The landscape system of the station areas: The Dian section of the Yunnan–Vietnam Railway. Unpublished masters thesis, Kunming Polytechnic University, Kunming, China.

Galla, A. (2005) Locating tourism in sustainable heritage development: Darjeeling Himalayan Railway (DHR). *Cultura y Desarrollo* 4, 1–14.

Gao, D. (2011) Driving along the Yunnan–Vietnam Railway. At http://www.caryouyou.com/note/news//2011-06-18/148676_2.html (accessed 21 July 2011).

Garrod, B. and Fyall, A. (2000) Managing heritage tourism. *Annals of Tourism Research* 27 (3), 682–708.

Halsall, D.A. (2001) Railway heritage and the tourist gaze: Stoomtram Hoorn-Medemblik. *Journal of Transport Geography* 9 (2), 151–160.

He, J. (2008) GIS-based cultural route heritage authenticity analysis and conservation support in cost-surface and visibility study approaches. Unpublished PhD thesis, Chinese University of Hong Kong, Hong Kong.

Hu, H. (2010) The 'living fossil' of railway anticipating role transformation. *People's Daily*, 1 April.

InKunming (2011) Abroad views: The Yunnan–Vietnam Railroad. At http://in.kunming.cn/abroad-views-the-yunnan-vietnam-railroad-t457.html (accessed 20 July 2011).

Inverted 'V' Bridge (2010) The project of the inverted 'V' Bridge. At http://www.hhzly.cn/P1013/ShowArticle.asp?ArticleID=1588 (accessed 18 July 2011).

Keeping Operation (n.d.) Keeping operation is the best way of preservation. At http://society.yunnan.cn/html/2010-12/20/content_1443975.htm (accessed 8 July 2011).

Label of the YVR (2011) Which label of the Yunnan–Vietnam Railway should be used in applying for world heritage status? At http://honghezhou.551.cn/Item/27232.aspx (accessed 6 August 2011).

Lee, R. (2003) *Potential Railway World Heritage Sites in Asia and the Pacific*. York: Institute of Railway Studies, University of York.

Li, C. and Peng, Z. (2009) On the 'heritabilization' of heritages through a study of Yunnan–Vietnam Railway. *Journal of Yunnan Nationalities University (Social Sciences)* 26 (1), 29–34.

Liu, Z. (2006) Yunnan–Vietnam: A world class heritage. *National Park of China* 11, 64.

Long, Y. and Long, Y. (1990) Is it a blessing? France's construction of the Yunnan–Vietnam Railway. *Southeast Asian Studies* 3, 67–71.

Luo, Z. (2010) Yunnan–Vietnam Railway: One sleeper at the cost of one life. *Creation* 2, 107–108.

Miao, C. (1986) Imperial France and the Yunnan–Vietnam Railway. *Journal of Honghe University* 2, 28–39.

Orbaşli, A. and Woodward, S. (2008) A railway 'route' as a linear heritage attraction: The Hijaz Railway in the Kingdom of Saudi Arabia. *Journal of Heritage Tourism* 3 (3), 159–175.

Peng, X. (2008) An objective evaluation of the Yunnan–Vietnam Railway: Afterword for an edited book. *Chinese Art Digest* 4, 17–19.

Pruszenski, A. (n.d.) Yunnan–Vietnam Railway: The end of its time. At http://scenery.cultural-china.com/en/158Scenery10792.html (accessed 20 July 2011).

Timothy, D.J. and Boyd, S.W. (2006) Heritage tourism in the 21st century: Valued traditions and new perspectives. *Journal of Heritage Tourism* 1 (1), 1–16.

VanBlarcom, B.L. and Kayahan, C. (2011) Assessing the economic impact of a UNESCO World Heritage designation. *Journal of Heritage Tourism* 6 (2), 143–164.

Wang, H. and Wang, Y. (2010) Discussing the history value, protection and development of the Yunnan–Vietnam Railway. *Journal of Honghe University* 8 (5), 9–11.

Wang, Y. and Fan, D. (2010) Yunnan–Vietnam Railway and industrialization of southeast Yunnan. *Journal of Honghe University* 8 (1), 12–15.

Wang, Y. and Wang, H. (2007) The railway between Yunnan and Vietnam that brings about development and progress in Yunnan Frontier where the minority live. *Journal of Honghe University* 5 (6), 28–31.

Wang, Y. and Zhao, J. (n.d.) The employment of institution and order in protecting the Yunnan–Vietnam Raiway: A perspective from laws and regulations. At http://wangyi.blshe.com/post/1334/541870 (accessed 21 July 2011).

Yang, F. (2010) My viewpoints on the preservation and development of the Yunnan–Vietnam Railway. At http://blog.sina.com.cn/s/blog_48a464120100hlwn.html (accessed 25 July 2011).

Yang, F. and Li, N. (2011) The impact of Dianyue Railroad on the social culture of Yi People along the route. *Guizhou Ethnic Studies* 32 (2), 46–51.

Yu, J. (1992) A note of the Yunnan–Vietnam Railway: The train from year 1910. At http://blog.tianya.cn/blogger/post_show.asp?idWriter=0&Key=0&BlogID=32132&PostID=29376578 (accessed 12 July 2011).

Zhang, Y. (2003) Historical memories of the Dian-Yue Railway: Buildings in the railway community of modern times along the route. *Development of Small Cities and Towns* 4, 57–59.

Zhao, S. (2009) The potential for cultural tourism development of Yunnan–Vietnam Railway. *Market Modernization* 579, 109–110.

Zhao, X. (2011) Yunnan–Vietnam Railway and Society of Yunnan in the semi-colonial context. *Journal of Chongqing Jiaotong University (Social Sciences)* 11 (2), 93–96.

Zhuang, X. (1992) The impact of Yunnan–Vietnam Railway on Yunnan's social economy. *Journal of Mengzi Teacher College* 9 (3), 64–72.

Zhuang, X. (1996) The role of Yunnan–Vietnam Railway in the late twentieth century Yunnan's economy development. *Journal of Mengzi Teacher College* 13 (3), 21–25.

17 The St Kitts Scenic Railway: A Journey into an Island's Heritage

William Found

Introduction

'The best tour in the Caribbean', says a passenger on the promotional video for the St Kitts Scenic Railway (Murray AdVentures, 2006). 'The BEST way to see the REAL Caribbean', says the Railway's website (St Kitts Scenic Railway, 2012). While these and other quotations extol the excitement and pleasure of riding the St Kitts Scenic Railway in the kind of rhetoric common for tourist destinations, they reflect a reality that is truly remarkable. The St Kitts Scenic Railway does provide unique access to a landscape of significant cultural value and natural beauty. Despite great technical challenges, the specially constructed passenger train provides comfortable, modern transportation along a narrow-gauge track, originally constructed for agro-industrial purposes. A combination of several elements – a splendid heritage landscape; inventive technical adaptations; off-shore investment by committed owners with heritage-railway experience; excellent local management, marketing and staffing; integration with the schedules of cruise ships landing at St Kitts; integration of the railway with bus transportation; essential cooperation with local government; and a strong sense of involvement and support by the people of St Kitts – all make the St Kitts Scenic Railway a fine tourist attraction and a commercial success.

The development of the St Kitts Railway is a story of local adaptation to global change. The initial construction of the railway led to the survival of sugar-cane production throughout the 20th century and the transformed railway is now an important focus for the St Kitts tourist industry. Both versions of the railway have required imagination, resources and commitment, and both have served their purposes well. The functions of the original and the transformed railways could not be more dissimilar, but the rail bed and the route have provided the continuity for effective transformation, and for the development of one of the Caribbean's most enjoyable journeys into an island's heritage (Found, 2005).

History of the Sugar-Cane Railway

By the late 19th century the days of the classical Caribbean sugar plantation economy were numbered, and islands that hoped to maintain cane production had to modernize in order to reach the efficiencies of large-scale production. Cuba had led the way, developing huge sugar estates of many thousands of acres, very large sugar factories and the latest in sugar-milling technologies. Essential to the functioning of the Cuban production system were steam-powered railways, which connected the fields and estates to regional factories (Galloway, 1989). Rising unemployment in those Caribbean islands with conventional, small-scale production led the British government, among others, to recommend that islands either modernize their industries in radical ways or abandon sugar-cane production entirely (West India Royal Commission, 1897).

St Kitts (the popular name for the British island of St Christopher) was one of the locations considered to have potential for modernization. Although a small island in the north-east Caribbean, only 18 miles long and an average of 5 miles wide, with a population of around 30,000, authorities realized that it could be modernized through the construction of a railroad that would transport all cane to a new central factory located just outside the capital city of Basseterre (Figure 17.1). A 30-mile railway, looping around the island near the coast, and serving the 26 privately owned plantations that previously processed their cane in small, uneconomical mills and boiling houses, would link approximately 15,000 acres of cane to emulate a single, large production unit. The physical geography of the island made this arrangement feasible, as the plantations occupied virtually all of a continuous belt of fertile land, stretching from the lower reaches of the mountainous interior to the coast. In short, the physical configuration of the island and its plantation landscape facilitated modernization, which allowed a small, disaggregated production base to attain economies of scale through the integration provided by the railway and a modern sugar factory.

Construction of the railway began in 1910, with a one-mile segment connecting the site for the new sugar factory to a port location at the eastern end of Basseterre Bay (Rollinson, 2001) (Figure 17.1). The first segments of the line were used to transport the heavy equipment required to build more of the railway and the factory. After the factory opened in 1912, raw sugar was transported along the route to the bulk storage facility at the port, awaiting export. Similarly, molasses was transported in tank cars. Rail lines

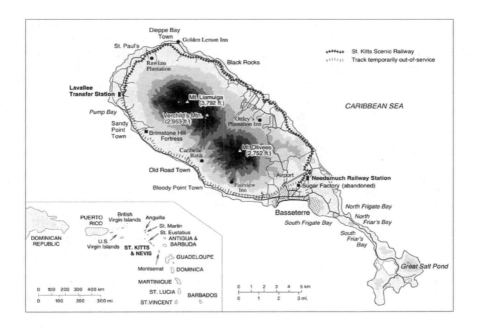

Figure 17.1 Map of St Kitts, showing the route of the St Kitts Scenic Railway
Source: Cartographic Unit, Department of Geography, York University

stretched in both directions from the sugar factory, gradually reaching more and more plantations to the north-east and the south-west. The complete route, circling the large, northern part of the island, was finished in 1926.

The single-track railway was of light construction and narrow gauge (30 inches), appropriate for the transport of small railway cars that each held three tons of cane. The original 30-pound rail sections were attached to two-inch steel trough sleepers about two feet apart (Dyde, 2008), laid directly on the road-bed, without ballast. Despite efforts to maintain minimum gradients and to avoid tight curves, some gradients reached 5%, and some curves greatly exceeded targeted standards. Twenty-six bridges spanned the ghuts (river beds, dry except during rain storms), the longest being 360 feet. Overcoming significant topographic challenges, the 16-year construction project produced a light railway that served its specific purpose well.

In addition to the marshalling yard at the factory, the line included passing loops and 12 sidings/transfer points (about 2.5 miles apart), where cane carts from plantations were unloaded and the cane was transferred into open railway cars. Coordinating railway traffic during the crop season (February to July) was a logistical challenge, as the sugar factory ran most efficiently with a continuous inflow of 900 wagon loads of cane per day. The transportation of cane was complex, involving two-way traffic along a single track, divided into regional segments (see Horsford, 2004, for a comprehensive and thorough description of the railway).

Development of the St Kitts Railway

By the turn of the 21st century the St Kitts sugar industry could no longer compete effectively with other world centres of production, and tourism had replaced agriculture as the nation's (St Kitts and Nevis) primary generator of revenue. The railroad that had saved the sugar-cane industry a century earlier would now serve a new purpose – as the roadbed for a scenic train, serving tourists (see Dodds & Jolliffe, 2013, for an excellent overview of the development of 'sugar heritage tourism' in St Kitts). The St Kitts Scenic Railway Company was formed in 2001 and operations began in December 2002. About the same time, the government announced the closing of the sugar industry, to take place at the end of the 2005 crop (the St Kitts Sugar Manufacturing Corporation ceased all forms of production on 31 July 2007). The numbers of tourists were increasing, partly due to the construction of hotels, but primarily because of vast improvements in the port facilities at Basseterre (beginning in the 1990s), which attracted more and more cruise ships. Port Zante, a large new development at the foot of a docking complex that could accommodate the world's largest cruise liners, opened in 2002. It dwarfed the previous entrance to the capital city, and became the cruise passenger's face of St Kitts. It also provided a perfect link, through specialized buses, for those passengers who wanted to ride the Scenic Railway. The early days of the 21st century marked the end of one era and the beginning of another, now focusing on mass tourism that included a unique feature – the Scenic Railway.

Ownership

Steve Hites, president and director of the St Kitts Scenic Railway, was an ideal proponent for the tourist railway project. Hailing from Skagway, Alaska, he was (and is) passionate about heritage trains, having helped to transform the White Pass and Yukon Railway (see Chapter 5) from a facility serving a collapsed mining industry to a highly successful passenger train for tourists from cruise ships arriving in Skagway. He is also president and owner of the Skagway Street Car Company, which provides rides through the town in a fleet of restored 1927 buses. Hites recently compared his experiences with railway transformation in Alaska and St Kitts: 'in both cases we found a way to keep a part of the old and ... to transition in the new' (Blishak & Blishak, 2011). Successful in business, and fully experienced from the ground up in running passenger trains, Hites is personable and charismatic, helping the government of St Kitts to develop its cruise ship activity through his contacts with the major cruise lines. For its part, the government provided the St Kitts Scenic Railway with a 30-year exclusive agreement to operate passenger trains on the tracks of the St Kitts Sugar Manufacturing Corporation (Schultz, 2003).

Hites's two business partners in the Scenic Railway were also good fits for the enterprise. Tom Rader (Colorado Railcar Manufacturing) and Jeff Hamilton (Hamilton Manufacturing) had designed and built the new tourist coaches for the transformed White Pass and Yukon Railway. They produced the innovative and unique coaches for the St Kitts train.

Technology

Building a comfortable passenger train for use on a light, 30-inch gauge track was a great technological challenge. Further, if passengers were to enjoy the scenic views of the St Kitts countryside, they had to experience a full 360-degree view over the top of the sugar cane which lined most of the route. Specially designed double-decked 'Island Series' railcars were built near Seattle. They are topped by an open upper deck, 13 feet above the ground from the base of the open side to 17.6 feet at the level of the canopy (Figure 17.2). In each coach, 28 passengers sit in cushioned, inward-facing seats, or stand. Alternatively, passengers can sit in the lower part of the carriages, connected to the upper storey by a circular stairway. Here they are provided with conventional railway seating in completely enclosed, air-conditioned and quiet comfort. Washrooms are adjacent.

A 600-horsepower 0–6–0 diesel locomotive, originally built in Romania for beet-sugar transportation in Poland, hauls three to five passenger carriages and a large generator car (Figure 17.3).

The narrow gauge of the track, the lack of ballast beneath the track and the height of the train create conditions that could have been unstable if mitigating actions had not been undertaken. The Scenic Railway made important improvements to the roadbed, first in a construction phase before the train began its journeys, and then in incremental stages ever since. Rails and sleepers have been replaced with heavier equipment, tight curves have been eliminated and the track has been fixed or cleared as dictated

Figure 17.2 View of the St Kitts heritage landscape from the upper deck of a passenger carriage. *Photo*: W. Found

by weather conditions and regular wear and tear. The track is inspected and maintained on a daily basis. The train is driven at slow speeds, which reduces the sway in the upper passenger deck (unavoidable with a rail gauge of 2 feet 6 inches; and a height of 17 feet 6 inches). The rolling stock squeaks as the heavy carriages manoeuver turns in the track; but the stately pace of the train and the sounds of stress and strain become part of the charm of the journey.

Figure 17.3 Locomotive, generator car and passenger carriages on the St Kitts Scenic Railway. *Photo*: W. Found

Modes of Operation

Originally the Scenic Train travelled the entire 30-mile length of the sugar-train track, beginning and ending at the Needsmuch Station, near the sugar factory. The journey took four hours in addition to the time taken to commute to the station from the cruise ship port or hotel. By 2005 the route was shortened, to cover only the 18-mile segment north from Needsmuch to Lavallee, a transfer station in the north-west (Figure 17.1). Nowadays trains travel between the two stations, running in alternate directions on the single track. Transportation between the train and the cruise ship port, source of the vast majority of passengers, is provided by specially constructed buses, each of which carries the passengers designated for a specific railway car. The buses, whose colourful paint and design match the train carriages, are operated by the Scenic Railway, and form an essential part of the integrated transportation system. The entire trip, including the train journey and the 12-mile road segment from Basseterre to Lavallee, takes three hours – the standard time for on-shore excursions for cruise ship passengers. The decision to reduce the length of the train trip in order to match the three-hour time limit for excursions was a critical adjustment that has allowed the Railway's business to flourish alongside increasing cruise ship tourism in St Kitts.

Management and Marketing

While the owners of the Scenic Railway play a vital role in large-scale decision-making and in international marketing, 75 local staff also play an indispensible role in running the railway. The executive vice president and general manager, the manager of sales and operations, and the manager of purchasing and maintenance are all Kittitians with a wealth of local experience. They know the country, its people and the railway; and from the company's head office in Basseterre they maintain the contacts and take the actions that allow the railway to thrive from day to day. As described below, the excursion on the Scenic Railway has a very local 'feel', attributable to the involvement of local people. This is no Disneyland. The ride provides an authentic voyage into the St Kitts landscape and into the lives of its people.

Coordination with Cruise Ship Tourism

The economic health of on-shore tourist attractions throughout the Caribbean has become highly dependent on cruise ship schedules and marketing (Found, 2004) and the operations of the Scenic Railway closely reflect the movements of ships in and out of Basseterre. Trains run five or six days a week during the winter (the peak months are November to April), when from one to five ships are berthed at the cruise port each day. Recently the train has run one day per week during the summer, when off-season cruise ship traffic has been limited to one large ship per week (thus leaving good time for track reconstruction and general maintenance). The economic welfare of the cruise ship companies and the railway are symbiotically linked, and each profits through the actions of the other. The ships are attracted to St Kitts in part because they share a portion of revenue from ticket sales on the railway.

Features of the Scenic Railway Tour

A trip on the Scenic Railway provides tourists and local citizens with a unique view of St Kitts, its landscape and its people. Most of St Kitts's small towns cling to the coast, connected by a road that loops around the north part of the island. The rail line rings the same area, sometimes crossing the road, but also travelling through areas that have been inaccessible to road traffic. The train journey, even the abbreviated 18-mile version, provides the visitor with unprecedented access to the countryside and island villages.

Authentic Interpretation

All of the people operating the railway are Kittitians, which provides a kind of authenticity sometimes missing in tourist attractions. An interpreter, well versed in the history and customs of St Kitts, provides almost constant commentary throughout the train trip – and with the lilt of a local dialect that is easy to understand by visitors from around the world (a majority are normally from North America). The content is highly informative, geared to the tastes of a curious and educated public, and gently mixed with humour. The commentary is a necessary part of the journey, as few tourists would recognize many of the local features.

Understanding the history of St Kitts, first the home of indigenous peoples, and later peoples from Africa (originally brought as slaves), Great Britain and France, is fundamental to appreciating the land and population. The route excludes Frigate Bay and the South-East Peninsula, home to the beaches, the large tourist hotels and new high-end developments of villas and yacht marina, so authentic interpretation for tourists is particularly important. The visitors may understand the features of modern golf courses and waterfront developments, but they need knowledgeable commentary to appreciate the large northern part of St Kitts and its landscape remnants from the rural past (Found & Berbés-Blázquez, 2012).

Interpreters explain both segments of the journey, the 18-mile train portion and the 12-mile bus trip from Lavallee Station to the Port. The bus portion includes a number of features not included on the train trip (e.g. the historic core of Basseterre), so the commentary by bus drivers/interpreters is a welcomed part of the journey.

The Plantation Landscape

The production and processing of sugar cane was the major economic activity on St Kitts from the middle of the 17th until the latter half of the 20th century. In the north part of the island almost all land from the coast to the 1000-foot contour was dedicated to the production of sugar; and the predominant landscape feature was the light green of the fields of cane. Beyond this agricultural belt was the mountainous interior, most of it forested. In many ways, today's landscape is little changed from the past, and the Railway provides access to views that are similar to those of 350 years ago. This gives the tourist an unprecedented image of the island's sugar-plantation heritage. Although no longer cultivated and harvested, the fields of cane survive, albeit with patches of intrusive bushes and a handful of new buildings. The landscape is still dominated by the remnant sugar-cane grass, often reaching heights of over 10 feet.

Prior to the building of the sugar-cane railway, cane was milled and the juice processed in a series of industrial buildings located on the separate plantations. Most prominent were the sugar mills, powered by animals, wind, water or steam (Hicks, 2007). The cane juice was evaporated and eventually transformed into sugar, molasses or rum in adjacent boiling houses. The train passes remnants of all of these buildings, which still form a significant part of the landscape. Few of the plantation houses, former homes of the plantation owners or managers, survive intact, but some remaining examples can be seen in the distance from the train carriages.

Small villages comprised of huts and food gardens, home to the large numbers of slaves who worked the plantations, were once a prominent component of sugar plantations. These tended to disappear after emancipation in 1834, but a few of the locations have developed into modern villages, some near the route of the Scenic Railway. But perhaps the most noticeable remnant from the days of slavery is the many descendants of Africans, who now form the basis of modern Kittitian society.

Plantation landscapes often evoke feelings in the minds of onlookers. Some view the quiet countryside, with its remnants from a previous era, as a romantic peek into the past. Others, perhaps descendants of those who worked the fields and factories in servitude, remember the harsh times, and view the landscape's heritage with sadness or indifference. Recently many Kittitians have tended to see the landscape as a kind of monument to their predecessors. They take pride in those who cleared the forests, planted and tended the cane, built the stone factories and great houses, and produced and processed the crops. No matter what the human response, the plantation landscape represents important heritage, and the Scenic Railway provides unprecedented access to this national and regional treasure.

Urban Centres

St Kitts has one major town, Basseterre, the capital city of St Kitts and Nevis, with population of around 13,000 in 2009 (Central Intelligence Agency, 2012). The bus portion of the Scenic Railway trip passes through the traditional centre of this former colonial town, providing a good view and interpretation of the old Treasury Building (former sea entrance to the town, now home to the St Christopher National Trust and Museum), the Berkeley Memorial Clock, and the town centre – the 'Circus' traffic centre. While the tour does not include an extensive exploration of the town, it provides a satisfying glimpse of the traditional architecture and the lively street life of this bustling capital.

As with other islands of the eastern Caribbean, the villages of St Kitts are coastal, originally connected by boat transportation or the coastal road. Consequently, both the bus and train portions of the Scenic Railway tour pass through or along the margins of most of the settlements. The bus travels up the south-west coastal road, through Bloody Point Town (site of a massacre of native Caribs during the first days of European settlement); through Old Road Town, original centre for British settlement, beginning in 1624; and past Sandy Point Town, the island's second largest town (population 3000). The bus trip also passes modern suburban developments, including modern housing (both private and government-sponsored), light industry on the edge of Basseterre, and a large veterinary school run by Ross University. The coastal road has high scenic value, with views of the Caribbean Sea, fishing villages and rural countryside between the few towns.

The train portion of the tour offers a unique view of St Kitts villages, a different perspective from that afforded even local residents. The train skirts a number of small settlements, often passing by the backyards of small properties, and generally avoiding the centres of towns served by the road. The train traveller sees people's gardens, some livestock, washing left out to dry and school playgrounds. Seen from atop the train carriages, these perspectives were made accessible for the first time when the Scenic Railway began operation.

People

The residents of St Kitts are a fundamental part of the landscape viewed from the Scenic Railway. They wave back and forth with the passengers, as they welcome the visitors to their domain. Children race excitedly as the train passes a school near the north end of the island. The train has become part of the local scene, in which Kittitians express obvious pride. The local management of the Railway, by people who are respected, and who involve many residents as staff members or passengers, has played a significant part in this pattern of local 'ownership'. No doubt the free ride offered to school students when the train began operations provided an excellent start to good relations with local residents.

Figure 17.4 Passing through an area of thick, jungle-like vegetation, viewed from the upper deck on the St Kitts Scenic Railway. *Photo*: W. Found

Bridges

The train passes over a number of bridges, which bring variety and a bit of excitement for passengers. The longest bridge, a compound girder structure stretching 360 feet over Lodge Ghut near the north coast, provides a slow, very smooth ride over a valley crammed with forest and gardens. A bit north of Basseterre the train passes under a passenger bridge; and at other points dense trees and bushes close to the track give passengers the impression of passing through a tunnel of jungle vegetation (Figure 17.4).

Other Views Along the Journey

Brimstone Hill Fortress, one of the Caribbean's largest historical military installations, and a UNESCO World Heritage site, is located a mile south of the Lavallee Station. Passengers onboard the Scenic Railway bus see the

800-foot hill looming above the surrounding fields, and hear the interpreter describe the construction and history of the fort complex. This is the most famous of the heritage sites in St Kitts and Nevis.

Looking inland from Brimstone Hill, tourists see the island's mountainous interior, a heavily forested complex of old volcanic peaks. This central spine of mountains is visible throughout the train's journey, and the highest peak, Mt Liamuiga (3792 feet), is particularly prominent. The highest elevations are often cloud-covered, precipitating rain that waters the fields of cane and occasionally floods the ghuts.

Some of the finest views from the train are offshore – seascapes to the north and east (the Atlantic side of St Kitts), and to the south and west (the Caribbean Sea). The volcanic peak of the sister island of Nevis is clearly visible from the railway just north of Basseterre, and views of the Dutch volcanic island of St Eustatius are prominent along the north coast. A combination of cane fields, small villages, enthusiastic local people, views of St Eustatius and a setting sun can make the north-coast portion of the train ride particularly stunning.

Heritage-train buffs are provided with occasional peeks of intriguing remnants of the previous sugar-cane railway – a few rusted cane railway cars on an old siding, parts of a diminutive diesel locomotive or the rusted remains of devices for loading cane onto the train cars. The unattractive junk from the early version of the railway has been gradually removed, but enough artifacts remain to satisfy the knowledgeable onlooker.

Sounds and Amenities

A trip on the Scenic Railway is filled with sound – the background growl of the diesel locomotive and generator (softer towards the back of the train); the squeaks, stresses and strains as the train rounds corners; and the continuing and well amplified voice of the interpreter. The Railway also features an *a cappella* choir of three-four Kittitians who sing old favourites in well practised harmony. Live singing is an important tradition in St Kitts, whether in churches, on work sites or in contemporary concerts, and this choir provides good entertainment of unmistakable local origins. The choir moves from carriage to carriage, providing each unit with its own live music.

No Caribbean excursion would be complete without refreshments, and the Scenic Railway offers complimentary (and unlimited) rum or non-alcoholic punch with a snack. The fruit punches, mixed in onboard blenders, are a welcomed treat in the tropical climate.

Demand and Future Prospects

The success of the Scenic Railway has been dependent on its ties to cruise shipping, and recent increases in the arrivals of cruise ship passengers have spurred the Railway's economic development. There were 165,542 cruise ship passengers arrivals in St Kitts in 2002, 247,393 in 2007, and 512,436 in 2010 (Statistics Division and Department of Tourism, 2012). At the same time, the number of passengers on the Scenic Railway has continued to increase, with a targeted number of 60,000 for 2011 (Hites, 2011).

The Railway has passed through an initial 10-year period of early growth, is now profitable and is making investments for an important second phase in its development. At the same time, the government has confirmed that the railroad property includes a total right of way of 50 feet, thus ensuring space and security for new construction and maintenance. New locomotives are under construction in the United States, and plans are in place to replace the rails and track with heavier and more stable construction. Initially, a five-mile section of track will be replaced during the summer days when cruise ships do not call at Basseterre. At the same time, the Railway is planning to refurnish and open the section of track that has been temporarily out of service, opening up opportunities for combining travel on the train with stops at various tourist/heritage sites. The Railway may once again carry some freight, or develop passenger service for local commuters. The possibilities are many.

The Railway will continue to face risks. Dependence on cruise ship passengers is always somewhat precarious, as tourism is highly sensitive to worldwide economic conditions and international security. While St Kitts and Nevis has made excellent progress in providing services for tourists, and in attracting good numbers of tourists since the 1990s, the islands of the eastern Caribbean are fiercely competitive with each other, and fluctuations in arrivals can be expected as different locations provide new incentives to the cruise ship companies. While natural disasters have never created long-term problems in St Kitts during historic times, the island is visited by occasional hurricanes and it sits in a geologically unstable zone. The risks of a disastrous natural event are slight, but real.

The end of the sugar industry in St Kitts means that one of the Scenic Railway's important attractions – the sugar-cane landscape – will eventually disappear, just as it has in other Caribbean islands (e.g. Antigua). The Scenic Railway and the government will need to plan for this eventuality and take whatever actions seem prudent to provide a landscape that retains vestiges of its previous form, and/or to provide alternative landscapes of interest and heritage value.

Conclusions

The St Kitts Scenic Railway is unique – the only commercial Caribbean railway operating outside of Cuba, and providing access to an island's heritage landscape that goes back 350 years. The original narrow-gauge St Kitts railway prolonged the island's sugar industry for a century, and the transformed Scenic Railway is part of the island's new role as a tourist destination. The Railway has continued to adapt and transform, the life-blood of its ongoing success. Enlightened and experienced investors, strong local management, a sense of 'ownership' by local citizens and wise govern-ment support have combined to create success. The Railway faces risks, including a heavy dependence on cruise ship tourism. But it has continued to plan and adjust with foresight, and provides the Caribbean with one of its most important heritage experiences.

Acknowledgements

I am very grateful to the following for providing interviews and feedback:
Carolyn James, Director, St Kitts Tourism Authority, Toronto.
Steve Hites, President and Director, St Kitts Scenic Railway.
David Rollinson, Author and Consultant.
Thomas Williams, Executive Vice President and Manager, St Kitts Scenic Railway.

References

Blishak, T. and Blishak, S. (2011) The railroad tycoon and the St Kitts Scenic Railway. At http://www.highonadventure.com/hoa11aug/sylvia/stkittsscenicrr.htm (accessed January 2014).

Central Intelligence Agency (CIA) (2012) St Kitts and Nevis. *The World Fact Book.* At https://www.cia.gov/library/publications/the-world-factbook/geos/sc.html (accessed January 2014).

Dodds, R. and Jolliffe, L. (2013) Developing sugar heritage tourism in St Kitts. In L. Jolliffe (ed.) *Sugar Heritage and Tourism in Transition* (pp. 110–127). Bristol: Channel View Publications.

Dyde, B. (2008) *St Kitts: Cradle of the Caribbean* (4th edition). Oxford: Macmillan Education.

Found, W.C. (2004) Historic sites, material culture and tourism in the Caribbean Islands. In D. Duval (ed.) *Tourism in the Caribbean: Trends, Development, Prospects* (pp. 136–151). London: Routledge.

Found, W.C. (2005) *St Kitts Scenic Railway: Journey into an Island's Heritage* (50-minute video). Toronto: St Christopher Heritage Society.

Found, W.C. and Berbés-Blázquez, M. (2012) The sugar cane landscape of the Caribbean Islands: Resilience and the changing plantation social-ecological system. In D. Plieninger and C. Bieling (eds) *Resilience and the Cultural Landscape: Understanding and Managing Change in Human-Shaped Environments* (pp. 164–184). Cambridge: Cambridge University Press.

Galloway, J.H. (1989) *The Sugar Cane Industry: An Historical Geography from Its Origins to 1914*. Cambridge: Cambridge University Press.

Hicks, D. (2007) *The Garden of the World: An Historical Archaeology of Sugar Landscapes in the Eastern Caribbean*. London: Archaeopress.

Hites, S. (2011) St Kitts Scenic Railway. At http://railroadfan.com/phpbb/viewtopic.php ?f=6&t=21158&p=182941&hilit=Hites – p182941 (accessed January 2014).

Horsford, J. (2004) *The St Kitts Railway: From Sugar Cane to Scenic Train*. St Teath: Locomotives International.

Murray AdVentures (2006) *St Kitts Scenic Railway – The Sugar Train* (commemorative video DVD).

Rollinson, D. (2001) *Railways of the Caribbean*. Oxford: Macmillan Education.

Schultz, T. (2003) St Kitts Scenic Railway. At http://www.trainorders.com/discussion/read.php?6,576763 (accessed January 2014).

St Kitts Scenic Railway (2012) At http://www.stkittsscenicrailway.com (accessed January 2014).

Statistics Division and Department of Tourism, St Kitts and Nevis (annual reports), *Cruise Passenger Arrivals and Tourist Arrivals (Stay-Over)*. Reported as online document by the Caribbean Tourist Organization. At http://www.onecaribbean.org/statistics/tourismstats (accessed January 2014).

West India Royal Commission (1897) *Report of the West India Royal Commission, Great Britain*. London: Her Majesty's Stationery Office.

18 The Future of Railway Heritage Tourism? The West Coast Wilderness Railway, Tasmania

Michael V. Conlin and Bruce Prideaux

Introduction

It is perhaps fitting that one of the final chapters in this book addresses the development and management of the West Coast Wilderness Railway (WCWR), located in the Australian state of Tasmania. The WCWR embodies many of the criteria presented in the railway heritage typologies introduced in Chapter 1 and which reflect the unusual characteristics of this particular niche of industrial heritage, particularly in the context of tourism. In stating this, it is not being suggested that the WCWR is necessarily a preferred model for the development of heritage railway tourism. Indeed, it is only one type of development model, one where a public–private form of partnership is a key element in its success. However, it is a particularly good example of how this particular form of development can be achieved. The initial result of this partnership was a superb example of a rejuvenated heritage railway attraction that formed part of a cohesive and comprehensive tourism attraction. As a result, one would think that the WCWR provides lessons and guidelines for the successful development and management of a railway heritage tourism attraction. Or does it?

On 4 February 2013, the Federal Hotels Group, a wholly owned subsidiary of Mulawa Holdings Pty Limited and the operator of the WCWR, announced it would stop operating the heritage railway attraction at the end of April 2013. The Federal Group indicated that it would break its 20-year agreement with the Tasmanian government to operate the WCWR after running the railway for the past 10 years. Daniel Hanna, a spokesman for the Group, stated that the railway was no longer financially viable: 'There was a critical need to invest in infrastructure and ..., of course, [there] has been reduced demand and a downturn in visitor numbers and passenger numbers' (ABC News, 2013a).

When the railway was formally opened in 2003 by the Prime Minister of Australia and the Premier of Tasmania, its future appeared very bright. It had benefited from an initial A\$20.45 million investment by the Australian government along with additional investment from the Tasmanian government of A\$18 million, and it enjoyed early success – in the fiscal year 2003/04, its first year of operation, the line carried 61,040 passengers (Tasmania Department of Infrastructure, Energy and Resources, 2004, 2012). A corporate structure had been established by the Tasmanian government through the Abt Railway Development Act 1999 to oversee the railway's development and management. The Abt Railway Ministerial Corporation (ARMC) was charged with ensuring that the development of the railway was achieved, that associated developments in the region supporting the railway also be put in place and that a commercially competent operator for the railway be identified and appointed. ARMC did all of this and as a result, in 2003, all stakeholders in this venture, both public and private, were confident of success.

Fast-forward 10 years and the outlook for the WCWR painted a very different picture. Because of the projected costs for maintenance and operating the railway, the Tasmanian government initially indicated that it would close the attraction following the Federal Group's announcement. The Tasmanian Infrastructure Minister, David O'Byrne, stated that the government could not afford to invest the approximately A\$15–20 million estimated to be necessary to perform past-due, current and future maintenance on the railway. Federal's David Hanna indicated that ridership on the railway had dropped significantly from the initial levels of over 60,000 annually to 45,000 by 2008 and 30,000 by 2012, a decline of 50% (ABC News, 2013a).

The complexities and challenges of developing railway heritage tourism attractions have been well documented and discussed in earlier chapters of this book. What becomes clear from this far-ranging discussion is that the scale of railway infrastructure, the complexities of land and property ownership particularly associated with rights of way, stations and equipment, and the provision of skilled human resources and adequate financial assets essential for effective and sustainable operation suggest that successful railway heritage tourism attractions are not well suited to projects or organizations driven only by amateur enthusiasts. Virtually all of the successful examples discussed in earlier chapters reveal the need for significant resources and planning in order to develop or repurpose existing railway infrastructure for touristic purposes. And as the following discussion will show, the WCWR is not simply an excellent example of how this has been recently accomplished but also one where tourism is a major element of the regional economy and in a location that is locally geographically challenged in terms of visitation (Australian Government, 2011).

Tasmanian Tourism

Tasmania is a state of the Commonwealth of Australia and consists of five main islands – Tasmania; Bruny; King; Flinders; and Macquarie – along with some 300 smaller islands. The majority of the population resides on the island of Tasmania and, being the largest of the five main islands, it is the principal site of economic activity in the state. By comparison with the rest of Australia, Tasmania is small in terms of both land mass and population. At 67,800 km², it is less than 1% of the Australian landmass and as of 2010 the resident population was just over 500,000 (Conlin 2002; Discover Tasmania, n.d.-a).

The state is somewhat isolated, being 240 km south-east of the mainland. All tourists arrive either by air, primarily through the airport at the capital city of Hobart, or by ship. Visitors arriving by ship primarily disembark either from the ferry services running between Melbourne and Devonport on the north coast of the island or from cruise ships which dock in Hobart, which is located in the south-east of the island.

The state has a relatively long history of tourism activity. The presence of a number of penal colonies built between the early 1800s and culminating with the closing of the notorious Port Arthur Prison in 1877 provided Tasmania with a range of heritage sites. The tourism potential for these sites was recognized even before the closing of Port Arthur and both it and the equally notorious Macquarie Harbor Penal Station, more commonly known as Sarah Island, began to see visitors in the second half of the 19th century. The lure of these iconic examples of 'dark tourism' has continued and grown and Port Arthur is now one of the 11 penal sites which comprise the Australian Convict Sites World Heritage listed property (UNESCO, n.d.). Sarah Island, located in Macquarie Harbour on the west coast, is, along with the WCWR, one of the prime tourism attractions of that region.

Tourism Tasmania (n.d.) reported a 4% drop in total visitor arrivals between June 2011 and June 2012, from 895,400 to 855,200, and a 1% decrease in length of stay by non-cruise visitors, from 10.1 nights to 10.0 nights. This downturn resulted in a significant 16% decrease in visitor expenditure, from $857 million to $717 million. The number of international visitors in this group was 143,000 through to September 2012, a slight decrease from the year before. Visitors coming to Tasmania on business and not specifically as tourists during this period numbered 173,300, an increase of 9% from the previous year.

The Tasmanian West Coast

A major challenge faced by the WCWR, and indeed any tourism attraction on the west coast, is the relative isolation of that part of the island. The region includes the Tasmanian Wilderness World Heritage Area (TWWHA), which occupies approximately 21% of the island (Conlin, 2002) and the Franklin-Gordon Wild Rivers National Park, which occupies approximately half of the west coast region and is not readily accessible to tourists other than by the main road that runs from Hobart to Queenstown. This road runs through the park for 56 km and provides opportunities for hikers to access the back-country. In addition, the park can be accessed by cruise boats that operate from Strahan (Tasmania Parks and Wildlife Service, n.d.). The distance from the airport at Hobart to the town of Queenstown where the eastern terminus of the WCWR is located is only 272 km and takes approximately 3½ hours to drive. However, in the context of tourism in Tasmania, this is widely considered to be a challenging distance. Fortunately, the region where the WCWR is located also includes a range of heritage, cultural and outdoor leisure activities, including Sarah Island discussed above, and these combined have allowed the area around Queenstown and Strahan to develop a tourism economy. Indeed, the region is the fifth most tourism-dependent region in Australia (Australian Government, 2011).

Nonetheless, the west coast region, which is called the Western Wilderness by Tourism Tasmania, due no doubt to its relative isolation, attracts the least number of visitors of any region on the island. In the 12-month period ending September 2012, some 215,000 of the island's visitors came to the Western Wilderness region and this represented a downturn from the previous year of 11%, when 242,000 of the island's visitors came west (Tourism Tasmanian, n.d.). This is consistent with the downturn of ridership on the WCWR.

The three principal centres in the region are the town of Queenstown, with a population of just over 2000, the village of Strahan, with a population of approximately 650, and the town of Zeehan, with a population of just over 700. Interestingly, Zeehan rivalled Hobart and Launceston at the start of the 20th century in terms of population and development, based on the wealth generated by various mining activities around the town (Discover Tasmania, n.d.-b). All three centres were active in the early development of west coast Tasmanian railways, as discussed below.

Railway Heritage in Tasmania

The industrial landscape that emerged after the industrial revolution provides a range of unique heritage opportunities that have been seized on by the tourism industry to provide a wide range of heritage-related activities and experiences, and Tasmania has been part of this movement. The state is home to 13 heritage railway attractions, including railways, museums and rolling stock (Rail Tasmania, n.d.). In some cases, disused industrial structures have been preserved as heritage attractions or recycled for new uses, such as shopping, recreation, accommodation and commercial precincts. In other areas, disused buildings have been demolished and new users including tourism have been found. As discussed in Chapter 1 and above, funding for rejuvenation and preservation of heritage infrastructure of this nature may be sourced from either the private or the public sector, or a combination of both.

Mining landscapes, particularly where mining activity has ceased, are some of the many heritage landscapes that have been targeted for redevelopment as tourism experiences. In Tasmania's Western Wilderness, the region's rich mining heritage can be experienced through a number of attractions, including tours of the West Lyell mining operation in Queenstown and a visit to the extensive West Coast Memorial Pioneers' Museum in Zeehan, 37 km north-west of Queenstown and 42 km north-east of the village of Strahan and the western terminus of the WCWR. This chapter examines the redevelopment of what was the largely demolished Mt Lyell railway as a commercial tourism attraction with a strong emphasis on its heritage values.

Preservation of heritage and operating a profitable heritage-themed experience are not always compatible. Where preservation is the overriding objective, commercial operations may not be possible and the public sector may be asked to assume financial responsibility for site operations. Contemporary operations are governed by a suite of legislative requirements, many of which may not have applied when the experience was first operated. In the case of the WCWR, many of the issues faced by organisations seeking to operate viable commercial operations at heritage sites do not apply. Most of the track and much of the associated infrastructure had been demolished well before the rebuilding of the line. For this reason, the current railway can be regarded as a replica operation that provides a commodified experience that has many parallels with the past. From a commercial perspective this is an important consideration and removes from the operator many of the impediments that may otherwise be encountered.

The following discussion commences with an overview of the construction of the line and a brief outline of railway operations during the period it functioned as a mineral line. The chapter then examines the line's resurrection as a heritage tourism venture and its current operations as a tourism attraction.

Railway Operations in the Mining Era

The construction and operation of mountain railways pose a range of problems not encountered in most railway operating environments. Typically, mountain railways need to ascend and descend steep slopes. This poses a number of problems, including building locomotives with sufficient horsepower to overcome steep gradients and with sufficient braking ability to overcome gravity and prevent trains from sliding down the track. The ruggedness of mountain terrains also poses engineering problems that require the construction of cuttings, tunnels, bridges and tight curves. Combined, the extra costs of track construction and of the acquisition, operation and maintenance of specialised locomotives and rolling stock pose burdens not encountered in other railway systems. Where the economics of construction and operations of railway systems of this nature are present, many operators adopt a narrow-gauge system (3 foot 6 inches, or 1067 mm) with tight curves as a cost-reduction measure. Where standard locomotives are not suitable because of slope issues, a rack railway system is required.

Intensive exploration for mineral deposits in the north-west region of Tasmania by the Mt Lyell Mining Company (renamed the Mount Lyell Mining and Railway Company in 1893) resulted in the discovery of a large copper and silver deposit in the Queenstown region. In the era before motorised transport, the only option available to the Company was to construct a railway to the coast. However the mountainous nature of the Queenstown area and local extreme weather events posed numerous construction problems.

The initial survey reports for a line from the mine site at Queenstown to the seaport of Strahan were not favourable. The steepest gradient was a climb of 1 m in 16 m (6.25%) and the need to construct tunnels, cuttings and embankments added to the cost of construction. Over 500 km of foot tracks were cut by survey teams as they searched for a favourable route for the railway (Rae, 2001). The obstacles included impassable mountains, dense rainforest, deep gouges and high rainfall. Eventually a decision was made to adopt a route that ran along the Queen and King Rivers.

The development of the Abt system of rack railway provided the technical solution required to overcome the problems posed by the gradient. The Abt system, devised by Roman Abt, a Swiss locomotive engineer, resolved many of the problems inherent in the earlier Riggenbach rack railway system. The Abt system, in common with other rack railway systems, uses a toothed cog wheel which engages a toothed rail track laid between the tracks. In effect, the engine uses the toothed cogs to pull itself up the slope. The Mount Lyell railway required 7 km of rack-and-pinion rail to be installed (Rae, 2001).

Construction of the narrow-gauge line was undertaken in two stages. Construction of the first stage, between Queenstown and Teepookana, began in 1895 and was opened 19 months later, in 1897. The second stage of the line, between Teepookana and Regatta Point on the coast, was constructed over the following two years. The entire system was officially declared open on 1 November 1899 (Rae, 2008). In the era before heavy earth-moving equipment was available, construction of the line posed numerous engineering problems, including the building of bridges, embankments and cuttings. By the time the line was completed, 58 bridges had been built, the combined length of which comprised 6% of the line. Just one example of the numerous engineering problems encountered was the construction of the iron bridge over the King River. Fabricated in England and shipped to Tasmania as a kit, the bridge weighted 110 tonnes. In an era when heavy lifting cranes had not been developed, the line's contractors assembled the bridge on a trestle pier mounted on a barge and floated the bridge to its required position before lowering the barge in the water, where it was able to float free from the bridge.

During the 67 years of its operation by the Mount Lyell Mining and Railway Company, the line also provided a link to the outside world. Indeed, until the opening of a highway to Hobart in 1932 the railway was Queenstown's only link to the world (Rae, 2008). During this period, the Company operated general freight and passenger services in addition to mineral trains. Children who lived in outlying fettlers' camps and small hamlets located adjacent to the railway travelled to school by train and regular passenger services were operated between Queenstown and Strahan. The Company established a picnic grounds at King River and regularly operated picnic trains to the area for Queenstown and Strahan residents. The final picnic train operated in 1963 and the final scheduled passenger train left Queenstown in mid-1963. The last ore train from Queenstown ran on 10 August 1963 and was pulled by Abe 1, which was also the first locomotive to steam into Queenstown (West Coast Wilderness Railway, n.d.).

By 1963 the line had become expensive to maintain and several of the larger bridges were in need of rebuilding. Moreover, the rolling stock was outdated and in need of replacement. From a shareholders' perspective, the Company had little option other than to shut the line down and switch to road transport. In the following years, the track was torn up and a number of bridges were swept away by the floods that periodically affect the region. By the 1980s, little remained of the original line except for its cuttings, embankments, a number of rapidly deteriorating bridges and several of the original buildings associated with the line.

Restructuring the Line

The reconstructed railway was designed to service a very different market to that which underpinned its first 67 years of operation. The winding down of mining and the closure of the Mount Lyell Company in 1994 left Queenstown with few options other than tourism to replace lost mining jobs. The mine's closure caused a rapid decline in population as families left the town in search of work. By 2006, the population of the town had contracted to 2117; of the 922 who were classified as being part of the labour force, 28.5% still classified their employment as being mining or mining related (Australian Bureau of Statistics, 2007).

The possibility of rebuilding the railway as a tourism attraction was first raised even before its 1963 closure. Those efforts were unsuccessful and the line quickly fell into disrepair. Further interest in rebuilding the line emerged in the early 1980s, led by a Tasmanian entrepreneur, Roger Smith. Funds for a study of the proposal were allocated by the Tasmanian government but the subsequent report by PA Management Consultants concluded that 'no significant additional benefit would flow to the state or region as a result of the restoration of the Abt as a tourism railway' (Rae, 2008). By the time the report was released, the track had been torn up and many of the bridges had either collapsed or were in an advanced state of decay. Nonetheless, interest in rebuilding the railway continued and in the mid-1990s a local business-man, Viv Crocker, along with other rail enthusiasts, established the Mount Lyell Abt Railway Society and began preliminary work on track reconstruc-tion. However, the task was far greater than the resources of the Society and a fund-raising campaign was undertaken, culminating in a successful application for A$20.45 million of funding under the federal government's Centennial of Federation programme.

The rebuilding programme faced a number of statutory reporting and approval processes that had not existed when the original line had been built. Among the various legislative requirements that had to be met were the need to provide an environmental impact assessment; in addition, it was necessary address the concerns of the West Coast Council and to meet various requirements of the Board of Environmental Management and Pollution Control and the Tasmania Heritage Council. Furthermore, the railway was also required to obtain approval from the Commonwealth government, in accordance with the Environmental Protection (Impacts of Proposals) Act, and to comply with the construction and operations provi-sions of the Tasmanian Rail Safety Act. As mentioned above, the Tasmanian government passed the Abt Railway Development Act 1999 to give planning approval to the project. A period of public consultation was also required, to allow members of the public to raise specific concerns they might have about the project (Rae, 2008). Three parallel projects were undertaken: restoration of the original steam and diesel locomotives and building replica rolling stock; refurbishment of the original stations and building of new workshops; and rebuilding the railway.

Following the line's closure, rolling stock was disposed of but two Abe locomotives were allocated as outdoor displays on the west coast. As part of the planning process for the railway, three of the five original locomotives were located and rebuilt to operational standard, including Abe No. 1, which commenced with the railway in 1887, Abe No. 3 and Abt No. 5, which was restored in 2005. Abt No. 4 was scrapped and used for parts for the other locomotives. Abt No. 2 remains on display at Hobart's Tasmanian Transport Museum. Several diesel locomotives that had been employed by the Mt Lyell Company were also located and restored. The original passenger carriages had been purchased by the Puffing Billy tourist railway in Victoria when the railway closed in 1963. Unable to negotiate their return, 12 replica carriages were built to the same specifications as the original carriages as part of the project.

By the time that the rebuilding programme began in 2000, little of the original building infrastructure associated with the railway remained, except for a small section of the Queenstown railway station that had been converted into a supermarket and later destroyed in a fire, the Station Master's Cottage in Queenstown, the Regatta Point Station in Strahan and the original locomotive sheds at Regatta Point. Both railway stations were rebuilt, while new workshops building were constructed in Queenstown. The Queenstown Station was specifically rebuilt as a tourism facility, with shops and catering facilities. The original turntable in Queenstown was also restored to operational status. New stations, including Rinadeena Station, were also built to serve as tourist viewpoints.

The most expensive part of the rebuilding programme was the reconstruction of the railway line. One of the many problems faced was the need to remove houses that had been built on or near to the original line near Queenstown. New water towers had to be built for the steam locomotives and 35 km of track laid. The trestle bridge at Dubbil Barril, 20 m high, was restored and bridges that had been destroyed by flooding, including the Quarter Mile Bridge near Teepoojana, were rebuilt. The steel Quarter Mile Bridge over the King River was also rebuilt. In all, 40 bridges needed reconstruction. The line reopened in December 2002 and the first full service between Queenstown and Strahan commenced on 27 December of that year. The restored railway operated under the name of the Abt Railway and was managed by Roger Smith's company, Honeybank Pty Ltd.

One of the many problems encountered in the reconstruction was relearning skills of a rail technology that had not been used for 40 years. By the late 1990s, many of the employees retrenched in 1963 had moved from the area or passed away, leaving few written records. Efforts were made to contact former staff for the information required to write manuals for the rail service. One of the former train drivers who was still living in the area at that time was Malcolm Powell, by then in his mid-80s. Mr Powell was able to provide invaluable advice for the new generation of locomotive drivers and was the first to drive one of the restored locomotives on the new line. Another former locomotive driver was able to assist in the writing of a manual on the responsibilities of guards, shunters, drivers and firemen.

While the rebuilt railway was a technical success, able to recreate the original rail journey, it was less successful from a financial perspective. The cost of the project escalated beyond the $20.45 million granted by the federal government, and both Smith and the Tasmanian government were forced to contribute extra funds (Rae, 2008). The rebuilding programme soon became a political issue and in August 2002 Smith handed over operation of the railway to the Federal Hotel and Resorts Group, which was at the time expanding its Tasmanian tourism portfolio. On the west coast, the Group had acquired the Strahan Village accommodation complex and Gordon River Cruises. Elsewhere in Tasmania, the Federal Group operated the West Point Casino in Hobart and the Country Club resort in Launceston. One of the objectives of the agreement to operate the railway was to integrate it into the suite of other tourism experiences the Company operated on the west coast.

Current Operations

One of the first things the Federal Group did upon acquiring the 20-year lease to operate the railway was to change the name from the Abt Railway to the West Coast Wilderness Railway. This change was motivated by marketing research. The line is currently operated six times weekly, with round-trip departures inclusive of lunch alternating between Strahan and Queenstown. Passengers have the choice of two classes, premier and standard. Premier class offers a range of gourmet foods and a selection of wines. Each departure includes stops at three locations to view various aspects of the line's heritage and spectacular scenery. Commentary given throughout the trip focuses on the heritage aspects of the line and its early operation, as well as the rainforest ecosystem through which the train runs.

However, as noted above, the operating climate for the WCWR has changed in the decade since its creation:

It is apparent to the ARMC and WCWR that the operating environment and market place of the railway have changed significantly from that envisaged when it was planned and reconstructed more than ten years ago. Both parties intend to undertake a joint process to assess all aspects of the railway and lease, identify appropriate amendments and instigate a more strategic approach to ensure the long-term viability of the railway. A review of legislation applying to the Abt Railway is also intended to identify any inconsistencies and possible need for amendments.... It is anticipated that following the above review, the Fund will be directed more effectively for railway improvements. The ARMC has not undertaken major asset improvement or funding the past reporting year, pending the review. The Office of the Valuer-General has recently undertaken a five yearly revaluation of the ARMC assets. In summary, the land value has declined in line with general property sale trends while other asset values remain fairly static. (Tasmania Department of Infrastructure, Energy and Resources, 2012: 73)

As mentioned above, ridership has fallen significantly since the WCWR recommenced operations in late 2002. In the fiscal year 2011/12, it totalled 29,700 compared with the approximately 60,000 passengers carried annually during the first several years of operation. Part of the decline is attributable to natural disasters such as the line blockage in March 2011 due to bad weather. This incident alone closed the line for some three months (Tasmania Department of Infrastructure, Energy and Resources, 2012).

The preceding commentary on the resurrection of a defunct railway operation as a tourism operation illustrates a number of factors that need to be considered when attempts are made to revive a former industrial operation. In circumstances such as the Mount Lyell railway line, where little of the original heritage remained, there may be scope for rebuilding in a manner that preserves the past in form if not substance. For example, the original passenger cars, if available, would not have conformed to contemporary operating requirements, nor would they have met contemporary occupational health and safety standards. Preservation in a strict heritage sense would require that original engineering standards of building and rolling stock be retained. However, if original engineering standards do not conform to contemporary standards, some modifications may be required before they can be used for operational purposes. This may pose a problem if heritage is the key determinate of a project. Where there is a need for attractions to operate commercially, there is likely to be pressure for changes that may compromise heritage values. In some cases such as the Mount Lyell railway line, the need to generate a return on investment can be expected to supersede heritage values. Other factors that need to be considered include the following:

- the manner and extent to which heritage values are to be retained;
- long-term economic sustainability;
- adherence to contemporary statutory requirements, including environmental impact assessments, adherence to occupational health and safety requirements, industry safety and operations standards, and consultation with the host community;
- retention of past knowledge;
- relearning past skill sets for technology and industrial processes not in contemporary use;
- commodification as a necessary element in developing commercial sustainability.

Many of these issues relating to authenticity and preservation are, in a sense, either mute or significantly challenged in heritage railways, particularly heritage railways that use steam locomotives. As discussed in Chapter 1, the wear and tear on equipment is such that the process of operating such equipment means that, at best, much of a heritage steam locomotive is a replication of the original engine and, as is the case with the WCWR, the rolling stock is either copied from the original equipment or so completely rejuvenated as to make it more a copy than the original piece (Schliephake & Sutton, 2007). As the above list demonstrates, this process of replication is a necessary aspect of using heritage railways for touristic purposes where revenue generation is a priority.

It is the last comment that is most compelling in this cautionary tale of heritage railway development. The WCWR, as has been mentioned several times in this chapter, is an example of a public–private partnership blessed with significant initial investment, broad community support, a stunning locale in a region where tourism is critically important, and a highly competent operator. Nonetheless, the project appears to have fallen victim to the costs of operating and, more importantly, maintaining a heritage rail line and the vagaries of the global economy. In this book, we have seen a number of examples of commercially operated heritage railways which have suffered in recent years as a result, presumably, of the global economic crisis – the Yukon and White Pass Railway (Chapter 5) and the Grand Canyon Railway (Chapter 12) – and some that have seemed immune to the economic downturn, namely the St Kitts Scenic Railway (Chapter 17). It is not clear what determines success or failure in such cases and it is this question that begs future research and examination.

Postscript

The current crisis faced by the WCWR underscores what so many of the chapters in this book have illustrated, namely that heritage railways have operated and increasingly do operate in a complex web of constituencies, stakeholders, legislation and regulations, and, in the case of those dependent upon tourism, an economic climate that can be a challenge to operating sustainability. As this book has shown, this web is challenging for enthusiasts, entrepreneurs and governments alike. However, it can also provide help in desperate situations.

Thus, it would appear that the WCWR, written off by its operators and its host government just several months before the time of writing, may get at least a short-term reprieve. The Tasmanian Minister of Infrastructure, David O'Byrne, who is quoted at the start of this chapter as saying the WCWR will be closed, is now saying, several weeks after that announcement, 'the government was working on a plan to keep the railway open.... We acknowledge time is of the essence.' He also said that the government had already had informal talks with potential new operators (ABC News, 2013b).

Time is of the essence in a situation like this. The mayor of Queenstown, Darryl Gerrity, points out that the accreditation to operate the line is held by some of the WCWR's staff and that they are already seeking new employment (ABC News, 2013b). If the railway loses their expertise and accreditation, the second resurrection of the Mt Lyell Railway will be even more challenging. Travel blogs are already discussing the closure of the railway and social media will no doubt spread the news faster than ever before (Tastetravel, n.d.). With all the challenges it now faces, it is hard to see how the WCWR can reclaim the sense of hope and success it had a mere 10 years ago. But it does seem to be the case that no matter what the challenges facing heritage railways, there is no shortage of enthusiasm for their continuation and success.

References

ABC News (2013a) End of the line for heritage railway, 4 February. At http://www.abc.net.au/news/2013-02-04/jobs-in-balance-as-tourist-railway-closes/4499832 (accessed 31 March 2013).

ABC News (2013b) Wilderness rail workers look for new jobs, 15 February. At http://www.abc.net.au/news/2013-02-15/wilderness-rail-workers-look-for-new-jobs/4520532 (accessed 31 March 2013).

Australian Bureau of Statistics (2005) 1384.6 – Statistics – Tasmania, 2005. At http://www.abs.gov.au/ausstats/abs@.nsf/0/8A47E9B5EB3632B8CA256C320024189B?opendocument (accessed 31 March 2013).

Australian Bureau of Statistics (2007) 2006 Census QuickStats: Queenstown. At http://
  www.censusdata.abs.gov.au/ABSNavigation/prenav/LocationSearch?collection=Ce
  nsus&period=2006&areacode=UCL613200&producttype=QuickStats&breadcrum
  b=PL&action=401 (accessed 20 February 2013).
Australian Government (2011) Economic importance of tourism in the regions, 12
  April.   At   http://minister2.ret.gov.au/MediaCentre/MediaReleases/Pages/Analysis
  HighlightstheEconomicImportanceofTourismintheRegions.aspx (accessed 31 March
  2013).
Conlin, M.V. (2002) Tourism in Tasmania: A model for environmentally sustainable
  tourism? Proceedings of the VII Islands of the World Conference, University of
  Prince Edward Island, Canada, June.
Discover Tasmania (n.d.-a) Tasmania general overview. At http://www.discovertasmania.
  com/about_tasmania/general_overview_of_tasmania (accessed 20 February 2013).
Discover Tasmania (n.d.-b) Tasmania Zeehan. At http://www.discovertasmania.com/
  western_wilderness/towns_and_places/zeehan (accessed 20 February 2013).
Rae, L (2001) The Abt Railway and Railways of the Lyell Region. Sandy Bay, Tasmania: Lou
  Rae.
Rae, L. (2008) The Abt Railway: Tasmania's West Coast Wilderness Railway. Sandy Bay,
  Tasmania: Lou Rae.
Rail Tasmania (n.d.) Railway preservation in Tasmania. At http://www.railtasmania.
  com/pres (accessed 20 February 2013).
Schliephake, K. and Sutton, K. (2007) Speed, steam and nostalgia: The heritage railways
  of northern England. In C. Ehland (ed.) Thinking Northern: Textures of Identity in the
  North of England (pp. 279–302). Amsterdam: Rodopi.
Tasmania Department of Infrastructure, Energy and Resources (2004) Annual Report.
  At   http://www.dier.tas.gov.au/publications/annual_reports/2004_annual_report/
  west_coast_wilderness_railway_and (accessed 31 March 2013).
Tasmania Department of Infrastructure, Energy and Resources (2012) Annual Report. At
  http://www.dier.tas.gov.au/__data/assets/pdf_file/0006/81951/dier_annual_report_
  2012.pdf (accessed 31 March 2013).
Tasmania Parks and Wildlife Service (n.d.) Wild Rivers National Park. At http://www.
  parks.tas.gov.au/?base=3937 (accessed 20 February 2013).
Tastetravel (n.d.) West Coast Wilderness Railway gets the shunt. At http://tastetravel.
  org/2013/02/20/west-coast-wilderness-railway-gets-the-shunt (accessed 31 March
  2013).
Tourism Tasmania (n.d.) Tasmanian tourism snapshot: Year ending September 2012. At
  http://www.tourismtasmania.com.au/__data/assets/pdf_file/0010/55378/tvs_sep
  12.pdf (accessed 20 February 2013).
UNESCO (n.d.) Australian convict sites. At http://whc.unesco.org/en/list/1306 (accessed
  20 February 2013).
West Coast Wilderness Railway (n.d.) Federal Hotels West Coast Wilderness Railway
  history. At http://www.westcoastwildernessrailway.com.au/history.asp (accessed
  10 June 2012).

Part 4
Conclusion

19 No Terminus in Sight: New Horizons for Heritage Railways

Geoffrey R. Bird and Michael V. Conlin

Lessons Learned and Future Directions

This book began with your editors recounting their early childhood experiences with railways. These anecdotes pointed to both a fascination with the physical artifacts of railway travel and also the more social elements associated with rail travel – the landscapes, cultures and people which rail travel opened up for so many, from the 19th century onwards. The subsequent 17 chapters described a special world full of both aspects: locomotives, carriages, hotels and right of ways, as well as journeys, change and exploration. Clearly, this collection of chapters demonstrates in detail how railway heritage in the context of tourism relies upon and responds to these elements.

Many of the chapters, however, also make it clear that there is a more mundane but nonetheless important element to railway heritage, namely economic sustainability. Chapter 5, by Lemky, Jolliffe and Conlin, along with Chapters 8, 12 and 17, by Porterfield, Collison and Found, and concluding with Chapter 18, by Conlin and Prideaux, all underscore the economic imperative that the use of railway heritage for touristic purposes imposes on the niche. This economic imperative is most profound when railway heritage is used to provide tourists and enthusiasts alike with a railway experience, either in the form of actually riding a train or, at the very least, observing, touching and smelling railway heritage's physical artifacts in museums and experiential displays and exhibits. It is perhaps less of a challenge where the railway heritage artifacts are simply the rights of way which are increasingly being converted to alternative uses, such as biking and hiking trails, an excellent example of which is found in Chapter 7, by Reis and Jellum.

So, after such a comprehensive and eclectic journey via these chapters through the world of railway heritage and tourism, what lessons can be derived from both the conceptual discussion and the examination of real examples railway heritage in action. And what does the future hold for the niche?

Heritage Railways and Tourism are Compatible

Railways maintain a unique position in tourism. Starting with the perspective of Frost and Laing (Chapter 4), they provide an interesting insight into railways from the perspective of children's books, capturing the essence of the heritage railway mystique: a mélange of nostalgia, magic and time travel, and the humanization of railways into personalities with identity and meaning. In Chapter 3, on 'railfan' tourism, Stefanovic and Koster explore the motivations and preferences of the niche railfan tourist, typically a middle-class male who is drawn to railway heritage destinations and less developed 'touristy' sites. These authors raise some interesting questions about this market, and whether by building infrastructure we attract more tourists at the cost of losing railfan tourists looking for a more authentic experience. This dichotomy raises many of the challenges that cultural heritage tourism faces when considering the issue of authenticity.

A number of the chapters spoke to the form in which railway heritage experience is packaged. For example, Lemky, Jolliffe and Conlin in Chapter 5 explore the relationship to cruise ships and the packaging of rail heritage for shore excursions. Indeed, railways are an appealing attraction for cruise tourists as shore excursions, encompassing natural landscapes, heritage and a comfortable setting in which to relax. In turn, the cruise ship visiting a small town such as Skagway, Alaska or Basseterre in St Kitts is a captive market that results in significant revenue generation, not just for the cruise operator but also for shore-based businesses, including, where they exist, heritage railway operators.

Hudson's exploration in Chapter 2 of the role of hotels in heritage railways is interesting from a number of perspectives. First, Hudson notes the awareness of hotel guests who not only know about the hotel's railway past but are knowledgeable about it. He goes on to note that these individuals may see themselves as rail enthusiasts, exemplifying the broad attraction of these grand hotels. Second, he calls for consideration of how hotels in the contemporary age employ or distance themselves from that railway past. In many cases, it is about striking a balance between the past and present-day branding. Not all markets are interested in heritage, and it may be seen as a detriment when attracting, for example, the Chinese market, to speak about an 'old railway hotel'. Certainly in the case of this nationality, railways in Canada do not represent simply an opportunity to explore the majesty of the wilderness, but rather the outcome of slave-like conditions resulting in the death of many Chinese labourers. Third, railway hotels also tie in historically with the cruise ship industry, such as the Canadian Pacific Steam Ship Company and its links not only to railway hotels in Canada, but also to Hong Kong's Peninsula Hotel and other grand hotels of the Pacific Rim. People forget that it was once popular to sail from Hong Kong on an Empress-class steamship, such as the *Empress of Japan*, and then transfer to the CP railway to traverse the North American continent, finally to cross the Atlantic on another CP steamship, all the while staying in CP hotels along the rights of way and termini. The scale of this mode of transportation, coupled with a series of hotels, seems quite extraordinary, even in today's context. Will that world ever occur again?

Finally, the hotel structures themselves are, in many cases, the last remaining vestige of the significance of the era when railways were the chief means of travel, and their hotels acted as a hub in the business of transport and, in some cases, such as the Banff Springs Hotel, as the destination itself. Whereas Hudson posits that these beautiful hotels will probably last into the next century, this may be a wish that is not financially feasible. The cost for upgrades can be prohibitive, as the magnificent refurbishment of St Pancras Station in London attests.

As with the challenges of maintaining the railway hotels and the actual running of steam trains and maintaining carriages, Pryce in Chapter 6 takes a very pragmatic perspective in the assessment of risk management and heritage railways. In her chapter, the challenge of operating preserved machinery in a 21st-century risk-management context adds another cost to operations. More importantly, it has the potential to detract from the overall visitor experience. Nonetheless, Pryce's discussion of risk management with heritage railways reinforces the attraction of train operations, in contrast to static displays, as part of the authentic experience.

Reis and Jellum in Chapter 7 explore the rails-to-trails phenomenon, an innovative adaptation of railway infrastructure. However, some may view the removal of rail lines as a mark of the demise of train traffic. In jurisdictions such as New Zealand, where there are a number of preserved railways, rail trails are simply good use of derelict lines. For other jurisdictions, it may mean the removal and ultimate forgetting of a region's railway history. This might be truer in North American jurisdictions, where railway beds have been destroyed to make way for trails and roadways. As passenger rail sees a resurgence as a green option in cities, the cost of establishing new corridors becomes prohibitive. We will be interested to observe whether, over time, these recycled greenways have served as a way to reserve rail corridors for future redevelopment.

Throughout the book, we have seen the combination of rail with other elements of the tourist experience. Porterfield's Chapter 8, on dining cars, is an example of this, where tourist trains become a unique setting for enjoying food and beverages. This clustering of services certainly repositions trains to other markets and uses, most notably local excursionist fund-raising events, reflecting the potential for train product innovation. Chaplin, in Chapter 9, highlights the significance of involving communities in tourism planning, and heritage railway preservation is no different. Indeed, there are clear benefits to the community in terms of providing local transportation, reflecting a dual value to the regeneration of rail systems. Including education as a key element in the policy and planning approach speaks volumes about the need to reintroduce and highlight the value of railways, not only as a means of transportation but also as a way to link communities both socially and economically.

In short, whether it is through static displays, operating railways, alternative uses or innovative product planning and community involvement, the value of railway heritage in the context of tourism seems to be viable. However, as is the case with any touristic activity, financial viability and sustainability are key elements that owners, both public and private, and volunteers, both organizational and individual, must constantly manage.

Railway Heritage Can Be Economically Sustainable

Heritage railways are, by their very nature and technology, expensive propositions. They involve large capital assets that are expensive to maintain and, where they are operated as railways, they require significant numbers of people, who add to the cost of operations and challenges in terms of skill retention, many of which are no longer commonly found in the working population. When coupled with the impact of seasonality, which quite often characterizes tourism, the financial challenges become even greater.

These fundamental issues can be illustrated by two of the examples presented here, in Chapter 5, by Lemky, Jolliffe and Conlin, on cruise and rail tourism, and, in contrast, in Chapter 18, by Conlin and Prideaux, on the West Coast Wilderness Railway in Tasmania, Australia. Both chapters discuss examples of heritage railways that received large injections of capital and which were integrated into more comprehensive touristic activities, either the cruise tourism sector or the major development of a cultural heritage and outdoor leisure destination. The White Pass and Yukon Railway, discussed in by Lemky, Jolliffe and Conlin in Chapter 5, demonstrates that large-scale heritage railway operations can be sustainable and profitable if the larger touristic venture into which it is integrated, namely cruise tourism, operates effectively to produce a significant level of ridership on the railway, notwithstanding any impact of seasonality. The West Coast Wilderness Railway discussed by Conlin and Prideaux in Chapter 18, also and somewhat unfortunately demonstrates this truth. In spite of significant public and private investment in the project and its incorporation into a larger-scale development of tourism in the Queenstown–Strahan–Macquarrie Harbor region of western Tasmania, the level of ridership was never sufficient to sustain the railway. As we know from Chapter 18, the railway is currently operating under heavy Australian federal government subsidy, a situation that is temporary at best.

This issue of ridership can be illustrated by an anecdote. One of your editors was lucky enough to find himself in Skagway, Alaska, in late July 2013. On Sunday 28 July, Skagway was enjoying what the locals consider to be a holiday, namely a day when no cruise ships entered the small port. This was one of only three Sundays in the 2013 cruise season when Skagway did not have any cruise ship arrivals. Residents and a small number of land-based visitors could wander through the shopping precinct, get a table in any of the restaurants and generally relax in the relative solitude of the small Alaskan town. But if they wanted to ride on the White Pass and Yukon Railway, they would have had to catch the morning train from Skagway to the top of the White Pass on the Canadian border; the train only made one run that day and it was far from full.

The next day, Monday 29 July, was another story. Your editor was camping at the end of what is called the White Pass Railroad Dock in Skagway. At 5 am, the first of many trains throughout the day began to run out onto the dock just as the Royal Caribbean's 2435-passenger *Rhapsody of the Seas* docked in the port. She was followed by Celebrity Cruises' 2138-passenger *Celebrity Millennium* a few minutes later and within the hour the Holland America 1380-passenger *Amsterdam* docked at an adjacent pier: in all, a potential railway ridership of almost 6000 persons. Starting at 8 am, trains seemed to run continually from both docks and the small terminal in town throughout the morning. It was not surprising, therefore, to see four trains at once working their way up the spectacular right of way in the early afternoon. What was all the more interesting was that one of those trains was pulled by the railway's heritage Mikado steam locomotive and that several of the others were pulled by railway's heritage shovel-nosed electro-motive diesels. It is worth noting that in the four days following 29 July, a total of 14 giant cruise ships tied up in Skagway – and they would have all contributed huge levels of ridership to the railway.

In Chapter 17 Found offers additional insight into the importance of ridership for sustainability in his examination of the gem that is the St Kitts

Scenic Railway. Clearly, this railway stands as an example of best practice in operating a commercially viable tourism business, a heritage railway that has certainly established itself in the community and as a tourism attraction. Still, the Railway is dependent upon the steady cruise ship traffic visiting the island, as we have seen in other chapters. Also interesting is the link Found makes between the Railway as a tourism attraction and its role in interpreting the history and society of St Kitts. It illustrates the larger context of industrial heritage that these railways represent: aside from the attraction of the train and surrounding infrastructure, the landscapes that visitors travel through and the accompanying interpretation educate visitors about the people whose lives depended on the railway in the past and the lives they lived on the sugar plantations.

Heritage Railways as Repositories of Cultural Industrial Heritage

As the chapters in this book attest, it is clear that railway heritage is compatible with tourism. It is also the case that in some tourism destinations, financial sustainability for heritage railways is both possible and predictable. Nonetheless, a third lesson can be drawn from the wide array of discussion and examples found in the preceding chapters: namely, the role of heritage railways as repositories of cultural industrial heritage.

Boksberger and Sturzenegger, in Chapter 14, on the Rhaetian Railway in Switzerland, illustrate the capacity of heritage railways to preserve and protect our cultural industrial heritage, in this case as one of the only three railways to be designated as a UNESCO World Heritage site, along with the Mountain Railways of India and the Semmering Railway in Austria. Yan and Zhuang, in Chapter 16, present a fascinating and compelling argument in support of designating the Yunnan–Vietnam Railway (YVR) a World Heritage site. Unfortunately, as it currently stands, the YVR is a stereotypical story of great heritage potential coupled with a lack of funds and political will that leaves the railway in a state of continuing decay. Certainly the Swiss example of the Rhaetian Railway, the famous cog railway that earns its World Heritage status through its technical wizardry coupled with stunning vistas of the Alps, emphasizes different heritage themes than those offered by the YVR. The YVR was built during the period of French colonialism in Vietnam and served as a main transportation artery through wars, revolutions and evolution over the past 140 years. While still a technical marvel in how and where it was constructed, it is the social and historical elements that Yan and Zhuang argue merit World Heritage designation and which, if attained, would help to preserve the railway. However, World Heritage designations do not necessarily translate into funding, although they may help with attractiveness and visitation. It seems that a key element in achieving that status would be gaining the support of appropriate government authorities and convincing them of the significance and value of preserving this stretch of history. If governments seem at times to be reluctant to invest in railway heritage in the context of a viable tourism business model, notwithstanding any cultural heritage value to the host country or nationalities, readers need only re-examine the discussion by Conlin and Prideaux in Chapter 18, on the Tasmanian West Coast Wilderness Railway, to see the dangers to economic viability. Railway heritage projects are, by their very nature, complex and expensive: governments and other funding sources need to be clear about why they would make such massive investments in cultural industrial heritage and what it is that would indicate a successful investment.

Railway Heritage and Volunteers

Finally, in addition to the tourism, economic and cultural aspects of railway heritage, the niche is also, again by its very nature, intrinsically connected with ordinary people. While much of the discussion in the book has focused on large-scale restoration and commercially operated projects and, indeed, businesses, it is also true that much of the allure and satisfaction of heritage railways is rather more small scale, involving ordinary people with an interest in one form or another in railways and their preservation.

Chapter 15, by Leanne White, on the Daylesford Spa Country Railway, presents an excellent example of one of the keys to success with many railways: the role of the volunteer. Is describes how the support and commitment of a local community to their heritage railway make the Daylesford operation feasible. The chapter offers a 'best practice' in terms of the operation of a heritage railway by way of the creation of a thriving and engaged railway volunteer community. Indeed, the world of heritage railways is in many ways the world of interested and committed railfans and volunteers.

Most of the small heritage railways operating in the United Kingdom and North America depend fundamentally on the investment of time, energy, skill and emotion by volunteers. Their roles are varied: the re-enactors who hold up the Kettle Valley train in British Columbia to the delight of the many riders as they travel through the Okanagan Valley during the summer season; the tradesmen who help to restore, repair and maintain the equipment of the Great Central Railway in the United Kingdom, billed as 'Britain's only mainline steam railway'; and the many volunteers of the New England

Railway in Australia who have been instrumental in the restoration and operation of the heritage railways around the Armidale-Glen Innes region of central New South Wales. In short, without volunteers, most railway heritage operations would likely not be sustainable.

The Future of Railway Heritage

This book presents some interesting groundwork in the study of heritage railways around the world. Particularly in Part 3, where we have been able to gather a variety of examples from around the world, we can see reflected the universal significance of railways in terms of community identity as well as tourism. Not surprisingly, funding is often seen as a key barrier to the redevelopment and maintenance of these lines and the infrastructure associated with them. Funding through ridership is important, as is public and private investment. Approaches to railway heritage management is a future area of research, particularly the ways in which local governments along with city and regional destination management organizations can partner and collaborate to share the burden of this valued tourism and community resource. In addition, approaches to assessing feasibility and railway business planning would be useful areas of study, in order to ascertain any specific elements or characteristics of rail heritage management and operations that require consideration.

The book provides the perspectives of both scholars and practitioners directly involved with railway heritage. More research, is required, though, partnering practitioners and academics, in order to gain further insight into topics such as the motivations of railway travellers, railway heritage management best practices, and successful policy and planning that have supported the regeneration of local railway lines.

Finally, for many government and communities, heritage railways offer an experience that integrates industrial heritage with picturesque landscapes, offering a comfortable journey through which to observe a region or country. Managing these products is clearly a challenge, given the expenses related to maintenance, upgrading to contemporary safety standards and marketing to changing audiences. It is no wonder that there is such a strong link between cruise ships and trains, given the benefit of a captured mass market that descends upon a given port. Other railways are less fortunate, pressed to attract visitors to the broader destination and then offering a schedule and service that maximize access to the market. Management of these railways, therefore, depends to a certain extent on collaborating with destination marketing agencies and tour operators to access the fragmented market. This potential key success element is noted by Fraga, de

Sequeira Santos and de Castro Ribeiro in Chapter 10, on Brazil, by Collison in Chapter 12, on the Grand Canyon Railway, and by White in Chapter 15, on the Daylesford Spa Country Railway of Victoria, Australia. These examples represent a level of sophistication in networking and promotion commensurate with the typically large scale of heritage railway operations.

Developed and developing destinations that are fully engaged in building a competitive advantage seem to tap into the necessary innovations to make heritage railway sustainable. Where there are competing investments, as in the case of Mexico, with its resorts and seaside towns, as outlined in Chapter 11, by Camargo, Morales and Garza, investing in railways requires a very strong business case. In addition, as exemplified by Henderson in Chapter 13, on the Singapore–Malaysia Railway, part of the battle in establishing railways is about building political support, gained in part by rekindling a sense an association, perhaps even a sense of identity, that is not only experienced but heralded and, indeed, celebrated. In short, the key to success in developing railway heritage in the context of tourism is to balance the goals and expectations of funding sources, operators, volunteers, and visitors and users with realistic management structures and business plans that have a reasonable chance of financial, social and political sustainability. This book has provided a number of examples where this has been done, both on a large scale and on a smaller scale. Where the balance has been achieved, railway heritage is successful and can look forward to a long and satisfying role in tourism and industrial heritage preservation.

Index